CONTEMPORARY IRISH POETRY

Edited, with Introduction and
Notes, by Anthony Bradley

An Anthology

UNIVERSITY OF CALIFORNIA PRESS
Berkeley • Los Angeles • London

University of California Press
Berkeley and Los Angeles, California

University of California Press, Ltd.
London, England

Copyright © 1980 by The Regents of the University of California

Library of Congress Cataloging in Publication Data

Main entry under title:

Contemporary Irish poetry.

  Includes indexes.
  1. English poetry—Irish authors. 2. English
poetry—20th century. I. Bradley, Anthony.
PR8858.C65   821'.9'1208   76-50244
ISBN 0-520-03389-2

Printed in the United States of America

CONTEMPORARY IRISH POETRY

for PATTY and MARY

CONTENTS

CONTENTS

CONTENTS

CONTENTS

CONTENTS

CONTENTS

CONTENTS

CONTENTS

INTRODUCTION

Irish poetry was for long dominated by a man and a movement —William Butler Yeats and the Irish Literary Revival. This anthology is devoted to a comprehensive representation of Irish poetry written in the last fifty years or so, since the waning of the Revival. It excludes the poems of Yeats's last period not because Yeat's genius can be contained within the bounds of the Revival (or any other literary movement, for that matter), but simply because their inclusion even in a brief selection would edge out another Irish poet whose work deserves to be better known. Yeats is in little danger of being neglected.

While it would be absurd to consider Yeats's mature work as merely an aspect of the Literary Revival, his influence on Irish writing often seemed calculated to encourage only the belated romanticism of that movement. A short time before his death, Yeats was still recommending Revival themes to Irish poets (though by this time no one was willing to take such advice literally):

Sing the peasantry, and then
Hard-riding country gentlemen,
The holiness of monks, and after
Porter-drinkers' randy laughter;
Sing the lords and ladies gay
That were beaten into the clay
Through seven heroic centuries.

The society reflected in these lines (from "Under Ben Bulben") is an idealized, anachronistic fantasy that has little or no relation to the political and social realities of life in modern Ireland. Of course, had Yeats restricted himself to the mythic version of Irish society and history he recommends here, and not taken a more complex attitude toward sex, old age, politics, philosophy, and art, he would hardly be accorded the status of a great modern poet. Yeats was, moreover, not above autocratically discouraging experiment that did not coincide with his ideas of what Irish literature should be: his rejection, as director of the Abbey Theatre, of O'Casey's *The Silver Tassie* is notorious, but he also excluded Austin Clarke from *The Oxford Book of Modern Verse*, despite the fact that Clarke was manifestly superior to the various Revival poets Yeats saw fit to include. (Ironically, Clarke's *Collected Poems* appeared in the same year, 1936!)

These Revival poets, AE (George Russell), Douglas Hyde, Katherine Tynan, F. R. Higgins, Lady Gregory, James Stephens, Padraic Colum, et al., though they helped gain acceptance for the idea of a national Irish literature in the English language, by now have assumed, for the most part, a historical as opposed to a literary importance. The distinguishing characteristic of Revival verse is a certain naiveté: simplicity of emotion, thought, and technique are joined to a preoccupation with Ireland's folk tradition and its mythological and heroic past, and a perception of Ireland's landscape as idyllic or picturesque. The Revival writers, at their worst, are products of a Victorian romanticism that idealizes remorselessly, manufactures Irishisms in archaic verse, and bowdlerizes the poetry in Irish that it translates or imitates.

The poetry represented in this anthology is almost invariably more moving and intelligent in the way it deals with human experience, more complex and accomplished in its art, and more universal in its implications than that written by the Revival poets. The writers included here have turned recognizably modern sensibilities toward the historical, political, and social realities of life in Ireland, toward the natural world, and toward the private world of personal experience. The anthology represents a half century of a poetry in English that has assimilated European and American influence as well as the influence of an ancient native tradition of poetry in the Irish language. This creative mingling of past and present, of national and international influences and concerns, has resulted in a body of poetry that is distinctively Irish in nature yet distinctively modern in its attributes and appeal.

Given the range and diversity of the poetry represented here, it seems best to introduce it in terms of its major themes as representative writers have handled them. Particularly since this body of poetry does not lend itself to discussion in terms of movements (with the possible exception of the work of the 1930s "European" Irish poets), or to a treatment of attributes that conveniently distinguish the poetic output of each decade, it does seem a useful simplification to introduce modern Irish poetry by saying what it is "about." The three major areas dealt with are the historical-social-political aspects of human existence, the natural world, and the world of personal experience. I realize, of course, that the work of some writers cuts across these divisions, and that the connotations of many poems transcend the boundaries of their subject matter. I am mindful, too, that to say what a poem is "about" in some measure distracts one from what a poem *is*, from the particular, complex linguistic structure that is the poem as art form. I can only hope that my division of these poems into three broad categories will serve as an admittedly imperfect bridge to the poems, one that will be made redundant by the reader's increasing familiarity with the poems themselves.

1

The poets of modern Ireland have had a rather oppressive political and social context in which to define themselves and their art. What Irish writers inherited in the postrevolutionary twenty-six county Republic of Ireland—that is, the Ireland that successively witnessed the Easter Rising (1916), assimilated the heroic spirit of its martyrs and fought the successful war for independence against England (1919-1921), and then split into the internecine strife of a civil war (1922-1923)—turned out to be a clericalist, bourgeois, narrowly nationalistic state. The special relationship between Church and state came to be enshrined in the constitution and has only fairly recently been repealed, its repeal a tardy and by now ineffectual concession to the principle that Church and state should be separated and to the fears of Northern Ireland Protestants that Irish political unity would mean a government dominated by the Catholic church. The constitution of the Republic still prohibits divorce; contraception and abortion are illegal; social welfare programs have been vigorously opposed by the Church (which still largely controls education); and censorship of literature, films, and drama is, even if exercised in an increasingly desultory fashion, still much in evidence.

The treaty of 1921 which ended the armed hostilities between Irish and English resulted in the partition of Ireland. The six-county state of Northern Ireland was administered by a local government that ruled for the fifty years of its existence essentially without the consent of one-third of its population. Since 1969 thousands of people have been maimed and killed in violence touched off by Catholic demands for civil rights.

In such circumstances it is not altogether surprising that there should exist in modern Irish poetry, both north and south of the border, a tradition of public verse that takes as its concern the historical, social, and political condition of the island.

The poet whose work initiates and most completely embodies this tradition is Austin Clarke, a writer who was, for most of his life, without honor in his native land. Apparently because of their sexual explicitness several of his early books were banned by the Irish censors, and his career as a university teacher was abruptly terminated when he married outside the Church. Clarke saw in the medieval monastic Irish culture of saints and scholars a political, religious, and artistic integrity conspicuously lacking in modern Ireland. There is some historical validity, at least, to Clarke's portrayal of the Celtic Romanesque period in Ireland as a period when religion was not so afflicted by the puritanical character it had assumed in Ireland of more recent date (there was no necessary conflict of love with morality, for example), and the church was not so dominated by Rome and the authoritarianism of an episcopal hierarchy. The art of the period was richly ornamental yet disciplined, as in the metalwork of Saint Patrick's Bell and Shrine and the Cross of Cong; the architecture of Cormac's Chapel at Cashel and the churches of the monastic settlements at Clonmacnois and Glendalough provided a similar blend of decoration and chaste design. Clarke found in this era of Irish history a way of life whose richness and energy and joy indicted the ignoble society he inhabited, and the penitential Christianity subscribed to by that society.

With the publication of *Ancient Lights* in 1955, Clarke began to confront directly the modern world and assume his role as satirical conscience of Ireland, as flayer of the bad morality and crippled hearts and minds of the Irish establishment. In many of his poems since the mid-fifties he has eloquently and often savagely inveighed against clerical domination in the state. (Clarke has, though, perceived that other countries have been afflicted, on occasion at least, with the same sort of complicity of Church and state, as in "Dirge," a poem inspired by Cardinal Spellman's sanction of the Vietnam War.) Clarke's satirical attacks on Irish society are clearly motivated by an outraged compassion for its victims: he sympathizes with the thwarted, guilt-ridden young in a puritanical society (in "The Envy of Poor Lovers") and he attacks the cold comfort enunciated by a Catholic bishop on the death by fire of sixty children in their firetrap orphanage (in "Three Poems About Children"). To read "Martha

Blake at Fifty-One" is to be made to feel dismay and pain. We are made to care about the ignominious suffering and death of a pious spinster, and to feel anger at the failure of her society and her religion to provide her (and many thousands like her) with the simplest consolation. Clarke's satire attains its emotional intensity in large part by his compassionate identification with other victims of his society. It is as though he realized that his own maiming at the hands of society—the sexual guilt deeply injected into his life, the proscription of his work, the punitive attitude of society toward him because of his marriage, the lifelong searching for spiritual values frustrated by clericalism—gives him common cause with those victims of society whose lot is so much worse than his. Unlike Yeats's satiric poems, then, Clarke's speak for the disenfranchised and from their viewpoint, rather than from identification with an aristocratic Anglo-Irish culture. It is this humble and deeply felt identification with those damaged by an unjust society that lends to Clarke's excoriation of modern Ireland so much of its moral force and intensity of emotion.

The strongly personal motivation for Clarke's satire leads him naturally into the realm of confessional poetry in *Mnemosyne Lay in Dust* (1966). This long poem documents with harrowing honesty and tenderness the poet's severe nervous breakdown, his hospitalization in the lunatic asylum Swift willed to the poor of Dublin, and his agonized search for a faith to live by. (That Mnemosyne is the Greek goddess of memory and mother of the muses suggests that the breakdown was connected with the temporary loss of creative powers):

One night he heard heart-breaking sound.
It was a sigh unworlding its sorrow.
Another followed. Slowly he counted
Four different sighs, one after another.
'My mother,' he anguished, 'and my sisters
Have passed away. I am alone, now,
Lost in myself in a mysterious
Darkness, the victim in a story.'

As with Clarke's satire, though, the experience is never allowed to damage the formal restraint of his craft: Clarke's experience in *Mnemosyne* is given an aesthetic distancing through his use of a persona, and more important than any mechanical device, through his utter commitment to the craft and integrity of writing—the poem is never, in any self-indulgent sense, merely confessional. At the same time as the horror and ignominy of the experience are preserved, human dignity and creativity are renewed.

One does not have to be bilingual, as Clarke was, to appreciate the way in which he grafts the assonantal patterning of verse in Irish onto verse in English. Admittedly, Clarke's poetry is occasionally marked by oddities as he employs the devices and rhythms of poetry in Irish, but most often an authentically Irish note is struck with little sense of strain, as in his mellifluous versions of eighteenth-century Irish harp songs, for example.

Louis MacNeice comes from a different background than Clarke's, a background that is Northern and Protestant. To characterize MacNeice as an Irish poet at all may seem strange to some, given that he is usually placed in the company of the British Thirties poets associated with Auden. But Ireland was not only MacNeice's birthplace and subject of some of his most memorable verse (in poems like "Dublin") but also an important influence on his psychic development and the philosophical skepticism that informs so much of his work. MacNeice is, moreover, an important model for some of the younger Ulster poets who share his identity problems and his *odi et amo* attitude toward Ireland; in his own life and work MacNeice found it hard not to return to the Ireland he left as a child and equally hard not to wish it yet another final good-bye. MacNeice's journalistic style is in keeping with his belief that poetry ought to speak to as large an audience as possible and that the concerns of poetry ought to be those of *l'homme sensuel moyen*. Yet MacNeice's genius for sharp, memorable images makes his poetry much more complex in its emotional and intellectual effect than any mere journalism, however brilliant, could be.

MacNeice's skepticism ultimately extended to the political cause endorsed by most of the liberal British writers of the 1930s—the support of the left in the Spanish civil war. The young poet Charles Donnelly, by contrast, died in Spain fighting in the International Brigade against Franco. (His death was the occasion of a moving elegy, included in this volume, by Donagh MacDonagh.) Donnelly's commitment did not result in simple-minded propaganda, however; it is the effect of imprisonment, war, and death on the human mind and emotions which interests him. "The Tolerance of Crows" bears witness to the abstract impersonality of modern warfare:

Death comes in quantity from solved
Problems on maps, well-ordered dispositions,
Angles of elevation and direction.

In "Heroic Heart," written shortly before his tragically early death, he reckons the human cost of political commitment in a very clear-sighted way, but without intimating that poets or other human beings can afford, in such circumstances, not to take sides.

The civil strife that has plagued Northern Ireland for the last decade has elicited a variety of responses from contemporary Irish poets. A number at first consciously resisted dealing with the situation in their writing, in part because they rejected the idea that a poet is a political creature, in part because they feared to seem to exploit human misery. But it was surely inevitable that writers living in the unrelenting pressure of such a crisis would, sooner or later, feel compelled to deal with it in their work in some manner.

In poems by John Montague and Seamus Heaney, among others, we are made to feel the uneasy, troubled sense of sleep broken by the sounds of an urban guerilla war that is waged virtually on one's doorstep, made to feel the inescapable way the violence penetrates one's personal life, and the gravity of what that violence portends for the society:

> While jungleclad troops
> ransack the Falls, race
> through huddled streets,
> we lie awake, the wide
> window washed with rain,
> your oval face, and tide
> of yellow hair luminous
> as you turn to me again
> seeking refuge as the
> cave of night blooms
> with fresh explosions.

> *Montague, "The Cave of Night"*

> And all shifts dreamily as you keen
> Far off, turning from the din
> Of gunshot, siren and clucking gas
> Out there beyond each curtained terrace

> Where the fault is opening.
> *Heaney, "A Northern Hoard"*

Montague has for long been conscious of the pathology of his native province (as one can see from such volumes as *Poisoned Lands*, first published before the outbreak of the present violence). In *The Rough Field*, however, he deals directly with the historical, social, and political roots of the conflict that make it tragically inevitable. In "A New Siege: An Historical Meditation" (dedicated to Bernadette Devlin), Montague conflates the siege of Derry in 1689, when the Protestant Loyalist garrison was besieged by the Catholic Jacobite forces, with the virtual siege to which the Catholic citizens of Derry were subjected early on in the present troubles. Montague's conclusion, in this historical meditation, is essentially right. Given the historical circumstances of the dispossession in the seventeenth century of the Ulster Catholics' land (and virtually their entire culture) by the Protestant English and Scots settlers, and the perpetuation of injustice and bigotry in subsequent centuries, recurrent violence is inevitable. In "A New Siege" Montague captures the incredulous revulsion of the squirearchy of Northern Ireland at the monstrous bigotry (personified in Ian Paisley and others like him) they have nourished for their own purposes for so long, thinking that they could control and exploit it for their own selfish ends of maintaining power:

> a Protestant parliament
> a Protestant people
> major this and
> captain that and
> general nothing
> the bland, pleasant
> face of mediocrity
> confronting in horror
> its mirror image
> bull-voiced bigotry

More sharply than any other Irish writer, Montague articulates the northern Catholic's view that the grievous losses of the seventeenth century are the root causes of his perennial sense of bitterness and disenfranchisement. Montague's "Lament for the O'Neills" and "A Grafted Tongue" give powerful elegaic expression to the grief and bitterness of the native Irish at the loss of their language, their leaders, their entire way of life. The exile of the Irish chieftains is

recalled by a fiddler's "intricate & mournful mastery" as he plays a
lament for the Ulster princes, the O'Neills:

> assuaging like a bardic poem,
> our tribal pain—
>
> Disappearance & death
> of a world, as down Lough Swilly
> the great ship, encumbered with nobles,
> swells its sails for Europe:
> The Flight of the Earls.
>
> ["*Lament for the O'Neills*"]

"A New Siege," "A Grafted Tongue," and "Lament for the O'Neills"
are all part of the long sequence entitled *The Rough Field*. The title is
a translation of the Irish place name Garvaghey, the townland in
Tyrone where Montague grew up, and is a metaphor for the
troubled province of Ulster. In this sequence of near-epic scope, too
rich to be reduced to paraphrase, Ulster's past and present are juxta-
posed, as are public and personal issues, rural and urban settings:
one has a sense of a whole way of life having been imaginatively
captured and expressed. Montague brings to this ambitious attempt
to depict the quintessential nature of experience in his native
province intelligence and compassion, and also a versatile poetic
technique in which can be seen the influences not only of traditional
Irish music and poetry in the Irish language but also of modern
American and European verse.

Seamus Deane has given the violence in Derry, the city where
the present troubles started, direct and sustained treatment in his
first volume, *Gradual Wars*. The symbolic rendering of the intuition
that the city's people are the victims of a malign historical destiny—
"History, the angel, was stirred / To turn her face upon us. Bird / Or
beast, as she turned / The streets split and burned"—is balanced by a
realistic diagnosis of the causes and effects of social malaise in
Northern Ireland:

> The unemployment in our bones
> Erupting on our hands in stones;
>
> The thought of violence a relief,
> The act of violence a grief;

Our bitterness and love
Hand in glove.

["*Derry*"]

While Montague's meditation on history directly addresses itself to the present situation in the North, the implications of poems on historical subjects apparently far removed in time from the present also bear more or less directly on the present. Richard Murphy's "The Battle of Aughrim," for example, which describes "the last decisive battle in Irish history" (July 12, 1691), between an Irish army led by the French, and an English army led by a Dutchman and composed of foreigners from seven different countries, is clearly an attempt to come to terms with the recurrent nightmare of Irish history by examining a confrontation that played an important part in shaping the political, social, and religious divisions of modern Ireland. The obtrusiveness of the past upon the present in an unredeemable continuum of time is occasioned by "a morass / Of godly bigotry and pride of race"; the common people are doomed forever to be losers—"Who cares which foreign king / Governs, we'll still fork dung." Seamus Heaney's "Requiem for the Croppies" commemorates the spirit of the rebels of 1798, Irish agricultural workers who died facing English artillery with scythes; their blood saturated the hillside where they fell, and the barley they carried in their pockets for food sprouted after their death. The redemptive beauty of these deaths is set against the pathos of their sacrifice. The great famine of the 1840s is still important for most Irishmen in that it forms part of their consciousness of being Irish. The Irish identity is formed in some measure by an awareness that the history of the Irish people has been one of oppression, an oppression that, at certain junctures in history, seems genocidal in nature. Brendan Kennelly's "My Dark Fathers" is a powerful poem about the great famine which eloquently gives voice to this sort of consciousness.

Derek Mahon has written directly about the present troubles in the North, but some of his best poems, while they are political in nature, transcend the immediate circumstances that may have inspired them. In his most recent volume, the title poem sets the aesthetic detachment of an imagined Japanese tea party, where the guests crowd to the window to watch the snow fall after the delicate "tinkling of china / And tea into china," against the brutality of historical event:

Elsewhere they are burning
Witches and heretics
In the boiling squares,

Thousands have died since dawn
In the service
Of barbarous kings—

> ["*The Snow Party*"]

To be in time, however, is to acknowledge one's affinity with "the dim / Forms that kneel at noon / In the city" whether in fear, prayer, or murderous intent, and specifically with those who suffer and inflict suffering in the present murderous conflict in Belfast ("Afterlives").

One of Mahon's finest poems, "A Disused Shed in County Wexford," sets the condition of life in Ireland into the context of other neglected, exploited, godforsaken places, "Indian compounds" and "Peruvian mines worked out and abandoned." The people of Ireland are the superfluous, lost souls, parasitic mushrooms existing in "a foetor of / Vegetable sweat since civil war days." Since their abandonment by the godlike mycologist they have been naively waiting for light and deliverance, but are doomed not only by the barbarity of political events (imperialist exploitation, firing squad, civil war, concentration camps, genocide) but by natural disaster and the death, or at least the disappearance, of God. The poem superbly portrays the condition of modern society in which a sense of victimization at the hands of history and politics merges with spiritual disappointment at abandonment by God.

In such poems as "Matthew V. 29-30" and "Ecclesiastes," Mahon's self-blame, coupled with accusation of the divinity, is an indictment of the joyless, puritanical Christianity that is such a depressing feature of existence in the North of Ireland, and at the same time a concession to its life-denying, fanatical appeal:

Yes you could
wear black, drink water, nourish a fierce zeal
with locusts and wild honey, and not
feel called upon to understand and forgive
but only to speak with a bleak

afflatus, and love the January rains when they
    darken the dark doors and sink hard
into the Antrim hills

             [*"Ecclesiastes"*]

The plight of the Ulster Protestant—his cultural uncertainty, basically—plagues several writers from the North, especially John Hewitt. If he rightfully insists on his Irishness, asserting that he is "as native in my thought as any here," he is still caught in that peculiar cultural predicament of a writer who feels neither fully English nor Irish, of one who succeeds naturally neither to "the graver English" nor to "the lyric Irish tongue" ("Once Alien Here").

For modern Irish poets, then, history is a meaningful if oppressive burden that bears very palpably on the significance of their present experience. The recent events in the North, in particular, have caused in many Irish writers a sharper awareness of the intransigent reality of the historical, social, and political conditions of their own existence, and of the manifold ways in which the private world is contingent on the public. The poetry they write is not always overtly political in nature, but it is, very often, discernibly linked to contemporary experience that is shaped by political exigency.

2

Despite the existence of large cities, notably Dublin and Belfast, and the increasingly evident encroachments of modern industry and commerce elsewhere in Ireland, the island is not yet, at least, merely another state in the overcrowded industrial and urban culture of western Europe. Most of Ireland is rural in character and the way of life for many of its citizens is still based on agriculture and direct contact with the natural world. Much of the countryside is breathtakingly beautiful, primitive, and remote from what characterizes modern society. Space and time blend frequently as one encounters in the elemental landscape the archaeological presences of a culture that goes back long before the birth of Christ.

The Revival writers' perception of the rural world often involved a rather cozy appreciation of the countryside's picturesqueness and a trivializing sense of its folklore manifested in their delight with fairies. Irish poets after the Revival have approached the natural scene with a sharper, more objective sense of its aesthetic properties, frequently with anthropological or archaeological awareness, and a much stronger sense of the earthiness of rural occupations. Many of them have, indeed, grown up actually experiencing the realities and exigencies of rural life, whereas the Revival writers lived at a considerable distance from the rural life they idealized.

Patrick Kavanagh is the genuine article, the peasant farmer oppressed and enthralled by his uneasy marriage to the unaccommodating "black hills" and "stony grey soil" of his native County Monaghan: though his pastoral vision is bleak and recriminating, it is also joyful and celebratory. His early poems of the 1930s are keen evocations of rural life loaded with sensuous images: "The seed like stars against the black / Eternity of April clay" ("To a Man After the Harrow"). *The Great Hunger* (1942) fell foul of the Irish censors when it first appeared apparently because of a few explicitly sexual images. One wonders whether the censors were sufficiently perceptive to be offended also by Kavanagh's powerful indictment of the spiritual deprivation of modern Ireland (which has succeeded the starvation of the 1840s, referred to colloquially as "the great hunger"). Kavanagh's artful simplicity is a constant feature of his work, but it is particularly admirable in his late poems, in such sonnets as "The Hospital." In this poem he derives solace and purpose from the unlikely surroundings of a hospital, realizing his task is to "record love's mystery without claptrap, / Snatch out of time the passionate transitory." This quasi-mystical impulse is joyfully at work in "October," "Canal Bank Walk" and "Lines Written On a Seat On the Grand Canal, Dublin," though the setting for these sonnets is, more characteristically than in "The Hospital," the natural world. Kavanagh was often betrayed into self-pity by his consciousness of having wasted his time and talent in his attempt to dominate Dublin's literary scene (he moved to the city after thirty years of country life), but poems like "If Ever You Go To Dublin Town" are humorous, moving, and controlled. The image of the poet that comes through in such poems is of a forceful man aware of defeat, but daring to reject the worldly virtues like commonsense that might have made his career more successful: that particular virtue he wittily describes as ". . . a bank [that] will refuse a post / Dated cheque of the Holy Ghost" ("To Hell With Commonsense").

The poems of Padraic Fallon have been published in book form only recently, though he was a contemporary and friend of Kavanagh. Like Kavanagh's poetry, Fallon's is much concerned with rural Ireland; and like his friend, Fallon was concerned to reject the

Revival's romanticizing of Ireland's rural life. He does this very explicitly and ironically in poems such as "For Paddy Mac." Fallon mocks the idealizing, mythologizing attitude toward Irish peasant life as "bunkum"—the reality was instead, the poet remembers:

> the homespun fellows
> Selling their spades on hiring days,
> For a year and a day the dear flesh off their bones
> From penury to slavery,
> The soul thrown in for a spare.

But Fallon's attitude is not, here or elsewhere, merely one of debunking: his demythologizing aims to purify language and to represent the ritual patterns that actually inhere in man's life, not those that are artificially imposed on it. Myth and ritual survive and are more important than the precise formulation we place on them. "Man lives; Gods die: / It is only the genuflection that survives."

Richard Murphy's heritage is an interesting contrast to Kavanagh's, and indeed to that of all the other modern Irish poets, in that he was born into the Anglo-Irish Ascendancy Yeats came to revere so much. In his outsider's interest in the people and customs of the remote west of Ireland where he lives and writes, Murphy appears at first sight to be a throwback to the days of the Revival. But Murphy's work is devoid of the condescension and romanticism of the Revival writers. His identification with the way of life he describes is balanced by an allegiance to his own tradition. His style is characterized by a sustained gravity of tone and by an attractive concrete imagery. The elegaic note that characterizes much of the earlier poetry has given way recently to a more astringent quality in such poems as *The Battle of Aughrim*, in which he seems to have come to a sharp sense of the bloody-mindedness of colonial history, and a vivid and energetic idiom that conveys a strong sense of elemental energy:

> The calamity of seals begins with jaws.
> Born in caverns that reverberate
> With endless malice of the sea's tongue
> Clacking on shingle, they learn to bark back
> In fear and sadness and celebration.
> The ocean's mouth opens forty feet wide
> And closes on a morsel of their rock.
>
> [*"Seals at High Island"*]

Seamus Heaney is probably the most impressive of the poets who take the natural world as their concern. His sensuous and felicitous images of rural life, embodied in finely-crafted verse, are meaningfully complex—the art of these poems is a vital extension of the genre of pastoral. There is something at once earthy and intellectual about Heaney. He does indeed, as he puts it himself, "dig" with his pen, emulating in his art the father and grandfather who delved in the soil and bogland of the Ulster farm where he grew up. Heaney invariably works toward significant complication of an apparently simple evocation of rural life. In "The Badgers," for example, Heaney adroitly moves his description of the animal toward its psychologically sophisticated conclusion:

How perilous is it to choose
not to love the life we're shown?
His sturdy dirty body
and interloping grovel.
The intelligence in his bone.
The unquestionable houseboy's shoulders
that could have been my own.

There is little that is naive about Heaney's treatment of nature, as the title of his first book, *Death of a Naturalist*, suggests, and his images of the natural world are frequently couched in the idiom of a distinctly modern and violent world. In "Trout" the fish is first a "fat gun-barrel," then it "darts like a tracer bullet"; in "Digging" the poet's pen rests between his finger and thumb, "snug as a gun"; in "In Small Townlands" the art of the painter to whom the poem is dedicated is described as making the spectrum burst, "a bright grenade, / When he unlocks the safety catch."

Heaney's bog poems retain this element of violence, though they use it in a more profound way. The bog (of which so much of Ireland is composed) is an ambiguous, potent symbol for Ireland as terrible Earth-mother, for racial memory, and the individual unconscious. The bogs of Northern Europe generally are a fearful storehouse of the past, and Heaney connects the victims of ritual murder found in the bogs of Denmark with the victims of political murder in modern Ireland. The tangle of emotions elicited by such powerful poems as "The Grauballe Man" mingles a sensuous appreciation of the artifact the victim has become, preserved and worked on over the centuries by the natural processes of the bog, with a painful sense of outrage and guilt. The Grauballe Man is "hung in the scales / With beauty and atrocity," the archaeological past of Northern Europe is connected with the present political reality of Northern Ireland and "with the actual weight / of each hooded victim, / slashed and dumped." By no means, though, do all of Heaney's poems involve violence in their depiction of the natural world. The painterly skill of his portrait of agricultural workers kneeling in the shelter of a hedge to cut seed potatoes suggests Breughel (whom he invokes in this poem), and his depiction of a countrywoman baking bread suggests the tranquillity and radiance of an interior by Vermeer:

> Now she dusts the board
> with a goose's wing,
> now sits, broad-lapped,
> with whitened nails
>
> and measling shins:
> here is a space
> again, the scone rising
> to the tick of two clocks.
>
> And here is love
> like a tinsmith's scoop
> sunk past its gleam
> in the meal-bin.

John Montague's concern with the natural world can manifest itself in such beautifully evocative portraits of the animistic Irish countryside as the neatly titled "Windharp"

> a hand ceaselessly
> combing and stroking
> the landscape, till
> the valley gleams
> like the pile upon
> a mountain pony's coat

though more often his sense of the natural world is of a landscape peopled with its inhabitants, of a rural society rather than a landscape.

3

Modern Irish poetry that deals with various aspects of personal experience—love, death, identity, and philosophic and religious experience—tends to be the most obviously modern in style, often showing the influence of Eliot, Pound, and their predecessors and successors on the Anglo-American and European scene. It is also the least obviously identifiable as Irish, and indeed, some writers, in reaction against the literary Revival, have very consciously rejected themes that are specifically Irish. It is probably this variety of Irish poetry that will seem most familiar to readers of modern English and American poetry.

Samuel Beckett, Thomas MacGreevy, Denis Devlin, and Brian Coffey constitute a lost generation of Irish poets who were self-exiled for a greater or lesser period of time from Ireland. They were conscious of themselves as the advance-guard (in the 1930s) of a new Irish poetic with a European identity, one that would administer the coup-de-grâce to the long-waning Revival movement. Writing of recent Irish poetry in 1934, Beckett categorically rejected the implicit assumption of the Revival writers and others that "the first condition of any poem is an accredited theme, and that in self-perception there is no theme." The Vertical Manifesto signed by Beckett and MacGreevy proclaimed "the hegemony of the inner life over the outer life." While it has not been necessary for later Irish poets (like Thomas Kinsella) to issue such manifestos, they have undoubtedly endorsed the assumption that it is in the inner life that the poet finds his theme. Though there is great diversity of style in their treatment of love, personal relationships, suffering, and death, what distinguishes all of the writers in this category is that they write about such themes not because they are "poetic" but because they are pressing aspects of the individual poet's intensely personal experience.

To deal first of all with the modernist poets mentioned above: Beckett's poems reveal the same savage, laconic, three-quarters despairing response to human misery one finds in his plays. In "Enueg I," the landscape of Dublin reflects his lover's fate (she seems

to be dying from tuberculosis) and his despair at the human
condition:

> . . . the stillborn evening turning a filthy green
> manuring the night fungus
> and the mind annulled
> wrecked in wind.

The title "Malacoda" refers to a demon in Dante's *Inferno*. Beckett
uses it, however, to refer to the undertaker at his father's funeral.
The last word and line of the poem—"nay"—starkly and uncompro-
misingly denies the efficacy of religious belief and, too, of the conso-
lations ritual proffers for the pain and grief of dying.

Thomas MacGreevy was a friend of Beckett and Joyce in the
Paris of the twenties and thirties, and also a longtime correspondent
of Wallace Stevens. Beckett praised his first book of imagistic
verse as possessing "a radiance without counterpart in the work of
contemporary poets writing in English." The images of icy landscape
in "De Civitate Hominum" and "Nocturne of the Self-Evident
Presence" suggest the metaphysical bereavement of MacGreevy's
world and the consequent indifference of nature to human existence.
The only color in the black and white ensemble of "De Civitate
Hominum" is the deathly, misleadingly beautiful "delicate flame, /
A stroke of orange in the morning's dress" of the aviator's plane
that has been shot down. The God invoked early in the poem
"makes no reply / Yet."

Brian Coffey was also a member of this group of Irish literary
expatriates who lived in Paris in the 1930s. He has translated Ver-
laine, Rimbaud, Mallarmé, Valery, Claudel, Apollinaire, Eluard, and
other French poets. His poetry is rather less abstract and cerebral
than that of the other European Irish writers, and interestingly,
despite his training as a philosopher, he shows an ironic sense of
the limitations of philosophical inquiry in the poem "Headrock."
The unusual shape of the poem (as well as the title) suggests
the headstone of a grave; the inscription is a series of unanswerable
questions ("What have you forgotten," "who are you, what are you,
when are you") whose absurdity is demonstrated with grim humor
by the shape of the poem and its conclusion—"NOESCAPE." More-
over, there is no living, the poem mockingly implies, if one neglects
the present in order to respond to a relentless series of insoluable
questions about the present and the future.

Yet Coffey's work is characterized by a certain philosophical bent, his attitude approximately described, perhaps, as Christian existentialism. His *Missouri Sequence* (1962), a long poem in four parts which derives from his sojourn in the United States, is a meditation on identity. The poem's theme is the coming and going of the exile, which is at once the defining, actual circumstance of the writer's life and also a metaphor for human existence, for birth and death: "Pain it was to come, / Pain it will be to go." The title of another late, long poem, *Advent,* suggests the poet's religious and philosophic preoccupation, his location of religious value in the experience of various kinds of preparation and anticipation. In Section V of this poem, man's voyage into space and his return to earth starts the poet speculating, comparing the brash assurance of technology's conquest of nature with the religious mystery of man's relation to the beautiful earth: "Earth could give one pause Earth strange / Like the stranger grown from one's child."

Denis Devlin's poetry of the thirties and forties looks startlingly sophisticated and difficult. Like the work of Beckett, MacGreevy, and Coffey, it often shows the influence of modern French poetry. Devlin's language is highly elliptical and his meaning emerges obliquely as he deals with the ambiguities of love and religious belief; yet his poetry as a whole is sensuous and profound. In the long religious poem "Lough Derg" (which has been compared with Crane's "The Broken Tower" and Stevens's "Sunday Morning"), the unquestioning faith of the pilgrims on retreat at St. Patrick's Purgatory is contrasted with the apprehension and uncertainty of the poet as Europe is engulfed by war: "With mullioned Europe shattered, this Northwest, / Rude-sainted isle would pray it whole again." "Ank'hor Vat" is a half-envious response to Eastern religion (so different from the penitential and Jansenist versions of Christianity that have influenced Irish Catholicism), to Buddha's smile which "holds in doubt / The wooden stare of Apollo / Our Christian crown of thorns." In "Wishes For Her" Devlin sounds the modernist note of lament for our spiritual desert, though with his own elegaic sympathy and melancholy, rather than with the typical modernist's air of chilling diagnosis. Devlin's inimitable imagery is one of his strongest points; in the suspended space and time of a suburban train station, in an ideal landscape briefly glimpsed before the train arrives, a cat watches a moth:

A white cat sacred dangerous within
Egyptian memories considers

Like a marksman a celluloid ball on a water-jet
A tigermoth's fatal rise and fall
On her rank breath.

[*"Daphne Stillorgan"*]

"Anteroom: Geneva" gives memorable expression to Devlin's experi-
ence of the ominous uncertainties of prewar Europe (he was a career
diplomat), the coming outrage surrealistically embodied in the
poem's last line: ". . . the private detective idly deflowered a rose."
The Heavenly Foreigner is a long poem in which the poet passionately
discusses human and divine love with a mysterious woman. The
imagery of the poem suggests, simultaneously, sacred and profane
love:

Last night on the gilded Bourbon bridge
The doom of Adam brought me down to earth
While the houses with their ruined freight
Filed down the soft, erotic river.

Devlin's characteristic "enwreathing language" (a phrase he uses in
"Renewal By Her Element") is still a feature of his style in *The
Heavenly Foreigner* (the revised version of the poem is dated 1959),
but over the course of his poetic career his involuted and dense style
had gradually moved toward a more simplified expression.

Thomas Kinsella, whose first notable poems were published in
the fifties, probably speaks more directly and authentically to the
modern alienated consciousness than any other Irish poet, evoking
as he does a powerful sense of psychological dismay and of the
various dark nights (and mornings) of the soul. In "A Mirror in
February" the poet, as he shaves, regards the pruned and lopped
trees outside his house and is austerely reminded of his own muta-
bility by the sight they present:

Below my window the wakening trees,
Hacked clean for better bearing, stand defaced
Suffering their brute necessities;
And how should the flesh not quail, that span for span
Is mutilated more?

Everywhere in his poetry there is evidence of, to paraphrase Donne, the subtle mind that loves to plague itself; but it would be a mistake to accuse Kinsella of self-indulgence in these repeated confrontations with his alienation, for there is too much evidence of pain and of courage at facing that pain. The psychological probing Kinsella is so adept at often finds its appropriate expression in surgical images, as in "Clarence Mangan" (the title is the name of a nineteenth-century Irish poet):

> Out of the shadows behind my laughter surgical fingers
> Come and I am strapped to a table.

> Ultimate, pitiless, again I ply the knife.

In a later poem, the disturbing, existential indifference of the universe (the language echoes Pascal) is alarmingly internalized by the self: in "Hen Woman" Kinsella refers to "the vast indifferent spaces / with which I am empty." Kinsella's anguish is qualified by a stoic determination to "Endure and let the present punish" ("Baggot Street Deserta"), and his morbidity by a saving, self-deprecatory irony—in the same poem he refers to his ennui as "educated boredom." The poet's Irishness is most explicit in poems like "Ritual of Departure" and "A Country Walk." The latter is a long contemplative work that connects the Irish countryside, history, and culture with his own role as poet in postrevolutionary Ireland. In this poem Kinsella deals with his "external" subject matter very appropriately and successfully, given the rather depressing nature of that subject matter, by assimilating it into his private anomie. Kinsella's imagery is at times emotionally draining, but its brooding sensuousness is an essential part of what makes him one of Ireland's most impressive and formidable poets.

We may find a salutary counterpart to alienation in the long tradition of love poetry in Irish literature. Frank O'Connor's translation of a medieval Irish poem by Murrough O'Daly gives us a sense of the passionate qualities of that tradition:

> And our first look was her first love;
>   No man had fondled ere I came
> The little breasts so small and firm
>   And the long body like a flame.

John Montague has written more poems on the subject of love than any of his contemporaries and has dealt most convincingly with the emotions of different kinds of loving. Montague's love poems are by turns elegant, joyful, and grave. They often attain a more than merely personal and lyric intensity from his habit of rendering love relationships with archetypal suggestiveness, as in "All Legendary Obstacles," and linking the fulfillment of love with that of the natural world, as in "Walking Late." Montague's frankness in treating the painful aspects of love, whether in individual poems such as "Special Delivery" (about an abortion), or in a whole collection (his most recent, *The Great Cloak*, details the breakdown of a marriage and the growth of a new relationship) is unparalleled in Irish poetry.

Other poets have also written memorably of love, marriage, and friendship. "Trilogy for X" provides us with a good example of the sophisticated, melancholy élan of MacNeice's erotic poems, which are usually neglected in favor of his more social and political verse: "And love hung still as crystal over the bed / And filled the corners of the enormous room." Michael Longley writes wittily and tenderly of love and marriage in his neo-metaphysical "Epithalamion" and in the less mannered "Desert Warfare." James Liddy rhapsodically and engagingly recommends love as the sovereign remedy to be employed against the deadening influence of middle-class life in Ireland and political repression, whether in Ireland or Spain—the sense of love here is that shared by the American counterculture of the 1960s. Eavan Boland's poems are notable in that they treat friendship (and love) with a particularly moving honesty and seriousness. In her most recent book, personal concerns are impressively and convincingly linked with the public issue of the terror, suffering, and death caused by Ireland's recurrent political violence. In such poems as "The War Horse" and "Child of Our Time," Boland's verbal exactness and admirable, restrained tone make the subject matter all the more affecting: "Child / Of our time, our times have robbed your cradle. / Sleep in a world your final sleep has woken."

There is, as well, a strain of poetry that is more or less consciously antiromantic, that portrays love and marriage as part of the quotidian reality of middle-class existence. The tone is restrained, wry, carefully eschewing any obscurities of thought or language, but subtle and pointed, as in Frank Ormsby's poem "Interim":

Six months of marriage sobered us. We found,
Not disenchantment, more a compromise
Charged with affection.

Anthony Cronin's "The Elephant to the Girl in Bertram Mills' Circus" strikes a comparable Larkinesque note of quiet disillusionment; its self-conscious and self-ironic lugubriousness, though, is touching and humorous at the same time. The imaginative qualities of this subdued and ironic mode should not be overlooked.

James Simmons is the most belligerent champion and chronicler of "liberated" middle-class existence—the joys and sorrows of love affairs, aging, working, drinking, and fighting are his characteristic subjects. All of Simmons's poems are permeated by a distinctly middle-class ambiance, though his sexual explicitness has (as indeed he intended) shocked many members of that social class in Ireland. Simmons often uses defiantly simple ballad-forms for his poems and is possessed of an engagingly unpoetic voice. There is something admirable about his attempt to celebrate what he feels is really life, as opposed to the deathliness and inauthenticity of life defined, as it so often is in Ireland, by abstract religious and political idealism.

Irish writers characteristically treat the subject of death with a vivid and compelling rendering of psychological and physical reality. Their portrayal of the depressive and obsessive experience of grief, coupled with the graphic and sensuous description of death, can be seen in poetry from the earliest times to the present. One can identify this note in as early a poem as "On the Death of His Wife," translated by Frank O'Connor,

> I parted from my life last night,
> A woman's body sunk in clay:
> The tender bosom that I loved
> Wrapped in a sheet they took away

but it is equally prevalent in the poetry of the modern period, from the work of Austin Clarke to that of Michael Hartnett. The tribal and ritualistic aspect of death, also a particularly Irish concern, is powerfully captured in Kinsella's "Death Bed":

> Motionless—his sons—
> we watched his brows draw together with strain.
> The wind tore at the leather walls of our tent;
> two grease lamps fluttered
> at the head and foot of the bed.

Other poems on death are especially moving because they are clearly grounded in the actual experience of specific, individual deaths: Clarke's "Martha Blake at Fifty-One"; Beckett's "Malacoda"; Kinsella's "Cover Her Face"; Iremonger's "This Houre Her Vigill"; Hartnett's "Death of an Irishwoman" and "For My Grandmother"; Maxton's "Waking"; and Carson's "Visiting the Dead." Hartnett's poems in particular are remarkable for their ability to convey the desolation of the deaths (and lives) of obscure country people.

Valentine Iremonger's "Hector" and "Icarus" put the violent, fated deaths of mythic heroes into a modern, Audenesque idiom. "Icarus" reflects the character of warfare in the twentieth century ("the airman, feeling the plane sweat"), and "Hector" humanizes the plight of the Trojan hero, making it that of any man who knows that the odds of time and death, personified here in Achilles, are insuperable:

> He slept well all night, having caressed
> Andromache like a flower, though in a dream he saw
> A body lying on the sands, huddled and bleeding,
> Near the feet a sword in bits and by the head
> An upturned, dented helmet.

Eiléan Ni Chuilleanáin has written poems that give a particularly brilliant and chilling sense of the preternatural stillness before and after violent death, as in "Site of Ambush" (which recreates an incident in the earlier Troubles).

The question of identity, of their Irishness, is predictably perplexing for a number of writers, particularly from the North. Louis MacNeice, John Hewitt, Michael Longley, Derek Mahon, and others treat this theme; the corollary theme of exile is also treated by these poets and others such as Desmond O'Grady, whose translation from the Irish of a nineteenth-century poem is engagingly melancholy and splenetic, and, for the Irish writer, perennial in its application:

> I shall leave this town as soon as I can
> for sharp is the stone here, deep the dung;
> there's nothing of value here for a man
> but the heavy word from everyone's tongue.
>
> ["If I Went Away"]

In more complex poems by O'Grady, Ireland and the past are not so much rejected as assimilated and transformed into a new synthesis of past and present, old and new, of Ireland and America, for example, in "Professor Kelleher and the Charles River." This sort of blending is very much in keeping with O'Grady's internationalism. His work is influenced by Pound (who was a personal friend) and he translates poetry from several languages in addition to the Irish.

O'Grady is one of a number of modern Irish writers whose work includes a substantial amount of translation and imitation of poetry in the Irish language. Clarke, O'Connor, Kinsella, Montague, MacIntyre, Hutchinson, Hartnett, Boland, Young and Carson are the most notable in this regard. Hutchinson and Hartnett also write poetry in Irish. Hartnett's "The Retreat of Ita Cagney" was published in a bilingual text. Moreover, if he means what he says in his "A Farewell to English," Hartnett intends to write henceforth primarily in Irish. A small number of Irish poets write only in Irish, but while the Irish linguistic and literary tradition is part of what gives much Irish poetry in English its distinctive qualities, particularly its characteristic music (and this may be as true of Yeats's metrics as of those of more contemporary poets), from the standpoint of an international English-speaking audience the importance of that tradition is one of influence only. If an Irish writer aspires to address the overwhelming majority of his own people, let alone a comparable audience to the ones Yeats and Joyce wrote for, he must surely write in English.

There is an interesting tradition of private presses in modern Ireland. The Cuala Press, founded and managed by Yeats's sisters, was guided by the preferences of the poet, and so its publications tended to perpetuate the ethos of the literary Revival. After his death the press published (in the 1940s) work by several of the older generation of poets included in this anthology—Patrick Kavanagh, Donagh MacDonagh, and Louis MacNeice. It was the Dolmen Press, founded in the early 1950s by Liam Miller, which was to provide Irish poets with an outlet for publication; from that time to the present the press has been committed to the publication of contemporary Irish poetry, indeed is almost synonymous with it. Though later arrivals on the scene, and smaller operations than Dolmen, Michael Smith's New Writers' Press, Peter Fallon's Gallery Books, The Goldsmith Press, and other small private presses have done much to help poetry flourish in contemporary Ireland. New Writers' Press has also published the work of those neglected Irish poets of an earlier generation, Brian Coffey and Thomas

MacGreevy. In the North, the Blackstaff and Ulsterman presses have opened up publishing possibilities for younger writers. On both sides of the border, literary magazines and journals flourish; perhaps the most noteworthy and influential at the present is *The Honest Ulsterman.*

But if Irish poets have been fortunate in the likelihood of being published in Ireland, much more so than novelists or dramatists, their work has generally not been easily accessible outside Ireland. In providing a comprehensive and representative selection from the work of a large number of contemporary poets, as well as a checklist of major published work, I have aimed to introduce the poets, as individual writers, to a larger reading audience than most of them have so far enjoyed, and to stimulate critical interest in the whole enterprise of modern Irish poetry. The reader, hopefully, will find the individual poems in this anthology to be emotionally and intellectually rewarding, and of significant interest collectively because they articulate imaginatively a complex consciousness of what it means to be Irish in the modern world.

THE POETRY

THOMAS MacGREEVY

Thomas MacGreevy was born in 1893 in County Kerry. He took degrees at University College, Dublin, and at Trinity College. He was an officer in the British Army during World War I, and was twice wounded at the Battle of the Somme. In 1925 MacGreevy went to London where he worked as a Lecturer at the National Gallery. He moved to Paris in 1927 and held a position as Lecteur at the Ecole Normale Superieure for seven years. During these years he was closely associated with the Irish expatriate writers living in Paris, especially Beckett and Joyce. His poetry and criticism appeared in many journals; critical studies of T. S. Eliot and Richard Aldington were published in 1931 and **Poems** in 1934. MacGreevy returned to London in 1935 when he was reappointed to his position at the National Gallery. In the early 1940s he moved back to Dublin where he established himself as an art critic, and in 1950 he was appointed Director of the National Gallery in Dublin, a position he held until his retirement in 1963. Mac-Greevy died in 1967. **Collected Poems** appeared in 1971.

DE CIVITATE HOMINUM

To A. S. F. R.

The morning sky glitters
Winter blue.
The earth is snow-white,
With the gleam snow-white answers to sunlight,
Save where shell-holes are new,
Black spots in the whiteness—

A Matisse ensemble.

The shadows of whitened tree stumps
Are another white.

And there are white bones.

Zillebeke Lake and Hooge,
Ice gray, gleam differently,

Like the silver shoes of the model.

The model is our world,
Our bitch of a world.
Those who live between wars may not know
But we who die between peaces
Whether we die or not.

It is very cold
And, what with my sensations
And my spick and span subaltern's uniform,
I might be the famous brass monkey,
The *nature morte* accessory.

Morte . . . !
'Tis still life that lives,
Not quick life—

There are fleece-white flowers of death
That unfold themselves prettily
About an airman

Who, high over Gheluvelt,
Is taking a morning look round,
All silk and silver
Up in the blue.

I hear the drone of an engine
And soft pounding puffs in the air
As the fleece-white flowers unfold.

I cannot tell which flower he has accepted
But suddenly there is a tremor,
A zigzag of lines against the blue
And he streams down
Into the white,
A delicate flame,
A stroke of orange in the morning's dress.

My sergeant says, very low, "Holy God!
'Tis a fearful death."

Holy God makes no reply
Yet.

AODH RUADH O'DOMHNAILL

To Stiefán MacEnna

Juan de Juni the priest said,
Each J becoming H;

Berruguete, he said,
And the G was aspirate;

Ximenez, he said then
And aspirated first and last.

But he never said
And—it seemed odd—he
Never had heard
The aspirated name
Of the centuries-dead
Bright-haired young man
Whose grave I sought.

All day I passed
In greatly built gloom
From dusty gilt tomb
Marvellously wrought
To tomb
Rubbing
At mouldy inscriptions
With fingers wetted with spit
And asking
Where I might find it
And failing.

Yet when
Unhurried—
    Not as at home
    Where heroes, hanged, are buried
    With non-commissioned officers' bored maledictions
    Quickly in the gaol yard—

They brought
His blackening body
Here
To rest
Princes came
Walking
Behind it

And all Valladolid knew
And out to Simancas all knew
Where they buried Red Hugh.

RECESSIONAL

In the bright broad Swiss glare I stand listening
To the outrageous roars
Of the Engelbergeraa
As it swirls down the gorge
And I think I am thinking
Of Roderick Hudson.
But, as I stand,
Time closes over sight,
And sound
Is drowned
By a long silvery roar
From the far ends of memory
Of a world I have left
And I find I am thinking:
Supposing I drowned now,
This tired, tiresome body,
Before flesh creases further,
Might, recovered, go, fair,
To be laid in Saint Lachtin's,
Near where once,
In tender, less glaring, island days
And ways
I could hear—
Where listeners still hear—
That far-away, dear
Roar
The long, silvery roar
Of Mal Bay.

HOMAGE TO MARCEL PROUST

To Jean Thomas

The sea gleamed deep blue in the sunlight
Through the different greens of the trees.
And the talk was of singing.
My mother, dressed in black, recalled a bright image from
    a song,
Those endearing young charms,
Miss Holly, wearing heliotrope, had a sad line,
The waves still are singing to the shore.
Then, as we came out from the edge of the wood,
The island lay dreaming in the sun across the bridge,
Even the white coastguard station had gone quietly to
    sleep—it was Sunday,
A chain on a ship at the pier
Rattled to silence,
Cries of children, playing, sounded faintly
And, musically, somewhere,
A young sailor of the island—

    He was tall
    And slim
    And curled, to the moustaches,
    And he wore ear-rings
    But often he was too ill to be at sea—

Was singing,
Maid of Athens, ere we part . . .

Looking suddenly like a goddess
Miss Holly said, half-smiling,
"Listen . . ."
And we stopped
In the sunlight
Listening . . .

The young sailor is dead now.
Miss Holly also is dead.
And Byron . . .
Home they've gone and

And the waves still are singing.

NOCTURNE OF THE SELF-EVIDENT PRESENCE

Fortunate,
Being inarticulate,
The alps
Rise
In ice
To heights
Of large stars
And little;
To courts
Beneath other courts
With walls of white starlight.
They have stars for pavements,
The valley is an area,
And I a servant,
A servant of servants,
Of metaphysical bereavements,
Staring up
Out of the gloom.

I see no immaculate feet on those pavements,
No winged forms,
Foreshortened,
As by Rubens or Domenichino,
Plashing the silvery air,
Hear no cars,

Elijah's or Apollo's,
Dashing about
Up there.
I see alps, ice, stars and white starlight
In a dry, high silence.

AUSTIN CLARKE

Austin Clarke was born in 1896 in Dublin. He was educated in Dublin at Belvedere College and University College, where he received his M.A. and was lecturer in English from 1918 to 1922. Clarke was a founding member of the Irish Academy of Letters and served as president from 1952 to 1954. He was married and had three children. During the course of a highly prolific writing career, Clarke produced numerous volumes of poetry, plays, novels, and criticism. His published collections of poetry include **The Vengeance of Fionn** (1917), **The Fires of Baal** (1921), **The Sword of the West** (1921), **The Cattledrive in Connaught and Other Poems** (1925), **Pilgrimage and Other Poems** (1929), **The Collected Poems of Austin Clarke** (1936), **Night and Morning** (1938), **Ancient Lights** (1955), **Too Great a Vine: Poems and Satires** (1957), **The Horse Eaters: Poems and Satires** (1960), **Collected Later Poems** (1961), **Forget-Me-Not** (1962), **Flight to Africa and Other Poems** (1963), **Mnemosyne Lay in Dust** (1966), **Old Fashioned Pilgrimage and Other Poems** (1967), **The Echo at Coole and Other Poems** (1967), **A Sermon on Swift and Other Poems** (1968), **Orphide** (1970), **Tiresias: A Poem** (1971), **The Wooing of Becfola** (after the Irish, 1973). Clarke died in 1974.

THE PLANTER'S DAUGHTER

When night stirred at sea
And the fire brought a crowd in,
They say that her beauty
Was music in mouth
And few in the candlelight
Thought her too proud,
For the house of the planter
Is known by the trees.

Men that had seen her
Drank deep and were silent,
The women were speaking
Wherever she went—
As a bell that is rung
Or a wonder told shyly,
And O she was the Sunday
In every week.

PILGRIMAGE

When the far south glittered
Behind the grey beaded plains,
And cloudier ships were bitted
Along the pale waves,
The showery breeze—that plies
A mile from Ara—stood
And took our boat on sand:
There by dim wells the women tied
A wish on thorn, while rainfall
Was quiet as the turning of books
In the holy schools at dawn.

Grey holdings of rain
Had grown less with the fields,
As we came to that blessed place
Where hail and honey meet.
O Clonmacnoise was crossed
With light: those cloistered scholars,
Whose knowledge of the gospel
Is cast as metal in pure voices,
Were all rejoicing daily,
And cunning hands with cold and jewels
Brought chalices to flame.

Loud above the grassland,
In Cashel of the towers,
We heard with the yellow candles
The chanting of the hours,
White clergy saying High Mass,
A fasting crowd at prayer,
A choir that sang before them;
And in stained glass the holy day
Was sainted as we passed
Beyond that chancel where the dragons
Are carved upon the arch.

Treasured with chasuble,
Sun-braided, rich cloak'd wine-cup,
We saw, there, iron handbells,
Great annals in the shrine
A high-king bore to battle:
Where, from the branch of Adam,
The noble forms of language—
Brighter than green or blue enamels
Burned in white bronze—embodied
The wings and fiery animals
Which veil the chair of God.

Beyond a rocky townland
And that last tower where ocean
Is dim as haze, a sound
Of wild confession rose:
Black congregations moved
Around the booths of prayer
To hear a saint reprove them;
And from his boat he raised a blessing
To souls that had come down
The holy mountain of the west
Or wailed still in the cloud.

Light in the tide of Shannon
May ride at anchor half
The day and, high in spar-top
Or leather sails of their craft,
Wine merchants will have sleep;
But on a barren isle,
Where Paradise is praised
At daycome, smaller than the sea-gulls,
We heard white Culdees pray
Until our hollow ship was kneeling
Over the longer waves.

NIGHT AND MORNING

I know the injured pride of sleep,
The strippers at the mocking-post,
The insult in the house of Caesar
And every moment that can hold
In brief the miserable act
Of centuries. Thought can but share
Belief—and the tormented soul,
Changing confession to despair,
Must wear a borrowed robe.

Morning has moved the dreadful candle,
Appointed shadows cross the nave;
Unlocked by the secular hand,
The very elements remain
Appearances upon the altar.
Adoring priest has turned his back
Of gold upon the congregation.
All saints have had their day at last,
But thought still lives in pain.

How many councils and decrees
Have perished in the simple prayer
That gave obedience to the knee;
Trampling of rostrum, feathering
Of pens at cock-rise, sum of reason
To elevate a common soul:
Forgotten as the minds that bled
For us, the miracle that raised
A language from the dead.

O when all Europe was astir
With echo of learned controversy,
The voice of logic led the choir.
Such quality was in all being,
The forks of heaven and this earth
Had met, town-walled, in mortal view
And in the pride that we ignore,
The holy rage of argument,
God was made man once more.

TENEBRAE

This is the hour that we must mourn
With tallows on the black triangle,
Night has a napkin deep in fold
To keep the cup; yet who dare pray
If all in reason should be lost,
The agony of man betrayed
At every station of the cross?

O when the forehead is too young,
Those centuries of mortal anguish,
Dabbed by a consecrated thumb
That crumbles into dust, will bring
Despair with all that we can know;
And there is nothing left to sing,
Remembering our innocence.

I hammer on that common door,
Too frantic in my superstition,
Transfix with nails that I have broken,
The angry notice of the mind.
Close as the thought that suffers him,
The habit every man in time
Must wear beneath his ironed shirt.

An open mind disturbs the soul,
And in disdain I turn my back
Upon the sun that makes a show
Of half the world, yet still deny
The pain that lives within the past,
The flame sinking upon the spike,
Darkness that man must dread at last.

THE STRAYING STUDENT

On a holy day when sails were blowing southward
A bishop sang the Mass at Inishmore,
Men took one side, their wives were on the other
But I heard the woman coming from the shore:
And wild in despair my parents cried aloud
For they saw the vision draw me to the doorway.

Long had she lived in Rome when Popes were bad,
The wealth of every age she makes her own,
Yet smiled on me in eager admiration
And for a summer taught me all I know,
Banishing shame with her great laugh that rang
As if a pillar caught it back alone.

I learned the prouder counsel of her throat,
My mind was growing bold as light in Greece;
And when in sleep her stirring limbs were shown,
I blessed the noonday rock that knew no tree:
And for an hour the mountain was her throne,
Although her eyes were bright with mockery.

They say I was sent back from Salamanca
And failed in logic, but I wrote her praise
Nine times upon a college wall in France.
She laid her hand at darkfall on my page
That I might read the heavens in a glance
And I knew every star the Moors had named.

Awake or in my sleep, I have no peace now,
Before the ball is struck, my breath is gone,
And yet I tremble lest she may deceive me
And leave me in this land where every woman's son
Must carry his own coffin and believe,
In dread, all that the clergy teach the young.

THE ENVY OF POOR LOVERS

Pity poor lovers who may not do what they please
With their kisses under a hedge, before a raindrop
Unhouses it; and astir from wretched centuries,
Bramble and briar remind them of the saints.

Her envy is the curtain seen at night-time,
Happy position that could change her name.
His envy—clasp of the married whose thoughts can be
    alike,
Whose nature flows without the blame or shame.

Lying in the grass as if it were a sin
To move, they hold each other's breath, tremble,
Ready to share that ancient dread—kisses begin
Again—of Ireland keeping company with them.

Think, children, of institutions mured above
Your ignorance, where every look is veiled,
State-paid to snatch away the folly of poor lovers
For whom, it seems, the sacraments have failed.

THREE POEMS ABOUT CHILDREN

I

Better the book against the rock,
The misery of roofless faith,
Than all this mockery of time,
Eternalising of mute souls.
Though offerings increase, increase,
The ancient arms can bring no peace,
When the first breath is unforgiven

And charity, to find a home,
Redeems the baby from the breast.
O, then, at the very font of grace,
Pity, pity—the dumb must cry.
Their tiny tears are in the walls
We build. They turn to dust so soon,
How can we learn upon our knees,
That ironside unropes the bell?

II

These infants die too quick
For our salvation, caught up
By a fatal sign from Limbo,
Unfathered in our thought
Before they can share the sky
With us. Though faith allow
Obscurity of being
And clay rejoice: flowers
That wither in the heat
Of benediction, one
By one, are thrown away.

III

Martyr and heretic
Have been the shrieking wick!
But smoke of faith on fire
Can hide us from enquiry
And trust in Providence
Rid us of vain expense.
So why should pity uncage
A burning orphanage
Bar flight to little souls
That set no churchbell tolling?

Cast-iron step and rail
Could but prolong the wailing:
Has not a Bishop declared
That flame-wrapped babes are spared
Our life-time of temptation?
Leap, mind, in consolation
For heart can only lodge
Itself, plucked out by logic.
Those children, charred in Cavan,
Passed straight through Hell to Heaven.

THE LAST REPUBLICANS

Because their fathers had been drilled,
Formed fours among the Dublin hills,
They marched together, countermarched
Along the Liffey valley, by larch-wood,
Spruce, pine road. Now, what living shout
Can halt them? Nothing of their faces
Is left, the breath has been blown out
Of them into far lonely places.
Seán Glynn pined sadly in prison. Seán
McNeela, Tony Darcy, John
McGaughey died on hunger-strike,
Wasting in the ribbed light of dawn.
They'd been on the run, but every dyke
Was spy. We shame them all. George Plant,
Quick fighter and a Protestant,
Patrick McGrath and Richard Goss,
Maurice O'Neill with Thomas Harte
Were executed when Dev's party
Had won the county pitch-and-toss,
Pat Dermody, John Kavanagh
John Griffith, John Casey, black-and-tanned.
At Mountjoy Gaol, young Charlie Kerins

Was roped; we paid five pounds to Pierpont,
The Special Branch castled their plans,
Quicklimed the last Republicans.

from MNEMOSYNE LAY IN DUST

One night he heard heart-breaking sound.
It was a sigh unworlding its sorrow.
Another followed. Slowly he counted
Four different sighs, one after another.
"My mother," he anguished, "and my sisters
Have passed away. I am alone, now,
Lost in myself in a mysterious
Darkness, the victim in a story."
Far whistle of a train, the voice of steam.
Evil was peering through the peep-hole.

Suddenly heart began to beat
Too quickly, too loudly. It clamoured
As if it were stopping. He left the heat
And stumbled forward, hammered
The door, called out that he was dying.
Key turned. Body was picked up, carried
Beyond the ward, the bedwhite row
Of faces, into a private darkness.
Lock turned. He cried out. All was still.
He stood, limbs shivering in the chill.

He tumbled into half the truth:
Burial alive. His breath was shouting:
"Let, let me out." But words were puny.
Fists hushed on a wall of inward-outness.
Knees crept along a floor that stirred
As softly. All was the same chill.
He knew the wall was circular

And air was catchcry in the stillness
For reason had returned to tell him
That he was in a padded cell.

The key had turned again. Blankets
Were flung into blackness as if to mock
The cringer on the floor. He wrapped
The bedclothes around his limbs, shocked back
To sanity. Lo! in memory yet,
Margaret came in a frail night-dress,
Feet bare, her heavy plaits let down
Between her knees, his pale protectress.
Nightly restraint, unwanted semen
Had ended their romantic dream.

Early next morning, he awakened,
Saw only greyness shining down
From a skylight on the grey walls
Of leather, knew, in anguish, his bowels
Had opened. He turned, shivering, all shent.
Wrapping himself in the filthied blankets,
Fearful of dire punishment,
He waited there until a blankness
Enveloped him . . . When he raised his head up,
Noon-light was gentle in the bedroom.

INSCRIPTION FOR A HEADSTONE

What Larkin bawled to hungry crowds
Is murmured now in dining-hall
And study. Faith bestirs itself
Lest infidels in their impatience
Leave it behind. Who could have guessed
Batons were blessings in disguise,

When every ambulance was filled
With half-killed men and Sunday trampled
Upon unrest? Such fear can harden
Or soften heart, knowing too clearly
His name endures on our holiest page,
Scrawled in a rage by Dublin's poor.

MABLE KELLY

   Lucky the husband
Who puts his hand beneath her head.
   They kiss without scandal
Happiest two near feather-bed.
He sees the tumble of brown hair
Unplait, the breasts, pointed and bare
   When nightdress shows
   From dimple to toe-nail,
All Mable glowing in it, here, there, everywhere.

   Music might listen
   To her least whisper,
Learn every note, for all are true.
   While she is speaking,
   Her voice goes sweetly
To charm the herons in their musing.
Her eyes are modest, blue, their darkness
Small rooms of thought, but when they sparkle
   Upon a feast-day,
   Glasses are meeting,
Each raised to Mabel Kelly, our toast and darling.

Gone now are many Irish ladies
Who kissed and fondled, their very pet-names
Forgotten, their tibia degraded.
She takes their sky. Her smile is famed.

Her praise is scored by quill and pencil.
    Harp and spinet
    Are in her debt
And when she plays or sings, melody is content.

    No man who sees her
    Will feel uneasy.
He goes his way, head high, however tired.
    Lamp loses light
    When placed beside her.
She is the pearl and being of all Ireland
Foot, hand, eye, mouth, breast, thigh and instep, all that
    we desire.
Tresses that pass small curls as if to touch the ground;
    So many prizes
    Are not divided.
Her beauty is her own and she is not proud.

(translation from the Irish)

GRACEY NUGENT

I drink, wherever I go, to the charms
Of Gracey Nugent in whose white arms
I dare not look for more. Enraptured
By a kiss or two, a little slap,
    Her virtue cannot harm me.

Delightful to share her company
Even with others. While she is speaking,
Music goes by and what she smiles at,
Would bring the swan back to the tide.
    Was ever plight so pleasing?

Her graceful walk, her pearly neck-lace,
And bosom so near, have made me reckless.
I want to sit, clasping her waist,
Upon her boudoir sofa, waste
    Hope. Days are only seconds.

Happy the young fellow, who wins
And can enjoy her without sinning.
Close in the darkness, they will rest
Together and when her fears are less,
    She'll take his meaning in

And know at last why he is seeking
Shoulder and breast, her shapely cheeks,
All that I must not try to sing of.
The modest may not point a finger
    Or mention what is best.

And so I raise my glass, content
To drink a health to Gracey Nugent,
Her absence circles around the table.
Empty the rummer while you are able,
    Two Sundays before Lent.

(translation from the Irish)

MARTHA BLAKE AT FIFTY-ONE

Early, each morning, Martha Blake
    Walked, angeling the road,
To Mass in the Church of the Three Patrons.
    Sanctuary lamp glowed
And the clerk halo'ed the candles
    On the High Altar. She knelt
Illumined. In gold-hemmed alb,
    The priest intoned. Wax melted.

Waiting for daily Communion, bowed head
    At rail, she hears a murmur.
Latin is near. In a sweet cloud
    That cherub'd, all occurred.
The voice went by. To her pure thought,
    Body was a distress
And soul, a sigh. Behind her denture,
Love lay, a helplessness.

Then, slowly walking after Mass
    Down Rathgar Road, she took out
Her Yale key, put a match to gas-ring,
    Half filled a saucepan, cooked
A fresh egg lightly, with tea, brown bread,
    Soon, taking off her blouse
And skirt, she rested, pressing the Crown
    Of Thorns until she drowsed.

In her black hat, stockings, she passed
    Nylons to a nearby shop
And purchased, daily, with downcast eyes,
    Fillet of steak or a chop.
She simmered it on a low jet,
    Having a poor appetite,
Yet never for an hour felt better
    From dilatation, tightness.

She suffered from dropped stomach, heartburn
    Scalding, water-brash
And when she brought her wind up, turning
    Red with the weight of mashed
Potato, mint could not relieve her.
    In vain her many belches,
For all below was swelling, heaving
    Wamble, gurgle, squelch.

She lay on the sofa with legs up.
  A decade on her lip,
At four o'clock, taking a cup
  Of lukewarm water, sip
By sip, but still her daily food
  Repeated and the bile
Tormented her. In a blue hood,
  The Virgin sadly smiled.

When she looked up, the Saviour showed
  His Heart, daggered with flame
And, from the mantle-shelf, St. Joseph
  Bent, disapproving. Vainly
She prayed, for in the whatnot corner,
  The new Pope was frowning. Night
And day, dull pain, as in her corns,
  Recounted every bite.

She thought of St. Teresa, floating
  On motes of a sunbeam,
Carmelite with scatterful robes,
  Surrounded by demons,
Small black boys in their skin. She gaped
  At Hell: a muddy passage
That led to nothing, queer in shape,
  A cupboard closely fastened.

Sometimes, the walls of the parlour
  Would fade away. No plod
Of feet, rattle of van, in Garville
  Road. Soul now gone abroad
Where saints, like medieval serfs,
  Had laboured. Great sun-flower shone.
Our Lady's Chapel was borne by seraphs,
  Three leagues beyond Ancona.

High towns of Italy, the plain
    Of France, were known to Martha
As she read in a holy book. The sky-blaze
    Nooned at Padua,
Marble grotto of Bernadette.
    Rose-scatterers. New saints
In tropical Africa where the tsetse
    Fly probes, the forest taints.

Teresa had heard the Lutherans
    Howling on red-hot spit,
And grill, men who had searched for truth
    Alone in Holy Writ.
So Martha, fearful of flame lashing
    Those heretics, each instant,
Never dealt in the haberdashery
    Shop, owned by two Protestants.

In ambush of night, an angel wounded
    The Spaniard to the heart
With iron tip on fire. Swooning
    With pain and bliss as a dart
Moved up and down within her bowels
    Quicker, quicker, each cell
Sweating as if rubbed up with towels,
    Her spirit rose and fell.

St. John of the Cross, her friend, in prison
    Awaits the bridal night,
Paler than lilies, his wizened skin
    Flowers. In fifths of flight,
Senses beyond seraphic thought,
    In that divinest clasp,
Enfolding of kisses that cauterize,
    Yield to the soul-spasm.

Cunning in body had come to hate
    All this and stirred by mischief
Haled Martha from heaven. Heart palpitates
    And terror in her stiffens.
Heart misses one beat, two . . flutters . . stops.
    Her ears are full of sound.
Half fainting, she stares at the grandfather clock
    As if it were overwound.

The fit had come. Ill-natured flesh
    Despised her soul. No bending
Could ease rib. Around her heart, pressure
    Of wind grew worse. Again,
Again, armchaired without relief,
    She eructated, phelgm
In mouth, forgot the woe, the grief,
    Foretold at Bethlehem.

Tired of the same faces, side-altars,
    She went to the Carmelite Church
At Johnson's Court, confessed her faults,
    There, once a week, purchased
Tea, butter in Chatham St. The pond
    In St. Stephen's Green was grand.
She watched the seagulls, ducks, black swan,
    Went home by the 15 tram.

Her beads in hand, Martha became
    A member of the Third Order,
Saved from long purgatorial pain,
    Brown habit and white cord
Her own when cerges had been lit
    Around her coffin. She got
Ninety-five pounds on loan for her bit
    Of clay in the common plot.

Often she thought of a quiet sick-ward,
    Nuns, with delicious ways,
Consoling the miserable: quick
    Tea, toast on trays. Wishing
To rid themselves of her, kind neighbours
    Sent for the ambulance,
Before her brother and sister could hurry
    To help her. Big gate clanged.

No medical examination
    For the new patient. Doctor
Had gone to Cork on holidays.
    Telephone sprang. Hall-clock
Proclaimed the quarters. Clatter of heels
    On tiles. Corridor, ward,
A-whirr with the electric cleaner,
    The creak of window cord.

She could not sleep at night. Feeble
    And old, two women raved
And cried to God. She held her beads.
    O how could she be saved?
The hospital had this and that rule.
    Day-chill unshuttered. Nun, with
Thermometer in reticule,
    Went by. The women mumbled.

Mother Superior believed
    That she was obstinate, self-willed.
Sisters ignored her, hands-in-sleeves,
    Beside a pantry shelf
Or counting pillow-case, soiled sheet.
    They gave her purgatives.
Soul-less, she tottered to the toilet.
    Only her body lived.

Wasted by colitis, refused
    The daily sacrament
By regulation, forbidden use
    Of bed-pan, when meals were sent up,
Behind a screen, she lay, shivering,
    Unable to eat. The soup
Was greasy, mutton, beef or liver,
    Cold. Kitchen has no scruples.

The Nuns had let the field in front
    As an Amusement Park,
Merry-go-round, a noisy month, all
    Heltering-skeltering at darkfall,
Mechanical music, dipper, hold-tights,
    Rifle-crack, crash of dodgems.
The ward, godless with shadow, lights,
    How could she pray to God?

Unpitied, wasting with diarrhea
    And the constant strain,
Poor Child of Mary with one idea,
    She ruptured a small vein,
Bled inwardly to jazz. No priest
    Came. She had been anointed
Two days before, yet knew no peace:
    Her last breath, disappointed.

DIRGE

He lies in state,
Though his robust
Soul left in a state
Of disarray
Scarlet robe, hat,
Humility raised.

Too late he had flown
The pyx from ice-floe
To jungle war, in
His seventy-ninth year
And dreaming of napalm,
(Dermatic warning),
Met in that nap
Saturnine
Spirits from Hell. Eyed
With helicopters,
He called for more raids
On occupied villages
When troops paraded
Before his lifted
Blessing. The lift
Fires down on devilish
Forests where monkey-
Folk whimper, herds of
Mad elephants
Blow up. He heard,
Far off, phantoms
Of Buddhist monks,
Still burning, sigh: "Gone!"
As he left Saigon.
Consoled by the Gospel, man
Fears no foe
Who turns to foliage.
Lauded by Church, State,
Cardinal Spellman
Lies in state.

from TIRESIAS

My mother wept loudly,
Crying, "Forgive me, Tiresias, the fault is
Mine alone for when I carried you in my womb, I
Prayed at the local temple that Our Lady Lucina
Might bestow on me a daughter." Tear-in-smile, she
    hugged me,
Kissing my lips and breasts, stood back with little starts of
Admiration, hugged me again, spread out our late supper:
Cake, sweet resin'd wine, put me to bed, whispered:
"Twenty-five years ago, I chose the name of Pyrrha
For you. Now I can use it at last." She tucked me in,
    murmured
"Pyrrha, my latecome Pyrrha, sleep better than I shall."
                                Next morning
Gaily she said:
                "I must instruct you in domestic
Economy, show you, dear daughter, how to make your
    own bed, lay
Table, wash up, tidy the house, cook every sort of
Meal, sew, darn, mend, do your hair, then find a well-off
Husband for you. As a young man you have spent too
    many
Hours in the study of history and science, never
    frequented
Dance-hall, bull-ring, hurried, I fear, too often to the
    stews."
Laughter-in-sigh, she handed me a duster.
                                One fine day
During siesta I gazed in reverence at my naked
Body, slim as a nespoli tree, dared to place my shaving
Mirror of polished silver—a birthday gift from my
    mother—
Between my legs, inspected this way and that the fleshy
Folds guarding the shortcut, red as my real lips, to Pleasure

Pass. Next day I awoke in alarm, felt a trickle of blood
    half-
Way down my thigh.
        "Mother," I sobbed,
                "Our bold Penates
Pricked me during sleep."
        "Let me look at it, Pyrrha."
                   She laughed,
    then
Said:
    "Why it's nothing to worry about, my pet, all women
Suffer this shame every month."
        "What does it mean?"
                "That you are
Ready for nuptial bliss."
        And saying this, she cleansed, bandaged,
Bound my flowers.
        When I recovered, a burning sensation
Stayed. Restless at night, lying on my belly, I longed for
Mortal or centaur to surprise me.

FRANK O'CONNOR

Frank O'Connor (the pseudonym of Michael Francis O'Donovan) was born in 1903 in Cork. He attended St. Patrick's National School where he was a pupil of the writer and critic Daniel Corkery. He left school at the age of fourteen, and shortly afterward joined the First Brigade of the Irish Republican Army; he later fought on the Republican side in the civil war, and was imprisoned in Gormanstown Internment Camp. After he was released in 1924, he became a teacher of Irish in rural schools, and then a librarian in Sligo, Wicklow, Cork, and Dublin. In 1935 he was appointed to the Board of Directors of the Abbey Theatre, and two years later was made Managing Director.

O'Connor wrote two novels, and numerous works of nonfiction, but his short stories—there are many collections—are what made him famous. O'Connor is also highly regarded as a translator of Irish poetry. His translations from the Irish include **The Wild Bird's Nest** (1932), **Lords and Commons** (1938), **The Fountain of Magic** (1939), **A Lament for Art O'Leary** (1940), **The Midnight Court, A Rhythmical Bacchanalia from the Irish of Bryan Merriman** (1946), **Kings, Lords & Commons** (1959), and **The Little Monasteries** (1963). He published one collection of his own poetry, **Three Old Brothers** (1936). In the 1950s O'Connor lectured at Harvard and the University of Chicago. He died in 1966.

THE END OF CLONMACNOIS

"Whence are you, learning's son?"
"From Clonmacnois I come.
My course of studies done,
    I'm off to Swords again."
"How are things keeping there?"
"Oh, things are shaping fair—
Foxes round churchyards bare
    Gnawing the guts of men."

(translation from the Irish)

HOPE

Life has conquered, the wind has blown away
Alexander, Caesar and all their power and sway;
Tara and Troy have made no longer stay—
Maybe the English too will have their day.

(translation from the Irish)

THE ANGRY POET

(Clonmacnois / c. 1100)

The hound
    Could never be called refined,
So push the tip of his nose
    Up the Master's behind.

The Master,
    May amend his scholarly air
If you screw the tip of his nose
    Up in the lackey's rear.

The lackey
    Will have the chance of his life
If you stuff his nose in turn
    In the tail of the Master's wife.

The wife—
    —Who is always sniffing around—
May sniff for the rest of her days
    Her nose in the tail of the hound.

(translation from the Irish)

ON THE DEATH OF HIS WIFE

I parted from my life last night,
    A woman's body sunk in clay:
The tender bosom that I loved
    Wrapped in a sheet they took away.

The heavy blossom that had lit
    The ancient boughs is tossed and blown;
Hers was the burden of delight
    That long had weighed the old tree down.

And I am left alone tonight
    And desolate is the world I see
For lovely was that woman's weight
    That even last night had lain on me.

Weeping I look upon the place
    Where she used to rest her head—
For yesterday her body's length
    Reposed upon you too, my bed.

Yesterday that smiling face
    Upon one side of you was laid
That could match the hazel bloom
    In its dark delicate sweet shade.

Maelva of the shadowy brows
    Was the mead-cask at my side;
Fairest of all flowers that grow
    Was the beauty that has died.

My body's self deserts me now,
    The half of me that was her own,
Since all I knew of brightness died
    Half of me lingers, half is gone.

The face that was like hawthorn bloom
    Was my right foot and my right side;
And my right hand and my right eye
    Were no more mine than hers who died.

Poor is the share of me that's left
    Since half of me died with my wife;
I shudder at the words I speak;
    Dear God, that girl was half my life.

And our first look was her first love;
    No man had fondled ere I came
The little breasts so small and firm
    And the long body like a flame.

For twenty years we shared a home,
    Our converse milder with each year;
Eleven children in its time
    Did that tall stately body bear.

It was the King of hosts and roads
    Who snatched her from me in her prime:
Little she wished to leave alone
    The man she loved before her time.

Now King of churches and of bells,
    Though never raised to pledge a lie
That woman's hand—can it be true?—
    No more beneath my head will lie.

(translation from the Irish)

PATRICK KAVANAGH

Patrick Kavanagh was born in 1905 in Inniskeen, County Monaghan. He left school at an early age and worked in turn as a hired hand, an apprentice shoemaker, and a farmer. In 1930 Kavanagh left Monaghan and set out on foot for Dublin (though he did not move there permanently until 1939). Kavanagh made a living in Dublin primarily by turning out reviews for the **Irish Times**, the **Irish Independent**, the **Irish Press**, and the **Standard**. He was editor, writer, and publisher (with his brother Peter) of **Kavanagh's Weekly**, a short-lived journal of literature and politics. In 1954, Kavanagh was found to have cancer and had to have one of his lungs surgically removed. He died in 1967, the same year he was married. Kavanagh's major collections of poetry are: **The Ploughman and Other Poems** (1936), **The Great Hunger** (1942), **A Soul for Sale** (1947), **Come Dance with Kitty Stobling** (1960), and **Collected Poems** (1964). **Complete Poems** appeared in 1972.

SHANCODUFF

My black hills have never seen the sun rising,
Eternally they look north towards Armagh.
Lot's wife would not be salt if she had been
Incurious as my black hills that are happy
When dawn whitens Glassdrummond chapel.

My hills hoard the bright shillings of March
While the sun searches in every pocket.
They are my Alps and I have climbed the Matterhorn
With a sheaf of hay for three perishing calves
In the field under the Big Forth of Rocksavage.

The sleety winds fondle the rushy beards of Shancoduff
While the cattle-drovers sheltering in the Featherna Bush
Look up and say: "Who owns them hungry hills
That the water-hen and snipe must have forsaken?
A poet? Then by heavens he must be poor."
I hear and is my heart not badly shaken?

STONY GREY SOIL

O stony grey soil of Monaghan
The laugh from my love you thieved;
You took the gay child of my passion
And gave me your clod-conceived.

You clogged the feet of my boyhood
And I believed that my stumble
Had the poise and stride of Apollo
And his voice my thick-tongued mumble.

You told me the plough was immortal!
O green-life-conquering plough!
Your mandril strained, your coulter blunted
In the smooth lea-field of my brow.

You sang on steaming dunghills
A song of cowards' brood,
You perfumed my clothes with weasel itch,
You fed me on swinish food.

You flung a ditch on my vision
Of beauty, love and truth.
O stony grey soil of Monaghan
You burgled my bank of youth!

Lost the long hours of pleasure
All the women that love young men.
O can I still stroke the monster's back
Or write with unpoisoned pen

His name in these lonely verses
Or mention the dark fields where
The first gay flight of my lyric
Got caught in a peasant's prayer.

Mullahinsha, Drummeril, Black Shanco—
Wherever I turn I see
In the stony grey soil of Monaghan
Dead loves that were born for me.

TO THE MAN AFTER THE HARROW

Now leave the check-reins slack,
The seed is flying far to-day—
The seed like stars against the black
Eternity of April clay.

This seed is potent as the seed
Of knowledge in the Hebrew Book,
So drive your horses in the creed
Of God the Father as a stook.

Forget the men on Brady's hill.
Forget what Brady's boy may say
For destiny will not fulfil
Unless you let the harrow play.

Forget the worm's opinion too
Of hooves and pointed harrow-pins,
For you are driving your horses through
The mist where Genesis begins.

from THE GREAT HUNGER

Maguire is not afraid of death, the Church will light him
    a candle
To see his way through the vaults and he'll understand the
Quality of the clay that dribbles over his coffin.
He'll know the names of the roots that climb down to
    tickle his feet.
And he will feel no different than when he walked
    through Donaghmoyne.
If he stretches out a hand—a wet clod,
If he opens his nostrils—a dungy smell;
If he opens his eyes once in a million years—
Through a crack in the crust of the earth he may see a
    face nodding in
Or a woman's legs. Shut them again for that sight is sin.

He will hardly remember that life happened to him—
Something was brighter a moment. Somebody sang in the
    distance.
A procession passed down a mesmerised street.
He remembers names like Easter and Christmas
By the colour his fields were.
Maybe he will be born again, a bird of an angel's conceit
To sing the gospel of life
To a music as flightily tangent
As a tune on an oboe.
And the serious look of the fields will have changed to the
    leer of a hobo
Swaggering celestially home to his three wishes granted.
Will that be? will that be?

Or is the earth right that laughs haw-haw
And does not believe
In an unearthly law.
The earth that says:
Patrick Maguire, the old peasant, can neither be damned
    nor glorified:
The graveyard in which he will lie will be just a deep-
    drilled potato-field
Where the seed gets no chance to come through
To the fun of the sun.
The tongue in his mouth is the root of a yew.
Silence, silence. The story is done.

He stands in the doorway of his house
A ragged sculpture of the wind,
October creaks the rotted mattress,
The bedposts fall. No hope. No lust.
The hungry fiend
Screams the apocalypse of clay
In every corner of this land.

TINKER'S WIFE

I saw her amid the dunghill debris
Looking for things
Such as an old pair of shoes or gaiters.
She was a young woman,
A tinker's wife.
Her face had streaks of care
Like wires across it,
But she was supple
As a young goat
On a windy hill.

She searched on the dunghill debris,
Tripping gingerly
Over tin canisters
And sharp-broken
Dinner plates.

EPIC

I have lived in important places, times
When great events were decided, who owned
That half a rood of rock, a no-man's land
Surrounded by our pitchfork-armed claims.
I heard the Duffys shouting "Damn your soul!"
And old McCabe stripped to the waist, seen
Step the plot defying blue cast-steel—
"Here is the march along these iron stones."
That was the year of the Munich bother. Which
Was more important? I inclined
To lose my faith in Ballyrush and Gortin
Till Homer's ghost came whispering to my mind.
He said: I made the Iliad from such
A local row. Gods make their own importance.

THE HOSPITAL

A year ago I fell in love with the functional ward
Of a chest hospital: square cubicles in a row,
Plain concrete, wash basins—an art lover's woe,
Not counting how the fellow in the next bed snored.
But nothing whatever is by love debarred,
The common and banal her heat can know.
The corridor led to a stairway and below
Was the inexhaustible adventure of a gravelled yard.

This is what love does to things: the Rialto Bridge,
The main gate that was bent by a heavy lorry,
The seat at the back of a shed that was a suntrap.
Naming these things is the love-act and its pledge;
For we must record love's mystery without claptrap,
Snatch out of time the passionate transitory.

CANAL BANK WALK

Leafy-with-love banks and the green waters of the canal
Pouring redemption for me, that I do
The will of God, wallow in the habitual, the banal,
Grow with nature again as before I grew.
The bright stick trapped, the breeze adding a third
Party to the couple kissing on an old seat,
And a bird gathering materials for the nest for the Word
Eloquently new and abandoned to its delirious beat.
O unworn world enrapture me, encapture me in a web
Of fabulous grass and eternal voices by a beech,
Feed the gaping need of my senses, give me ad lib
To pray unselfconsciously with overflowing speech
For this soul needs to be honoured with a new dress
        woven
From green and blue things and arguments that cannot be
        proven.

LINES WRITTEN ON A SEAT ON THE GRAND CANAL, DUBLIN

"Erected to the Memory of Mrs. Dermot O'Brien"

O commemorate me where there is water,
Canal water preferably, so stilly
Greeny at the heart of summer. Brother

Commemorate me thus beautifully.
Where by a lock niagarously roars
The falls for those who sit in the tremendous silence
Of mid-July. No one will speak in prose
Who finds his way to these Parnassian islands.
A swan goes by head low with many apologies,
Fantastic light looks through the eyes of bridges—
And look! a barge comes bringing from Athy
And other far-flung towns mythologies.
O commemorate me with no hero-courageous
Tomb—just a canal-bank seat for the passer-by.

IN MEMORY OF MY MOTHER

I do not think of you lying in the wet clay
Of a Monaghan graveyard; I see
You walking down a lane among the poplars
On your way to the station, or happily

Going to second Mass on a summer Sunday.
You meet me and you say:
"Don't forget to see about the cattle—"
Among your earthiest words the angels stray.

And I think of you walking along a headland
Of green oats in June,
So full of repose, so rich with life;
And I see us meeting at the end of a town

On a fair day by accident, after
The bargains are all made and we can walk
Together through the shops and stalls and markets
Free in the oriental streets of thought.

O you are not lying in the wet clay,
For it is a harvest evening now and we
Are piling up the ricks against the moonlight
And you smile up at us—eternally.

TO HELL WITH COMMONSENSE

More kicks than pence
We get from commonsense
Above its door is writ
All hope abandon. It
Is a bank will refuse a post
Dated cheque of the Holy Ghost.
Therefore I say to hell
With all reasonable
Poems in particular
We want no secular
Wisdom plodded together
By concerned fools. Gather
No moss you rolling stones
Nothing thought out atones
For no flight
In the light.
Let them wear out nerve and bone
Those who would have it that way
But in the end nothing that they
Have achieved will be in the shape up
In the final Wake Up
And I have a feeling
That through the hole in reason's ceiling
We can fly to knowledge
Without ever going to college.

OCTOBER

O leafy yellowness you create for me
A world that was and now is poised above time.
I do not need to puzzle out Eternity
As I walk this arboreal street on the edge of a town.
The breeze too, even the temperature
And pattern of movement is precisely the same
As broke my heart for youth passing. Now I am sure
Of something. Something will be mine wherever I am.
I want to throw myself on the public street without caring
For anything but the prayering that the earth offers.
It is October over all my life and the light is staring
As it caught me once in a plantation by the fox coverts.
A man is ploughing ground for winter wheat
And my nineteen years weigh heavily on my feet.

IF EVER YOU GO TO DUBLIN TOWN

If ever you go to Dublin town
In a hundred years or so
Inquire for me in Baggot Street
And what I was like to know.
O he was a queer one,
Fol dol the di do,
He was a queer one
I tell you.

My great-grandmother knew him well,
He asked her to come and call
On him in his flat and she giggled at the thought
Of a young girl's lovely fall.
O he was dangerous,
Fol dol the di do,
He was dangerous
I tell you.

On Pembroke Road look out for my ghost,
Dishevelled with shoes untied,
Playing through the railings with little children
Whose children have long since died.
O he was a nice man,
Fol dol the di do,
He was a nice man
I tell you.

Go into a pub and listen well
If my voice still echoes there,
Ask the men what their grandsires thought
And tell them to answer fair.
O he was eccentric,
Fol dol the di do,
He was eccentric
I tell you.

He had the knack of making men feel
As small as they really were
Which meant as great as God had made them
But as males they disliked his air.
O he was a proud one,
Fol dol the di do,
He was a proud one
I tell you.

If ever you go to Dublin town
In a hundred years or so
Sniff for my personality,
Is it Vanity's vapour now?
O he was a vain one,
Fol dol the di do,
He was a vain one
I tell you.

I saw his name with a hundred others
In a book in the library,
It said he had never fully achieved
His potentiality.
O he was slothful,
Fol dol the di do,
He was slothful
I tell you.

He knew that posterity has no use
For anything but the soul,
The lines that speak the passionate heart,
The spirit that lives alone.
O he was a lone one,
Fol dol the di do
Yet he lived happily
I tell you.

PADRAIC FALLON

Padraic Fallon was born in 1905 in Athenry, County Galway, and was educated at St. Joseph's College, Roscrea. Fallon was employed as a customs official for many years, first in Dublin, then in Wexford (he also worked a small farm outside Wexford). He was married in 1930 and had six sons. Fallon wrote numerous verse plays that were broadcast on Radio Eireann. But while many of his poems were published in journals and periodicals from the early thirties onward, it was not until 1974, the year of Fallon's death, that an extensive collection, **Poems**, was published in book form.

ODYSSEUS

Last year's decencies
Are the rags and reach-me-downs he'll wear forever,
Knowing one day he'll sober up inside them
Safe in wind and wife and limb,
Respected, of unimpeachable behaviour.

Meanwhile he goes forward
Magniloquently to himself; and, the fit on him,
Pushes his painful hobble to a dance,
Exposing in obscene wounds and dilapidation
The naked metre of the man.

His dog will die at sight of him,
His son want fool-proof, and his lady-wife
Deny his fingerprints; but he
With his talent for rehabilitation
Will be his own man soon, without ecstasy.

FOR PADDY MAC

I

Once, so long ago,
You used to probe me gently for the lost
Country, sensing somehow in my airs
The vivid longlipped peasantry of
Last century

And those bronze men pushed
With their diminishing herds far out on
The last ledge of original earth,
Fomorian types
In the big one-eyed sky

All messed up with sundogs and
Too many rainbows, and that wishwashing head of Bran
In the toppling arches seaward sailing and singing
On his weathered maypole from
A caved-in skull.

Ours were the metres
Of early waters, the first argosy hardly home
With new women, orgies
When the moon rode round
Stone circles counting her twelve.

Homer's people.
And wasn't I lucky, born with
Boundaries floating, language still making
Out of the broadlands where my fathers
Tended their clouds of ewes?

Bunkum, Dear P. The thing was gone, or
Never was. And we were the leftovers,
Lord-ridden and pulpit-thumped for all our wild
Cudgels of Gaelic. Ours was Lever's
One-horse country; the bailiff at the bighouse door.

And hags hung all day
In turfsmoke among the fowl where I was licked.
That was a town
Walled and towered as Troy, and never sieged for a
    woman:
Trading bullocks and pennies for glory gone;

And watched from the top of a shilling the homespun
    fellows
Selling their spades on hiring days,
For a year and a day the dear flesh off their bones
From penury to slavery,
The soul thrown in for a spare.

That was my country, beast, sky and anger:
For music a mad piper in the mud;
No poets I knew of; or they mouthed each other's words;
Such low powered gods
They died, as they were born, in byres.

Oh, maybe some rags and tatters did sing.
But poetry, for all your talk, is never that simple,
Coming out of a stone ditch in the broadlands
Newborn, or from
The fitful pibroch of a lonely thorn,

Or old saws at winter fires.
Muted the big words. Love was left
To eloping earls or such
Lest the snake creep up, usurping the ancient timber
And some odd bloom come bursting from the Cross.

II

And you speak of Raftery, that bold tongue, the tramp
In borrowed bootleather, those rainy eyes
Lifted to empty heaven from a blind man's stick;
I sang like him you say, and praised women,
And I had the true cow's lick;

You who should know how every poet must
Baptize first the font and the very waters,
And have no godfathers but this great thirst
For what is not;
And no mothers;

Who must quote Ambrose crookedly (Nam quid divinius
Isto ut puncto exiguo culpa cadet
Populi), bog Latin for
The bit of earth we tread
Into metaphor

Knowing we're just another civilisation
To be dumped, but go on, say it you,
We've eaten all the Gods yet bow the knee,
And are only really at home
In the larger toleration of the poem.

Carefully, now that you are dead,
I must amend the scribbles of the tribe
Lest sheepman and bullhead
Become a frieze of fathers like stone man,
Hieratic, almost Egyptian,

And from the uncreated, with arms widespread,
From puncto exiguo, beyond the dead
And Lazarus rising, where God is making still
Release the flood
Of living images for good and ill.

Dear P. I'll never know
What you brought over and passed on,
But this seems certain as I grow:
Man lives; Gods die:
It is only the genuflection that survives.

POT SHOT

I tell words that talk in trees, this hill
Is my vocabulary, and when I lie down
The sky seizes me so very quietly
I reflect the sunset, the river and I are one.
And then the gun goes off. Am I that, too?
Thunder and blast? And when the hooves of the echoes
Have galloped over the grass and the field aloofly
Returns to itself and silence on its toes
Cranes to hear a rabbit squeal, am I
The wound that I give, the hurt I hurt, the shiver
That talks so tall in trees, that is the sky,
That explodes in death, yet walks like the wide river
So calmly through the evening that I tame
The world around me till it names my name.

WEIR BRIDGE

The lodestoned salmon, hurtling
Always in the right direction, find
The trickle of their birth,
Stand fantailed on the falls
And somersault into the milting weather.

Whole gravels are in rut.
The ocean has come home to melt away
The salt, to lie under
A maybush and almost tenderly
Suck from the lazy heavens a blue-green fly.

On love's seething house,
Rocking the thousand cradles the first fresh
Will fall and the spent bulls
Drop with it down the slow river spirals;
Aching for space now the once rampant males;

Caught here in their bored
Congregations, while the wandering nerve
Twitches towards Norway. How many years
Since I first saw the stones waver,
The river paving turn to fins and tails?

Loafing a lunch hour in the sun,
And here's the wheel come round again;
So much to do, so little done;
The tiny trickle of my birth
Dwindling back into the earth.

THE HEAD

I

The day after decapitation
Was no wound yet. Noon found the head
Excited still and still singing
The visionary woman, still exalting
The woman in measures to which no words came
Off the black tongue. The river flies
Were busy on specks of blood, in clouds upon the hair;
But where her praise was fixed upon his face
No one had died, the flesh was adequate;
And on a mouth that seemed alive
Only the smile was anti-clockwise;
But no wound yet.

That night it drifted on
Through stars that buzzed no brighter, inches
Of radiance before it and around
That felt no wound;
And this was dyed with a flutter of vague moths,
And overhead where a curious white owl
Dilated, there was some reflection too;
And down below
More of it and stranger for the eels
Had scented blood and wavered under the wicker;
This was a head that trickled down many tails
Into the deeps, eddying without end;
And still was felt no wound.

The slow morning came
Back to the eyes and brought the labouring crow
(Corvus corax corax) who discharged himself
Upon the skull unskilfully and cawed

Once, twice, and there for long was still.
The gulls disturbed him when the eyes were gone
And over the bloody mess rose such confusion
Three salmon fishers rowed out from a draft
Only to retch their morning stirabout:
That noon the skull gaped
And still was felt no wound.

The second afternoon it rained;

Rinsing the ruin the nozzled drops removed
Sundry strips, tissues, barber's clippings,
Odds of nerves, bits, leaving such scrags, jags
And rags as still clung and dripped
To shine strangely when the sun came out.
The waters steamed a little before night
And from the skull where little pools remained
There oozed a smoke, a vagrant and hairlike smoke;
And in the hollow eyes the rain
Was bright as sight, and so it seemed
The nose put forth its bridge again,
And from the earholes arched two tufts of fawn,
Two gilded wisps, the ears. The face had dreamed
Itself right back again.
And still no pain;
Still the exultant thing was fixed, and dawn
Found the bare teeth beautiful.

II

The third day repeated as before
Washed out the skullhouse and refurnished it
With the changeable midsummer weather:
The head alone at last
Was bonebare and beaming; and where it floated
Down the broad vowel of the river, once
Its song was heard;

Snatches only, faint upon the ripple
And weirs of the water-word: A thin
Piping.

The reeds heavytopped tipped to it
As to a breeze.

       So it was the wind
That used the tattered wizen of the throat
As well as the sockets of the eyes, the earholes
And the pit behind the nose for hollow music,
Not overlooking the jewels of the mouth
That still smiled
For yet no wound was felt.

So time stopped
Outwardly, but there was still this woman
In the weather of the head
Who was all time to it no longer human.
And in that time the head came

By stages of water world
From green granaries, tilled, from fat uddered
Cow-lawns by river houses, woods that spoke in oak
And heavy roots and clumped along the banks,
To a country narrow low and cold
And very thin like a wire,
Where the head sang all day.

There the seas fell inland almost vacantly
Over a sieve of sand;
There the head lay
While the coracle under it of sally withes
Dried, withered in sunlight, salt sealight,
Rotted till the ashen thwart that held the head
Rigid and singing, sprung the spent lashings,
Tipping over;

This, one day when the set from the southwest
Piled up an equinoctial on the coast;
On the white shore with no one to notice
The head fell.

And broke

In a separation of its major and distinct parts.
Two.

And from the still centre where was the true
Bubble or heartbeat, came the tiny whimper
Of some unhouselled thing;
The head's first cry
At last and never heard

By gull, gale, sandpiping bird
Or gannet in the tall and touselled blue,
Nor the wader on two pins nearby,
Though the cry was human,
The pain spreading greatly, going
Towards blood in every direction

But never arriving
Near and away where the woman was
Doing the usual things to men and clothes
Afraid of the glass,
Groundswell and undertows,
What happens and the happening
That will never come to pass.

BRIAN COFFEY

Brian Coffey was born near Dublin in 1905. He attended Clongowes Wood College, then University College, Dublin, where his father was president. His poems appeared first in student publications, then in **Poems** (1930) which was coauthored by his friend Denis Devlin. Coffey graduated from University College, Dublin, with an M.Sc., and did research in Paris in the early thirties in physical chemistry. Later he completed his doctoral studies at Paris in philosophy. He continued to write poetry during his studies, encouraged by Beckett, Devlin, and MacGreevy. He married in 1938, the year his collection **Third Person** was published. He spent the war years in England. After the war he taught philosophy for five years at St. Louis University, Missouri, then returned to England with his family. He taught mathematics in London schools until 1972. His translation of Mallarmé s **Coup de Dés** was published in 1965, and of Neruda's love poems in 1973. Coffey's **Selected Poems** was published in 1971; his long poem **Advent** was published in the **Irish University Review** in 1975. **Death of Hektor**, a poem with illustrations by S. W. Hayter, was published in 1978.

from MISSOURI SEQUENCE

Nightfall, Midwinter, Missouri

To Thomas McGreevy

Our children have eaten supper,
play Follow-my-Leader,
make songs from room to room
around and around;
once each minute
past my desk they go.

Inside the house is warm.
Winter outside blows from Canada
freezing rain to ice our trees
branch by branch, leaf by leaf.
The mare shelters in the barn.

On the impassable road no movement.
Nothing stirs in the sky against the black.
If memory were an ice-field
quiet as all outside!
Tonight the poetry is in the children's game:
I am distracted by comparisons,
Ireland across the grey ocean,
here, across the wide river.

          *   *   *

We live far from where
my mother grows very old.
Five miles away, at Byrnesville,
the cemetery is filled with Irish graves,
the priest an old man born near Cork,
his bloss like the day he left the land.

People drifted in here from the river,
Irish, German, Bohemians,
more than one hundred years ago,
come to make homes.

Many Irish souls have gone back to God from Byrnesville,

many are Irish here today
where cedars stand like milestones
on worn Ozark hills
and houses white on bluegrass lawns
house people honest, practical and kind.

All shows to a long love
yet I am charmed
by the hills behind Dublin,
those white stone cottages,
grass green as no other green is green,
my mother's people, their ways.

France one loves with a love apart
like the love of wisdom;
Of England everyday love is the true love;
there is a love of Ireland
withering for Irishmen.

Does it matter where one dies,
supposing one knows how?

Dear Tom, in Ireland,
you have known
the pain between
its fruiting and the early dream
and you will hear me out.

          *   *   *

Our children have ended play,
have gone to bed,
left me to face
what I had rather not.

They know nothing of Ireland,
they grow American.
They have chased snakes through the couch-grass
in summer, caught butterflies and beetles
we did not know existed,
fished for the catfish,
slept on an open porch
when Whip-poor-Will and tree-frog
work all night,
observed the pupa of the shrill cicada
surface on dry clay,
disrobe for the short ruinous day.
The older ones have helped a neighbour, farmer,
raise his field of ripe corn
in heat that hurt us to the bone,
paid homage to dead men
with fire-crackers in July,
eaten the turkey in November.
Here now they make their friendships,
learn to love God.

Yet we must leave America,
bitter necessity no monopoly
of Irish soil.
It was pain once to come,
it is pain now to go.

How the will shifts from goal to goal
for who does not freely choose.
Some choose, some are chosen
to go their separate paths.
I would choose, I suppose, yet would be chosen
in some equation between God's will and mine,
rejecting prudence to make of conflict
a monument to celtic self-importance.

The truth is, where the cross is not
the Christian does not go.

         *   *   *

Return home takes on while I dream it
the fictive form of heaven on earth,
the child's return to motherly arms
for fright at frogs disturbed among iris leaves.

One poet I admire has written:
wherever the soul gives in to flesh
without a struggle is home.
Would one want home like that,
rest, supine surrender
to oneself alone,
flight from where one is?

There is no heaven on earth,
no facile choice for one
charged with care of others,
none for one like me
for whom no prospect opens
fairly on clear skies.

It grows late and winter
lays its numbing pall.
Doubts restless like what you see
when you lift a flat damp stone
exasperate my warring wishes
until wrenched apart by desperate extremes
I am back where I started.

Pain it was to come,
Pain it will be to go.

        *   *   *

Not just to go,
not just to stay,
but the act done in wisdom's way—
not impossible
if one is wise.

Our William Butler Yeats
made island flowers grow
that need as much
the local rain
as wind from overseas
to reach their prime.
He struggled towards the exact muse
through a sunless day.

No servant, the muse
abides in truth,
permits the use of protest
as a second best
to make clean fields,
exults only in the actual
expression of a love,
love all problem,
wisdom lacking.

        *   *   *

How near the surface of the pool
sunfish play, distract
us from where down deep
real reasons impose their rule.

The room is filled with children's lives
that fill my cares who turn again
to sudden starting words
like birds in cages.
Without all is silent,
within I have no peace at all,
having failed to choose
with loving-wise choice.

Midnight now.
Deepest winter perfect now.
Tomorrow early we shall make lunches
for the children to take to school,
forgetting while working out the week
our wrestling with the sad flesh
and the only Ireland we love
where in Achill still
the poor praise Christ aloud
when the priest elevates
the Saviour of the world.

ODALISQUE

The fog-horns bellow across the fields of fog.
Firm the beat of my heart. Do you hear the steps,
Long lean steps, the watchman pacing the night?

What matter now that you were stupid to-day,
What matter that I saw all that you saw.
Your talk pleased you. So much, I smiled.

At least you did remark the tented seas,
Waves we saw jumping like antelopes,
And clouds, roan horses charging mountains.

Tonight do not tell me I am beautiful.
Do not say: You are beautiful with such eyes.
My dog tells me as much as well.

Be silent. Let me suppose I am alone,
No light in my eyes, no voice in my ears, with night
That draws down, draws down closer, closer comes.

H E A D R O C K

IpsofactopaperAnswerallquesti
onstakingallyourtimeONEWhatha
veyouforgottenAreyoubeyonddou
btingyourmotives'honestyWhomd
idyousupposeinwhoseskinlastti
meyoumadeitTWOIsyourmotherath
omedearieordoyoumentallyreser
ve/prudentlydissimulateWho'sl
yingnowTHREECandamnationbeama
tterofroutineadminCouldyouorg
aniseandmaintainaninquisition
wouldyouAreyouthatstrongreall
yFOURAreyoupushedfortimeyetDi
dyoutakeyourpillAndhaveyoufou
ndaplacetohideintohidefromFIV
EWhataboutyourmotherDoyoudrin
kunusallymuchwaterthesedaysS
IXWhenyouwerebeatingyourwifed
idshesmileandifsowhySEVENWhoa
reyouWhereareyouWhenareyouWha
tdidthenthGadareneswinesaytot

he(n + 1)thonthewaydownEIGHTWas
yourMaagoodchapyourfatherwors
hippedwhenhechasedyourlittles
istertothetoolshedNINEActuall
yAkchelliFranklyspeakingManto
man/Womantowomandidyoueverlov
eanyonedeadEverownedabodTENDo
youagreethatitisfaircommenton
FUZZ'Sviewoftheevilthatisabro
adinourlandthatManthereisMant
hereisabsolutelyManManthereis

N   O   E   S   C   A   P   E

from ADVENT

Awakening like return to Earth from Moon
Splashdown to difference

Point-light-studded velvet-black
to sapphire sea
Start into conjecture

One had been programmed for any case whatever
naught unmanageable assumed
Like ballet-dancer each step as if remembered
Cave cave   All in the bag   Cave cave

Never the unforeseen
Even on rocking yielding water
a destined helping hand is awaited

Victor in the now no longer
could one fail in the not yet now

Home base and
how behind summer heat-veil
Earth could give one pause   Earth strange
like the stranger grown from one's child

From Northleigh to Southleigh
from the Flats to Farwood
wide one stretched one's arms
in standing greeting
across mocking plains of contentment

A day so perfect one found oneself
asking   of whom   for a cloud in the sky

Beyond concrete apron trees summerly
branches supple green with crowding leaves
How their quietude does arrest movement
as when one remembers
what one had not failed to forget

Trees grasses carpet and shelter earthly home
stretch fingers in turned soil soil welcomes warm

What sky-blue pollen-haze slight-swallows-high
feel and touch intensified by wind out of nowhere
One remembers from Samothrace fields of butterflies
scattered like scraps by screech-wind from sea

As if uncounted years of waiting had fruited
for Earth in unrepeatable day and pang of longing
to show her very best her fields of ripest corn

We had forgotten Earth Earth's muted murmur anguished
Earth since early savannahs ours   all ours

　　　　　*　　　　　*　　　　　*

How strange they are frail dry-leafly
small need terminal cares
lackless here to die

Each mirrors self in other right or left
counts gifts callers shows off flowers
gropes as if for sweets for memories blurred

Sister trails one "Happying profiting
soon he will fetch you home"
Soon for us to find no eye-flash no faint pulse
soon their grey unhoping undespairing ended we say
weathercocks no longer no naked need to assuage
all sealed back to shore receding forward
expectant will they descry an opened sky

Rooms furniture servants ready for dismissal from years
     back
before Sister began her watch for signs of ending
And how it came about
General ward for a half-year soon acclimatised
among scraps of habit to new ways
Others like oneself in one's glass grey and near to sleep
One could not withhold oneself eat peach alone
one began to share goods and memories eroded
month after month until life seemed whole again

Daughters one's children's children chattered by the bed
but one mused and judged and said
"Just like the others I am weary of walls"
"Where is son now So long since I have seen him"
and Sister smiled Sister moved one's bed
One had entered a ward for two

Two was very old talked not at all
One saw Two die ritual candles steady in deep night
What Sister said to one "He won't delay now"

Candles water chrism prayer-words priest
body sealed from world-pain
"He is coming" Sister said

We saw her eyes open as in greeting
She said "I knew son could not come"
Her face wore son's his image
She smiled at her silver cross
Blue flame her eyes winked out
"She is home" Sister said
Over shoulder on way to Three throws
"Seek what will find you"

Small bundles of skin and bone
who bruise as easily as small girl's neck
their questions sought no answer within

Not weird   strange strange like everyday
they had never put on masks never moved by indirection
did not dissemble forthright faced occasion event

Such a one I have known orphaned young and left
to be robbed of fortune by guardian yet came through
to clear laughing eyes skill in telling tales

Her house she ran without waste entertained
taught new maids how tables are laid stairs dusted
in words a loved grandmother had used

Grey eyes her song   Blue eyes her own
friendly greeted dark hawk visiting
warmed when children left to song of canary
its death she wept at buried it said
"Let us waste no more time"

As much unlike as like each one of them gets ready to die
so matter-of-fact in preparation they are pieces of jade
each one different in each one the green glowing heart

No archetype exerted fearful sway over them in dream
Their strength a style of saying "They have no wine"
Existentialists in day by day in need
as naked as thirst in drought how they comforted
the lost child praised the clumsy one
For them was written "All tears shall be wiped from their
    eyes"

Little they claimed to know about great affairs
They would say "God is good" in fair times or foul
their children
    they bore them reared them sent them out to live
and at the end blessed them with dying grace

"THE NICEST PHANTASIES ARE SHARED"

Whence let us go to
what is shared is nicest
and begin

Taking her garments
while she takes his
does not make theirs
a single robe

Their holding hands leaves each
aware of self and other
Their touching skins
breast to mouth mouth to breast
their planting kisses in hair
sunders uniting if he in her
unmatched is by a her in him

And when a pair bereft of day
and movement into night are sunk
how would it suit her her hell him
or suit his will with his hell her

What then is love
for lovers mating
with nought spoiled
though all uprooted
but completing natural skill
forever giving him to her
giving forever her to him
for them joying
in every difference
love decrees

SAMUEL BECKETT

Samuel Beckett was born in 1906 near Dublin. He was educated at Portora Royal School, County Fermanagh, and at Trinity College, Dublin, where he received his B.A. in French and Italian in 1927 and his M.A. in 1931. He was Lecturer in English at the Ecole Normale Superieure in Paris from 1928 to 1930, during which time he met and became friends with Joyce. He then was Lecturer in French at Trinity for several years. After wandering over the continent for five years, he settled in Paris in 1937, renewing his earlier friendship with Joyce. In 1938 he narrowly escaped death when he was stabbed on a Paris street by a complete stranger. In 1940 he joined the Resistance and had to flee Paris in 1942 to avoid arrest by the Gestapo. Beckett received the Nobel Prize for Literature in 1969; his international reputation rests chiefly on his plays, particularly on **Waiting for Godot**. Beckett has also written numerous novels and volumes of short stories. Of his collections of poems, the most complete to date is **Collected Poems in English and French** (1977).

MALACODA

thrice he came
the undertaker's man
impassible behind his scutal bowler
to measure
is he not paid to measure
this incorruptible in the vestibule
this malebranca knee-deep in the lilies
Malacoda knee-deep in the lilies
Malacoda for all the expert awe
that felts his perineum mutes his signal
sighing up through the heavy air
must it be it must be it must be
find the weeds engage them in the garden
hear she may see she need not

to coffin
with assistant ungulata
find the weeds engage their attention
hear she must see she need not

to cover
to be sure cover cover all over
your targe allow me hold your sulphur
divine dogday glass set fair
stay Scarmilion stay stay
lay this Huysum on the box
mind the imago it is he
hear she must see she must
all aboard all souls
half-mast aye aye

nay

ENUEG 1

Exeo in a spasm
tired of my darling's red sputum
from the Portobello Private Nursing Home
its secret things
and toil to the crest of the surge of the steep
       perilous bridge
and lapse down blankly under the scream of the
       hoarding
round the bright stiff banner of the hoarding
into a black west
throttled with clouds.

Above the mansions the algum-trees
the mountains
my skull sullenly
clot of anger
skewered aloft strangled in the cang of the wind
bites like a dog against its chastisement.

I trundle along rapidly now on my ruined feet
flush with the livid canal;
at Parnell Bridge a dying barge
carrying a cargo of nails and timber
rocks itself softly in the foaming cloister of the
       lock;
on the far bank a gang of down and outs would
       seem to be mending a beam.

Then for miles only wind
and the weals creeping alongside on the water
and the world opening up to the south
across a travesty of champaign to the mountains
and the stillborn evening turning a filthy green
manuring the night fungus
and the mind annulled
wrecked in wind.

I splashed past a little wearish old man,
Democritus,
scuttling along between a crutch and a stick,
his stump caught up horribly, like a claw, under
          his breech,
smoking.
Then because a field on the left went up in a
          sudden blaze
of shouting and urgent whistling and scarlet
          and blue ganzies
I stopped and climbed the bank to see the game.
A child fidgeting at the gate called up:
"Would we be let in Mister?"
"Certainly" I said "you would."
But, afraid, he set off down the road.
"Well" I called after him "why wouldn't you
          go on in?"
"Oh" he said, knowingly,
"I was in that field before and I got put out."
So on,
derelict,
as from a bush of gorse on fire in the mountain
          after dark,
or, in Sumatra, the jungle hymen,
the still flagrant rafflesia.

Next:
a lamentable family of grey verminous hens,
perishing out in the sunk field,
trembling, half asleep, against the closed door
          of a shed,
with no means of roosting.
The great mushy toadstool,
green-black,
oozing up after me,
soaking up the tattered sky like an ink of
          pestilence,

in my skull the wind going fetid,
the water . . .

Next:
on the hill down from the Fox and Geese into
        Chapelizod
a small malevolent goat, exiled on the road,
remotely pucking the gate of his field;
the Isolde Stores a great perturbation of sweaty
        heroes,
in their Sunday best,

come hastening down for a pint of nepenthe or
        moly or half and half
from watching the hurlers above in Kilmain-
ham.

Blotches of doomed yellow in the pit of the
        Liffey;
the fingers of the ladders hooked over the
        parapet,
soliciting;
a slush of vigilant gulls in the grey spew of the
        sewer.

Ah the banner
the banner of meat bleeding
on the silk of the seas and the arctic flowers
that do not exist.

I WOULD LIKE MY LOVE TO DIE

I would like my love to die
and the rain to be falling on the graveyard
and on me walking the streets
mourning the first and last to love me

(translated from the French)

JOHN HEWITT

John Hewitt was born in 1907 in Belfast. He was educated at Methodist College, and Queen's University, Belfast, where he received his B.A. and M.A. From 1930 to 1957 he was assistant and then deputy director of the Belfast Museum and Art Gallery. For the next fifteen years he was director of the Herbert Art Gallery and Museum in Coventry, England. Hewitt is a member of the Irish Academy of Letters, and has been associate editor of the magazine **Lagan** and poetry editor of **Threshold**. His major collections of poetry are: **Collected Poems 1932–1967** (1968), **The Planter and the Gael** (with John Montague, 1970), **An Ulster Reckoning** (1971), **Out of My Time** (1974), and **Time Enough: Poems New and Revised** (1976).

IRELAND

We Irish pride ourselves as patriots
and tell the beadroll of the valiant ones
since Clontarf's sunset saw the Norsemen broken . . .
Aye, and before that too we had our heroes:
but they were mighty fighters and victorious.
The later men got nothing save defeat,
hard transatlantic sidewalks or the scaffold . . .

We Irish, vainer than tense Lucifer,
are yet content with half-a-dozen turf,
and cry our adoration for a bog,
rejoicing in the rain that never ceases,
and happy to stride over the sterile acres,
or stony hills that scarcely feed a sheep.
But we are fools, I say, are ignorant fools
to waste the spirit's warmth in this cold air,
to spend our wit and love and poetry
on half-a-dozen peat and a black bog.

We are not native here or anywhere.
We were the keltic wave that broke over Europe,
and ran up this bleak beach among these stones:
but when the tide ebbed, were left stranded here
in crevices, and ledge-protected pools
that have grown salter with the drying up
of the great common flow that kept us sweet
with fresh cold draughts from deep down in the ocean.

So we are bitter, and are dying out
in terrible harshness in this lonely place,
and what we think is love for usual rock,
or old affection for our customary ledge,
is but forgotten longing for the sea
that cries far out and calls us to partake
in his great tidal movements round the earth.

BECAUSE I PACED MY THOUGHT

Because I paced my thought by the natural world,
the earth organic, renewed with the palpable seasons,
rather than the city falling ruinous, slowly
by weather and use, swiftly by bomb and argument,

I found myself alone who had hoped for attention.
If one listened a moment he murmured his dissent:
this is an idle game for a cowardly mind.
The day is urgent. The sun is not on the agenda.

And some who hated the city and man's unreasoning acts
remarked: He is no ally, he does not say that
Power and Hate are the engines of human treason.
There is no answering love in the yellowing leaf.

I should have made it plain that I stake my future
on birds flying in and out of the schoolroom window,
on the council of sunburnt comrades in the sun
and the picture carried with singing into the temple.

AN IRISHMAN IN COVENTRY

A full year since, I took this eager city,
the tolerance that laced its blatant roar,
its famous steeples and its web of girders,
as image of the state hope argued for,
and scarcely flung a bitter thought behind me
on all that flaws the glory and the grace
which ribbons through the sick, guilt-clotted legend
of my creed-haunted, Godforsaken race.
My rhetoric swung round from steel's high promise
to the precision of the well-gauged tool,
tracing the logic in the vast glass headlands,
the clockwork horse, the comprehensive school.

Then, sudden, by occasion's chance concerted,
in enclave of my nation, but apart,
the jigging dances and the lilting fiddle
stirred the old rage and pity in my heart.
The faces and the voices blurring round me,

the strong hands long familiar with the spade,
the whiskey-tinctured breath, the pious buttons,
called up a people endlessly betrayed
by our own weakness, by the wrongs we suffered
in that long twilight over bog and glen,
by force, by famine and by glittering fables
which gave us martyrs when we needed men,
by faith which had no charity to offer,
by poisoned memory and by ready wit,
with poverty corroded into malice
to hit and run and howl when it is hit.

This is our fate: eight hundred years' disaster
crazily tangled as the Book of Kells,
the dream's distortion and the land's division,
the midnight raiders and the prison cells.
Yet like Lir's children banished to the waters
our hearts still listen for the landward bells.

ONCE ALIEN HERE

Once alien here my fathers built their house,
claimed, drained, and gave the land the shapes of use,
and for their urgent labour grudged no more
than shuffled pennies from the hoarded store
of well rubbed words that had left their overtones
in the ripe England of the mounded downs.

The sullen Irish limping to the hills
bore with them the enchantments and the spells
that in the clans' free days hung gay and rich
on every twig of every thorny hedge,
and gave the rain-pocked stone a meaning past
the blurred engraving of the fibrous frost.

So I, because of all the buried men
in Ulster clay, because of rock and glen
and mist and cloud and quality of air
as native in my thought as any here,
who now would seek a native mode to tell
our stubborn wisdom individual,
yet lacking skill in either scale of song,
the graver English, lyric Irish tongue,
must let this rich earth so enhance the blood
with steady pulse where now is plunging mood
till thought and image may, identified
find easy voice to utter each aright.

THE SPECTACLE OF TRUTH

A masterly lens-polisher,
pride of his guild in Amsterdam,
once linked two crystals rim by rim
whose mutual strength should make all clear;
and when he clapped them to his eyes
they proved so purging to the sight
that all seemed as the last Assize,
in the strict justice of the light.

He saw the burgomaster stand
beneath the towering Westkirk's porch,
and like a candle in a church
he held his small soul in his hand:
one housewife bent above her tub,
one pinned white linen on the line,
and whether shift or bridal robe
bright as their sheets their spirits shone.

He saw the flowering barges glow,
the men aboard seemed bowed in prayer,
and at the stalls across the square
where nameless figures come and go,
all stood for judgment, stirring not,
hand held to mouth or hand at side;
and he could tell from where he sat
that this was wicked, this was good.

Then while he marvelled at the sight
a breathless moment or an hour,
his rocking heart grew still and sure
that charity was more than light,
that, gazed at through the perfect glass,
this shining scene was bright and false,
the men, the houses and the trees,
mere patterned shapes on painted tiles;

and while he fixed his mind on truth
time and the world were ice and stone,
so if he'd have them move again
and air thaw out in noisy breath,
he'd have to lay the lenses by,
and turn once more upon the street
his old decaying mortal eye,
desiring it, despising it.

A MINOR VICTORIAN PAINTER

A bright scene; a summer morning,
dew on the deep grass. The bearded man
in corduroy, stands before his easel
and as he paints, he sings;
at the bend of a Warwickshire stream
heavy with foliage and reflections
green, its surface still, except
for dip of swallow, broken ring.

At intervals he lays down his brush
beside the paint-box on the stool
and pads across to one or other
of the young men at their canvasses,
the brush-stroke demonstrated,
the difficult transition resolved,
the encouraging nod, he strides
back to his own adventure.

Then bread and beer under cool oak;
pipes are lit, and the smoke drifts
among the hanging leaves, as they talk
of Ruskin and truth to nature;
and the high sun moves over,
puts the shadows on the other side,
making ready the subjects
for the long afternoon.

LOUIS MacNEICE

Louis MacNeice was born in Belfast in 1907 and educated in England at Marlborough and at Oxford, where he received a B.A. degree. Before the outbreak of World War II, he lectured on Classics at the University of Birmingham, the University of London, and Cornell University in the United States. On his return to England in 1940, he became a producer for the BBC. Besides his radio plays, translations, critical and autobiographical prose, he published sixteen collections of poetry. His **Collected Poems** appeared in 1966, three years after his death in London.

DUBLIN

Grey brick upon brick,
Declamatory bronze
On sombre pedestals—
O'Connell, Grattan, Moore—
And the brewery tugs and the swans
On the balustraded stream
And the bare bones of a fanlight
Over a hungry door
And the air soft on the cheek
And porter running from the taps

With a head of yellow cream
And Nelson on his pillar
Watching his world collapse.

This was never my town,
I was not born nor bred
Nor schooled here and she will not
Have me alive or dead
But yet she holds my mind
With her seedy elegance,
With her gentle veils of rain
And all her ghosts that walk
And all that hide behind
Her Georgian façades—
The catcalls and the pain,
The glamour of her squalor,
The bravado of her talk.

The lights jig in the river
With a concertina movement
And the sun comes up in the morning
Like barley-sugar on the water
And the mist on the Wicklow hills
Is close, as close
As the peasantry were to the landlord,
As the Irish to the Anglo-Irish,
As the killer is close one moment
To the man he kills,
Or as the moment itself
Is close to the next moment.

She is not an Irish town
And she is not English,
Historic with guns and vermin
And the cold renown
Of a fragment of Church latin,

Of an oratorical phrase.
But oh the days are soft,
Soft enough to forget
The lesson better learnt,
The bullet on the wet
Streets, the crooked deal,
The steel behind the laugh,
The Four Courts burnt.

Fort of the Dane,
Garrison of the Saxon,
Augustan capital
Of a Gaelic nation,
Appropriating all
The alien brought,
You give me time for thought
And by a juggler's trick
You poise the toppling hour—
O greyness run to flower,
Grey stone, grey water,
And brick upon grey brick.

SNOW

The room was suddenly rich and the great bay-window
        was
Spawning snow and pink roses against it
Soundlessly collateral and incompatible:
World is suddener than we fancy it.

World is crazier and more of it than we think,
Incorrigibly plural. I peel and portion
A tangerine and spit the pips and feel
The drunkenness of things being various.

And the fire flames with a bubbling sound for world
Is more spiteful and gay than one supposes—
On the tongue on the eyes on the ears in the palms of
    one's hands—
There is more than glass between the snow and the huge
    roses.

from TRILOGY FOR X

And love hung still as crystal over the bed
    And filled the corners of the enormous room;
The boom of dawn that left her sleeping, showing
    The flowers mirrored in the mahogany table.

O my love, if only I were able
    To protract this hour of quiet after passion,
Not ration happiness but keep this door for ever
    Closed on the world, its own world closed within it.

But dawn's waves trouble with the bubbling minute,
    The names of books come clear upon their shelves,
The reason delves for duty and you will wake
    With a start and go on living on your own.

The first train passes and the windows groan,
    Voices will hector and your voice become
A drum in tune with theirs, which all last night
    Like sap that fingered through a hungry tree
Asserted our one night's identity.

DENIS DEVLIN

Denis Devlin was born of Irish parents in 1908 in Greenock, Scotland. He grew up in Dublin and was educated at Belvedere and University College, Dublin, where he took his M.A. in 1930. Devlin continued his studies in Munich and Paris, before accepting a position in the English department at University College, Dublin (1933–1935). Devlin then joined the Irish Foreign Service, in which he had a very distinguished career. He held important diplomatic posts in the United States, was minister plenipotentiary to Italy, then to Turkey, and ambassador to Italy. Devlin published three collections of translations of the French poet St. John Perse: **Rains** (1945), **Snows** (1945), and **Exile and Other Poems** (1949). His own published collections of poetry include **Poems** (with Brian Coffey, 1930), **Intercessions** (1937), **Lough Derg and Other Poems** (1946), and the posthumous **Selected Poems** (1963), **Collected Poems** (1964), and **The Heavenly Foreigner** (1967). When Devlin died in Dublin in 1959, an award for poetry was set up to commemorate him.

LOUGH DERG

The poor in spirit on their rosary rounds,
The jobbers with their whiskey-angered eyes,
The pink bank clerks, the tip-hat papal counts,
And drab, kind women their tonsured mockery tries,
Glad invalids on penitential feet
Walk the Lord's majesty like their village street.

With mullioned Europe shattered, this Northwest,
Rude-sainted isle would pray it whole again:
(Peasant Apollo! Troy is worn to rest.)
Europe that humanized the sacred bane
Of God's chance who yet laughed in his mind
And balanced thief and saint: were they this kind?

Low rocks, a few weasels, lake
Like a field of burnt gorse; the rooks caw;
Ours, passive, for man's gradual wisdom take
Firefly instinct dreamed out into law;
The prophets' jeweled kingdom down at heel
Fires no Augustine here. Inert, they kneel;

All is simple and symbol in their world,
The incomprehended rendered fabulous.
Sin teases life whose natural fruits withheld
Sour the deprived nor bloom for timely loss:
Clan Jansen! less what magnanimity leavens
Man's wept-out, fitful, magniloquent heavens

Where prayer was praise, O Lord! the Temple trumpets
Cascaded down Thy sunny pavilions of air,
The scroll-tongued priests, the galvanic strumpets,
All clash and stridency gloomed upon Thy stair;
The pharisees, the exalted boy their power
Sensually psalmed in Thee, their coming hour!

And to the sun, earth turned her flower of sex,
Acanthus in the architects' limpid angles;
Close priests allegorized the Orphic egg's
Brood, and from the Academy, tolerant wranglers
Could hear the contemplatives of the Tragic Choir
Drain off man's sanguine, pastoral death-desire.

It was said stone dreams and animal sleeps and man
Is awake; but sleep with its drama on us bred
Animal articulate, only somnambulist can
Conscience like Cawdor give the blood its head
For the dim moors to reign through druids again.
O first geometer! tangent-feelered brain

Clearing by inches the encircled eyes,
Bolder than the peasant tiger whose autumn beauty
Sags in the expletive kill, or the sacrifice
Of dearth puffed positive in the stance of duty
With which these pilgrims would propitiate
Their fears; no leafy, medieval state

Of paschal cathedrals backed on earthy hooves
Against the craftsmen's primary-colored skies
Whose gold was Gabriel on the patient roofs,
The parabled windows taught the dead to rise,
And Christ the Centaur, in two natures whole,
With fable and proverb joinered body and soul.

Water withers from the oars. The pilgrims blacken
Out of the boats to masticate their sin
Where Dante smelled among the stones and bracken
The door to Hell (O harder Hell where pain
Is earthed, a casuist sanctuary of guilt!).
Spirit bureaucracy on a bet built

Part by this race when monks in convents of coracles
For the Merovingian centuries left their land,
Belled, fragrant; and honest in their oracles
Bespoke the grace to give without demand,
Martyrs Heaven winged nor tempted with reward.
And not ours, doughed in dogma, who never have dared

Will with surrogate palm distribute hope:
No better nor worse than I who, in my books,
Have angered at the stake with Bruno and, by the rope
Watt Tyler swung from, leagued with shifty looks
To fuse the next rebellion with the desperate
Serfs in the sane need to eat and get;

Have praised, on its thunderous canvas, the Florentine
     smile
As man took to wearing his death, his own,
Sapped crisis through cathedral branches (while
Flesh groped loud round dissenting skeleton)
In soul, reborn as body's appetite:
Now languisht back in body's amber light,

Now is consumed. O earthly paradise!
Hell is to know our natural empire used
Wrong, by mind's molting, brute divinities.
The vanishing tiger's saved, his blood transfused.
Kent is for Jutes again and Glasgow town
Burns high enough to screen the stars and moon.

Well may they cry who have been robbed, their wasting
Shares in justice legally lowered until
Man his own actor, matrix, mold and casting,
Or man, God's image, sees his idol spill.
Say it was pride that did it, or virtue's brief:
To them that suffer it is no relief.

All indiscriminate, man, stone, animal
Are woken up in nightmare. What John the Blind
From Patmos saw works and we speak it. Not all
The men of God nor the priests of mankind
Can mend or explain the good and broke, not one
Generous with love prove communion;

Behind the eyes the winged ascension flags,
For want of spirit by the market blurbed,
And if hands touch, such fraternity sags
Frightened this side the dikes of death disturbed
Like Aran Islands' bibulous, unclean seas:
Pietà: but the limbs ache; it is not peace.

Then to see less, look little, let hearts' hunger
Feed on water and berries. The pilgrims sing:
Life will fare well from elder to younger,
Though courage fail in a world-end, rosary ring.
Courage kills its practitioners and we live,
Nothing forgotten, nothing to forgive,

We pray to ourself. The metal moon, unspent
Virgin eternity sleeping in the mind,
Excites the form of prayer without content;
Whitethorn lightens, delicate and blind,
The negro mountain, and so, knelt on her sod,
This woman beside me murmuring My God! My God!

ANK'HOR VAT

The antlered forests
Move down to the sea.
Here the dung-filled jungle pauses

Buddha has covered the walls of the great temple
With the vegetative speed of his imagery

Let us wait, hand in hand

No Western god or saint
Ever smiled with the lissome fury of this god
Who holds in doubt
The wooden stare of Apollo
Our Christian crown of thorns:

There is no mystery in the luminous lines
Of that high, animal face
The smile, sad, humoring and equal
Blesses without obliging
Loves without condescension;
The god, clear as spring-water
Sees through everything, while everything
Flows through him

A fling of flowers here
Whose names I do not know
Downy, scarlet gullets
Green legs yielding and closing

While, at my mental distance from passion,
The prolific divinity of the temple
Is a quiet lettering on vellum.

Let us lie down before him
His look will flow like oil over us.

WISHES FOR HER

Against Minoan sunlight
Slight-boned head,
Buildings with the thin climb of larks
Trilling off whetstone brilliants,
Slight head, nor petal nor marble

Night-shell
Two, one and separate.

Love in loving, all
A fledgling, hard-billed April,
Soil's gaudy chemistry in fission and fuse.
And she
Lit out of fire and glass
Lightning
The blue flowers of vacant thunder.

In the riverlands
Stained with old battlefields, old armor
In which their child, rust, sighs,
Strangers lost in the courtyard,
I lie awake.
The ice recedes, on black silk
Rocks the seals sway their heads.

No prophet deaths
In the webbed tensions of memory,
No harm
Night lean with hunters.
I wish you well, wish
Tall angels whose rib-freezing
Beauty attend you.

DAPHNE STILLORGAN

The stationmaster is garrulous in
The modest station set in the glen
Bushes wink with brown birdwings
The benches spread their knees, present
Drowsy laps to the sun.
A white cat sacred dangerous within

Egyptian memories considers
Like a marksman a celluloid ball on a water-jet
A tigermoth's fatal rise and fall
On her rank breath.

One shadow makes the whole sky shake
But I flick with instantaneous eyes
The next quick change before the change begins.
The water spouts are dried
Laurel leaves
Shine in the waxen summer.

The clean metronome of horses' feet on the road
Made anguish with clocks and rules which now
Silence beyond measure floods again
Through the trees' green bazaar and patches
Of light like muslin girls in forest lost.
And lost, but after noisy pebble wrinkling
This scene became a pool in air limpid
Restoring to the inimitable Images
Reflections paled but smooth as smooth as smooth.

Fuchsias revive and breathe through scarlet mouths
Rumors on wind
Far-off the humid pounding of a train
Wind-cylinders boom along
Steel wires, the rails drone,
Far-off thudding, trampling, thud
Of thousand pink-soled apes, no humorous family god!

Southward, storm
Smashes the flimsy sky.

Vines, virgins, guard your red wine
Cross branching arms frail on breasts
Small showers will fall before the rain crowds:

Use them to cool your rind-stiffening flesh
Writhing with blood for sap
To suck the insect-pointed air, the first threat
Of eager ravishers.

Scared faces lifted up
Is the menace bestial or a brusque pleiad
Of gods of fire vagabond?
Quick just in time quick just in time; ah!
Trees in light dryad dresses

Birds (O unreal whitewashed station!)
Compose no more that invisible architecture.

ANTEROOM: GENEVA

The General Secretary's feet whispered over the red carpet
And stopped, a demure pair, beside the demure
Cadet, poor but correct,
Devoted menial of well-mannered Power.
"A word with you." "Yes, your Excellency."
Excellency smiled. "Your silk shirt is nice, Scriptor.
But listen. Better not let these private letters
Reach the President. He gets worried, you know,
About the personal misfortunes of the people;
And really, the Minister is due to arrive.
It is surely most unseemly
To keep the State in the waiting-room
For God knows what beggars,
For totally unnecessary people."

Their mutual shirtfronts gleamed in a white smile
The electorate at breakfast approved of the war for peace
And the private detective idly deflowered a rose.

RENEWAL BY HER ELEMENT

The hawthorn morning moving
Above the battlements,
Breast from breast of lover
Tears, reminds of difference
And body's raggedness.

Immune from resolution
Into common clay
Because I have not known you;
Self-content as birdsong
Scornful at night-breakage
You seem to me. I am
Fresh from a long absence.

O suave through surf lifting
My smile upon your mouth;
Limbs according to rhythm
Separating, closing;
Scarcely using my name,
Traveller through troubling gestures,
Only for rare embraces
Of prepared texture.
Your lips amused harden
My arms round you defiant,
You shirk my enwreathing
Language, and you smile,
Turning aside my hand
Through your breath's light leafage,
Preferring yourself reflected
In my body to me,
Preferring my image of you
To you whom I achieved.
Noise is curbed attentive,
The sea hangs on your lips:
What would I do less?

It is over now but once
Our fees were nothing more,
Each for use of the other
In mortgage, than a glance.
I knew the secret movements
Of the blood under your throat
And when we lay love-proven
Whispering legends to sleep
Braceleted in embrace
Your hands pouring on me
Fresh water of their caresses,
Breasts, nests of my tenderness,
All night was laced with praise.

Now my image faded
In the lucid fields
Of your eyes. Never again
Surprise for years, years.

My landscape is grey rain
Aslant on bent seas.

from THE HEAVENLY FOREIGNER

Chartres

The spires, firm on their monster feet rose light and thin
    and trembling in the tracery of bird-motion and
    bell-echo;
A woodshaving sailed on the calm, vernal water.
Now, fixing our secret in my eyes, that's what is there,
That's what is there, she said, all this is more
Beautiful than Chartres.
Again, again protesting
Like those who will not surrender a small liberty

Which they cannot cultivate in any case.
Rebellion is imperfection, like all matter:
Mirror without reflection, I am helpless,
As if I were watching a wooden beam pushing up through
    the soil
As if I were the soft-voiced people forever against the
    people with hard voices.

Whereas, O my term, my unavoidable turnstile
In the cathedral porch, I call you these things,
Term itself, apse itself, had you but come,
Our absolute Lord had not been me, not me or you,
But an instant preconising eternity
Borne between our open eyes,
With no perceptible bank of land between,
Nor oblique eyesight deciding other objects were there.

Ile-St-Louis

It goes on all night, the sorceresses whispering
Wind in the wood, and when you listen
Vanishing like a whistle downriver. Then, Oh, cling
Close to the world and her; she crowns
This moment with the diadem of her Time, and waves
The floral barge into a frame of trees;
Her eyes darken with the music,
Darkness lies against her mouth,
There is a sharp wind between laugh and cry.

Last night on the gilded Bourbon bridge
The doom of Adam brought me down to earth
While the houses with their ruined freight
Filed down the soft, erotic river.
I was not guilty, had I but known it!
For now and then the royal pall of peace
Can fall without prayer, without need,

Love's earnest gift being frivolously given;
And as the lucid, pagan music
Blows with brown leaves over the asphalt,
Guilt slips off like a wet coat in the hall.

. . . And past her ivory head
Stream the pebble notes like a run of deer;
A shy god moves across the terrace,
A being born among the flowers of her mind
Beautiful, loving and beloved.

In all these one-room flats, while the street-lamps,
    unseasonably awake all night long,
Mutter their proverbs—that it's not worth it, it makes no
    difference—
How many white-collar clerks sit alone over a thin drink
Singing ballads out of anthologies,
Reading, in a spurt and laze, the provincial eyebrow
    raised,
The Essays of Sorel, the novels of Maxim Gorky! and
    brush their teeth,
Take two aspirins and fall between the soiled sheets,
Thinking of the good brother and sister who have stayed
    at home
In the country where the trucks are loading now
With greens and tuberose and cackle;
And fall asleep and resume the dream
Of the fern and roses altar in childhood,
Of the campaigns of childhood
Against the fortress of the Snow Princess.

W. R. RODGERS

W. R. Rodgers was born in 1909 in Belfast and educated at Queen's University, Belfast. From 1934 to 1946 Rodgers was a Presbyterian minister in County Armagh. He worked as a BBC producer and scriptwriter from 1946 to 1952, during which time he produced a number of lively radio discussions of the major literary figures of modern Ireland. Rodgers was elected to the Irish Academy of Letters in 1951. His first wife died in 1953, and in that year he remarried; there are two children from his first marriage and one from his second. In 1966 Rodgers moved to Claremont, California, to become writer-in-residence at Pitzer College, and in 1968 he accepted a position at the California State Polytechnic College. He died the following year in Los Angeles. His published collections of poetry are **Awake and Other Poems** (1941), **Europa and the Bull** (1952), and the posthumously published **Collected Poems** (1971).

THE NET

Quick, woman, in your net
Catch the silver I fling!
O I am deep in your debt,
Draw tight, skin-tight, the string

And rake the silver in.
No fisher ever yet
Drew such a cunning ring.

Ah, shifty as the fin
Of any fish this flesh
That, shaken to the shin,
Now shoals into your mesh,
Bursting to be held in;
Purse-proud and pebble-hard,
Its pence like shingle showered.

Open the haul, and shake
The fill of shillings free,
Let all the satchels break
And leap about the knee
In shoals of ecstasy.
Guineas and gills will flake
At each gull-plunge of me.

Though all the Angels, and
Saint Michael at their head,
Nightly contrive to stand
On guard about your bed,
Yet none dare take a hand,
But each can only spread
His eagle-eye instead.

But I, being man, can kiss
And bed-spread-eagle too;
All flesh shall come to this,.
Being less than angel is,
Yet higher far in bliss
As it entwines with you.

Come, make no sound, my sweet;
Turn down the candid lamp
And draw the equal quilt
Over our naked guilt.

PAIRED LIVES

Though to strangers' approach
(Like swing doors cheek to cheek)
Presenting one smooth front
Of summed resistance and
Aligned resentment, yet,
On nearer view note how,
At the deflecting touch
Of intervening hand,
Each in its lonely arc
Reaches and rocks inward
(Retires and returns
Immediately to join
The other moiety).
Each singly yields to thrust,
Is hung on its own hinge
Of fear and hope, and in
Its own reticence rests.

SCAPEGOAT

God broke into my house last night
With his flying-squad, narks, batmen, bully-boys,
Proctors, bailiffs, aiders and abettors—
Call them what you will—hard-mouthed, bowler-hatted.
Hearing a lack of noise I had gone downstairs
To let the dog out.
The tall figure with his obedient shadows

Pushed past me into the light and turned
With the accusing document; all my fears.
It seemed I had for years out of mind
Owed him a sum of money and had paid
Nothing. "Lord," I said reluctantly, looking
Into his implacably-forgiving face,
"I would have called it a lie, but if you
Say so, it must be so."
I do not know—
It being a dream of sorts—I do not know
If it were His son or my son
The doomsmen laid upon the floor then,
The knife to his throat.
I saw no more. But the dog of the house
Fled howling through the open door.

DONAGH MacDONAGH

Donagh MacDonagh, the son of Thomas MacDonagh, poet and leader of the Easter Rising, was born in 1912 in Dublin. He was educated at University College, Dublin, and was admitted to the Irish Bar in 1936. He pursued a legal as well as a literary career, becoming a justice of the district courts. MacDonagh wrote several successful plays. His published collections of poetry are: **Veterans and Other Poems** (1941), **The Hungry Grass** (1947), and **A Warning to Conquerors** (1968).

THE VETERANS

Strict hairshirt of circumstance tears the flesh
Off most delicate bones;
Years of counter and office, the warped mesh
Of social living, dropping on stones,
Wear down all that was rough and worthy
To a common denominator of dull tones.

So these, who in the sixteenth year of the century
Saw their city, a Phoenix upturned,
Settle under her ashes and bury
Hearts and brains that more frantically burned
Than the town they destroyed, have with the corrosion of
    time
Spent more than they earned;

And with their youth has shrunk their singular mystery
Which for one week set them in the pulse of the age,
Their spring adventure petrified in history,
A line on a page,
Betrayed into the hands of students who question
Oppressed and oppressor's rage.

Only the dead beneath their granite signatures
Are untroubled by the touch of day and day,
Only in them the first rich vision endures;
Those over clay
Retouch in memory, with sentiment relive,
April and May.

from CHARLES DONNELLY

Dead in Spain 1937

Of what a quality is courage made
That he who gently walked our city streets
Talking of poetry or philosophy,
Spinoza, Keats,
Should lie like any martyred soldier
His brave and fertile brain dried quite away
And the limbs that carried him from cradle to death's
    outpost
Growing down into a foreign clay.

Gone from amongst us and his life not half begun
Who had followed Jack-o'-Lantern truth and liberty
Where it led wavering from park-bed to prison-cell
Into a strange land, dry misery;
And then into Spain's slaughter, sniper's aim
And his last shocked embrace of earth's lineaments.
Can I picture truly that swift end
Who see him dead with eye that still repents?

What end, what quietus can I see for him,
Who had the quality of life in every vein?
Life with its passion and poetry and its proud
Ignorance of eventual loss or gain . . .
This first fruit of our harvest, willing sacrifice
Upon the altar of his integrity,
Lost to us. Somewhere his death is charted,
A signature affixed to his brief history.

        *   *   *

They gave him a gun,
A trigger to pull that any peasant finger
Could have pulled as well, a barrel to keep sweet
That any eye from Valencia to Madrid
Could have looked through.
His body stopped a bullet and little else,
Stopped no tank or French 75
From crunching over roads of human bones.
His brain might have done that
But it has melted into Spanish soil,

But speaks into my brain in parody
Of the voice that was its servant,
And speaks only what it spoke before.
The intricate cells, the labyrinthine ways,
The multicoloured images that lurked and shone,
The dreams betrayed into expression,
Melted into a red earth, richer for olive crop.
And through the pleasant European landscapes
The legions march; theodolite and map
Plan out the tactical approach, the gun emplacement,
The unencumbered field for cemetery.

JUST AN OLD SWEET SONG

The pale, drooping girl and the swaggering soldier
The row-dow-dow-dow of the stuttering drum,
The bugles, the charges, the swords are romantic
For those who survive when the bugles are dumb.

The lice of the trenches, the mortars, machine-guns,
The prisoners exchanged and the Christmas Day lull,
The no-man's-land raid and the swagger-stick rally
Are stirring, for when was a finished war dull?

The road-block, the ambush, the scrap on the mountain,
The slouch-hat, the trench-coat, the raid in the night,
The hand-grenade hefted, police-barracks burning
Ah, that was the life, and who's hurt in a fight?

The blitzkreig, the landings, the victories, the losses,
The eyes blind with sand, the retreat, the alert,
Commando and D-Day, H-Hour and Block-buster
Have filed through the glass, and was anyone hurt?

A flash and a mushroom, a hole in the planet,
Strange growth in the flora, less fauna to feed
Peace enters, the silence returns and the waters
Advance on the earth as the war tides recede.

A WARNING TO CONQUERORS

This is the country of the Norman tower,
The graceless keep, the bleak and slitted eye
Where fear drove comfort out; straw on the floor
Was price of conquering security.

They came and won, and then for centuries
Stood to their arms; the face grew bleak and lengthened
In the night vigil, while their foes at ease
Sang of the stranger and the towers he strengthened.

Ragweed and thistle hold the Norman field
And cows the hall where Gaelic never rang
Melodiously to harp or spinning wheel.
Their songs are spent now with the voice that sang;

And lost their conquest. This soft land quietly
Engulfed them like the Saxon and the Dane—
But kept the jutted brow, the slitted eye;
Only the faces and the names remain.

CHARLES DONNELLY

Charles Donnelly was born in 1914 in County Tyrone, and raised in Dublin. Donnelly received his education at University College, Dublin, where he was a contemporary of Flann O'Brien, Denis Devlin, and Donagh MacDonagh. Donnelly left home when his Marxist political activities involved him in difficulties with the authorities. He lived and worked for some time in London, then, in 1936, joined the Republican forces in Spain as a volunteer in the James Connolly centuria attached to the Abraham Lincoln Brigade. He was killed on the Jarama Front in Spain on February 27, 1937. A number of Donnelly's poems were published in journals in the 1930s, but a collection has yet to appear.

POEM

Between rebellion as a private study and the public
Defiance is simple action only which will flicker
Catlike, for spring. Whether at nerve-roots is secret
Iron, there's no diviner can tell, only the moment can
    show.
Simple and unclear moment, on a morning utterly
    different
And under circumstances different from what you'd
    expected.

Your flag is public over granite. Gulls fly above it.
Whatever the issue of the battle is, your memory
Is public, for them to pull awry with crooked hands,
Moist eyes. And villages' reputations will be built on
Inaccurate accounts of your campaigns. You're name for
    orators,
Figure stone-struck beneath damp Dublin sky.

In a delaying action, perhaps, on hillside in remote parish,
Outposts correctly placed, retreat secured to wood, bridge
    mined
Against pursuit, sniper may sight you carelessly
    contoured.
Or death may follow years in strait confinement, where
    diet
Is uniform as ceremony, lacking only fruit
Or on the barracks square before the sun casts shadow.

Name, subject of all considered words, praise and blame
Irrelevant, the public talk which sounds the same on
    hollow
Tongue as true, you'll be with Parnell and with Pearse.
Name alderman will raise a cheer with, teacher make
    reference
Oblique in class, and boys and women spin gum of
    sentiment
On qualities attributed in error.

Man, dweller in mountain huts, possessor of colored mice,
Skilful in minor manual turns, patron of obscure subjects,
    of
Gaelic swordsmanship and medieval armory,
The technique of the public man, the masked servilities
    are
Not for you, Master of military trade, you give
Like Raleigh, Lawrence, Childers, your services but not
    yourself.

THE TOLERANCE OF CROWS

Death comes in quantity from solved
Problems on maps, well-ordered dispositions,
Angles of elevation and direction;

Comes innocent from tools children might
Love, retaining under pillows
Innocently impales on any flesh.

And with flesh falls apart the mind
that trails thought from the mind that cuts
Thought clearly for a waiting purpose.

Progress of poison in the nerves and
Discipline's collapse is halted.
Body awaits the tolerance of crows.

HEROIC HEART

Ice of heroic heart seals plasmic soil
Where things ludicrously take root
To show in leaf kindnesses time had buried
And cry music under a storm of 'planes,
Making thrust head to slacken, muscle waver
And intent mouth recall old tender tricks.
Ice of heroic heart seals steel-bound brain.

There newer organs built for friendship's grappling
Waste down like wax. There only leafless plants
And earth retain disinterestedness.
Though magnetised to lie of the land, moves
Heartily over the map wrapped in its iron
Storm. Battering the roads, armoured columns
Break walls of stone or bone without receipt.
Jawbones find new way with meats, loins
Raking and blind, new way with women.

THE FLOWERING BARS

After sharp words from the fine mind,
protest in court,
the intimate high head constrained,
straight lines of prison, empty walls,
a subtle beauty in a simple place.

There to strain thought through the tightened brain,
there weave
the slender cords of thought, in calm,
until routine in prospect bound
joy into security,
and among strictness sweetness grew,
mystery of flowering bars.

VALENTIN IREMONGER

Valentin Iremonger was born in 1918 in Dublin. He was educated at Synge St. Christian Brothers School, at Colaiste Mhuire, and at the Abbey Theatre School of Acting (1938–1940). He was associated with the Abbey and the Gate theaters as actor and producer until 1946, when he entered the Irish Foreign Service. Iremonger has had an impressive career in the Foreign Service: he was Irish ambassador to Sweden, Norway, and Finland (1964–1968), then ambassador to India (1968–1973), and since 1973 ambassador to Luxembourg. Iremonger has also managed to pursue the vocation of man of letters: he was poetry editor of **Envoy** magazine in Dublin from 1949 to 1951, and is author of many articles and reviews in Irish and British journals. He received the AE Memorial Award in 1945. His poems are collected in **On the Barricades** (1944), **Reservations** (1950), and **Horan's Field and Other Reservations** (1972). Iremonger has translated two novels from the Irish; **Beatha Mhuire** (1955) is his translation into Irish of Rilke's **Das Marienleben**.

HECTOR

Talking to her, he knew it was the end,
The last time he'd speed her into sleep with kisses:
Achilles had it in for him and was fighting mad.
The roads of his longing she again wandered,
A girl desirable as midsummer's day.

He was a marked man and he knew it,
Being no match for Achilles whom the gods were backing.
Sadly he spoke to her for hours, his heart
Snapping like sticks, she on his shoulder crying.
Yet, sorry only that the meaning eluded him.

He slept well all night, having caressed
Andromache like a flower, though in a dream he saw
A body lying on the sands, huddled and bleeding,
Near the feet a sword in bits and by the head
An upturned, dented helmet.

ICARUS

As, even to-day, the airman, feeling the plane sweat
Suddenly, seeing the horizon tilt up gravely, the wings
    shiver,
Knows that, for once, Daedalus has slipped up badly,
Drunk on the job, perhaps, more likely dreaming, high-
    flier Icarus,
Head butting down, skidding along the light-shafts
Back, over the tones of the sea-waves and the slip-stream,
    heard
The gravel-voiced, stuttering trumpets of his heart

Sennet among the crumbling court-yards of his brain the
    mistake
Of trusting somebody else on an important affair like this;
And, while the flat sea, approaching, buckled into oh!
    avenues
Of acclamation, he saw the wrong story fan out into
    history.
Truth, undefined, lost in his own neglect. On the hills,
The summer-shackled hills, the sun spanged all day;
Love and the world were young and there was no ending:

But star-chaser, big-time-going, chancer Icarus
Like a dog on the sea lay and the girls forgot him,
And Daedalus, too busy hammering another job,
Remembered him only in pubs. No bugler at all
Sobbed taps for the young fool then, reported missing,
Presumed drowned, wing-bones and feathers on the tide
Drifting in casually, one by one.

THIS HOURE HER VIGILL

Elizabeth, frigidly stretched,
On a spring day surprised us
With her starched dignity and the quietness
Of her hands clasping a black cross.

With book and candle and holy water dish
She received us in the room with the blind down.
Her eyes were peculiarly closed and we knelt shyly
Noticing the blot of her hair on the white pillow.

We met that evening by the crumbling wall
In the field behind the house where I lived
And talked it over, but could find no reason
Why she had left us whom she had liked so much.

Death, yes, we understood: something to do
With age and decay, decrepit bodies;
But here was this vigorous one, aloof and prim,
Who would not answer our furtive whispers.

Next morning, hearing the priest call her name,
I fled outside, being full of certainty,
And cried my seven years against the church's stone wall.
For eighteen years I did not speak her name

Until this autumn day when, in a gale,
A sapling fell outside my window, its branches
Rebelliously blotting the lawn's green. Suddenly, I thought
Of Elizabeth, frigidly stretched.

PADRAIC FIACC

Padraic Fiacc (the pseudonym of Patrick Joseph O'Connor) was born in 1924 in Belfast. His father emigrated in 1930 to New York City and Fiacc was educated at St. Joseph's Seminary in Calicoon, New York. He returned to Belfast in 1946. In 1957 he won the AE Memorial Award for poetry. He has edited an anthology of contemporary Ulster poetry, **The Wearing of the Black** (1974), and has published three collections of his own poetry, **By the Black Stream** (1969), **Odour of Blood** (1973), and **Nights in the Bad Place** (1977).

HAEMORRHAGE

"I bleed by the black stream
for my torn bough."
       James Joyce

Entries patent leather with sleet
Mirror gas and neon light.

A boy with a husky voice picks a fight
And kicks a tin down home in pain

To tram rattle and ship horn
In a fog from where fevers come

In at an East Wind's
Icy burst of black rain . . .

Here I was good and got and born
Cold, lost, not predictable

Poor, bare crossed in grain
With a shudder no one can still

In the damp down by the half-dried river
Slimy at night on the mudflats in

The moon light gets an un-
earthly white Belfast man.

THE POET

I am the chaunt-rann of a Singer
Who has sung to heart at night
How the rust-loch's hazel waters
Mirror the stars all right:
Christ on a tree for you and me
And the moon-dark worlds between!

I am the chaunt-rann of a Singer
Who has sung to heart by day
How the grey rain on the wet street
Washes our lives away:
Christ on a tree for you and me
And the sun-bright worlds between!

I am the chaunt-rann of a Singer
Who does not cease chaunt with loam
As the crouched lime of the good earth
Eats us away on home:
Christ on a tree for you and me
And none of the worlds between!

GLOSS

Nor truth nor good did they know
But beauty burning away.
They were the dark earth people of old
Restive in the clay.

Deirdre watched Naisi die
And great King Conor of himself said
'Did you ever see a bottomless bucket
In the muck discarded?'

And comradely Dermot was destroyed by Fionn
Because of the beauty of a girl.
Because of the beauty of a girl
The sky went raging on fire

And the sea was pushed out into rage.
They were the dark earth people of old
And Deirdre pitched herself into the sea.
Turn the page. Turn the page.

BRENDAN GONE

for Derek Mahon

Man seasick with drink
Steadying himself against a lamp post
Before he is game to risk: chance
The long street's precipice brink

Like a very fleshy ghost
Doing a St. Vitus dance
In night's depth, the disappearing
Act, the deep, death-fearing, lost
Irish bachelor in a New York flat

PADRAIC FIACC

After money-making years of waste
Blown up with beer false fat
Losing one's boy taste
For life, woman, or
Enemy encounter during war
At night bolts his apartment door

Alone, window-hurtling to the street

A corpse once young and sweet.

ANTHONY CRONIN

Anthony Cronin was born in 1925 in County Wexford. He was educated at Trinity College, Dublin, and later lived for some years in London and in Spain. Cronin has been editor of the important Irish magazine, **The Bell**, literary editor of the London weekly review **Time and Tide**, and a columnist for the **Irish Times**. A very perceptive literary critic, he wrote a collection of critical essays called **A Question of Modernity** (1966). Cronin's published collections of poetry include **Poems** (1958) and **Collected Poems 1950–1973** (1973).

APOLOGY

It was proper for them, awaking in ordered houses,
Among russet walls where fruit grew ripe to the hand,
Walking on lawns where fountains arched in the summer,
To praise through their gentle days the dwelling virtues
And architect epics to honour the good and the brave.
And easy perhaps for the desert-maddened preacher,
With his withered loins and the dirt hard in his pores,
To lash with his locust-tongue the uncertainly happy
And call on the townsmen to shrive and to shrivel for
    God.
But we who have climbed to the top of tall houses in
    winter

And heard in the gathering silence the limp of the clock,
Who dunned by our need through the days are unfailingly
    traitors
In sad and undignified ways to each circle of friends,
How can we praise in our poems the simplified heroes,
Or urge to the truth we can never be true to ourselves?
O love that forgives because needing forgiveness also
Forgive us that we have not lived through a virtuous day,
That we ask to be judged in the end by our own
    compassion,
Thief calling to thief from his cross with no Christ in
    between.

ANARCHIST

With dirty collar and shoes unpolished,
Dodging the traffic he crosses the street.
Thoughts of loose ends and unfinished poems
Drag at his indeterminate feet.

Now warm by the railings he saunters unhurried
Regarded by workers who fear to be late.
They have achieved like the ant to action,
His is a gloomier, lazier fate.

The bank will grow grimier, office blocks crumble,
The cinemas gleam in the April day,
But he has no part in the organization,
For drainage or water-works he will not pay.

A bus shudders past him, he steps off the pavement,
Blood and world ageing as onward he walks,
Now seated again at the marble-topped table
The dream flickers round him, he lives as he talks.

Tomorrow again perhaps wonder will wake him
And words like tame pigeons will flock to his call,
He will rise from the dead, this disconsolate lover,
And proudly and carelessly ride for a fall.

AUTUMN POEM

With fires and lights we ward the winter off,
The damp that falls on Hampstead and the heart,
Indoors, who live alone, inconstant lovers,
Hear creaking threats in every empty room.

And leaving parks where summer crumples over
And leaves are slowly burning in the rain
The heart a hungry gull wheels off at nightfall
To snatch for food on any lighted shore.

For as before with winter here grows harsher
The law we suffer under in the streets,
The self-sufficient south withdrawn, not caring
What wounds have marked the north, sincere and raw.

We know who chance on poverty fall poorer,
Splintering their sticks of hope to make a fire
In that queer stillness of October evenings
As autumn gutters out behind the trees.

And growing out of summer's cast-off clothing,
Too awkward and too hopeful for our age,
We pawn to pay for sleeping space this winter
Out of the fog and traffic of the brain.

SURPRISE

Since we are told it we believe it's true,
Or does as it's intended. Birds eat worms,
The water flows downhill and aunts depart.
Sea heaves, sky rains and can be blue.
Always love cherishes and firelight warms.
That knocking sound you hear is just your heart.

Nothing is angry long and all surprises
Are well provided for. The dog that died
Became a legend and then had its day.
Sooner or later someone realizes
That a mistake occurred and no one lied.
If it is said to be then that's the way.

But soon when doors are opened hints are found
Of strange disorders that have no because.
In one room on the ceiling is a stain.
Someone is missing who should be around.
Some games are stopped by arbitrary laws
And an odd I does things it can't explain.

Nothing is order now and no forecast
Can be depended on since what's declared
To be may not be so and each face wears
A false expression. Yet the very last
Surprise of all still finds us unprepared:
Although we say I love you no one cares.

THE ELEPHANT TO THE GIRL
IN BERTRAM MILLS' CIRCUS

I, like a slow, morose and shabby fatalist,
Unfitted for presumption, trousers too loose,
Shamble towards you, scented, delicate,
Your eyes glittering myopically back at the front rows,
Shoulder blades bared to me,
Imagining, although I cannot see
Your faintly trembling lips, white teeth, those fixed bright
    eyes,
Your desperate smile and stare.
I stoop, mournful that this should be
Over your lacquered hair,
My soft tongue touches it,
My loose pink lips enclose
Your closing eyes and nose,
Between the inside of your thighs
And the front rows' avid gaze
I drop my trunk.
Then you lean back, breasts taut
And grip my ears,
Abandoned to decision now you raise
Your legs and close them round my forehead bone
And we proceed on circuit, we alone,
You in my dark, my gravity, my space
Waiting for your release.
You are my victim, yes, but all my care,
Your face invisible and your shining hair
Within my mouth's pink softness,
My foul breath
Your fierce preoccupation.
The rest possess
Only your white long arms and legs,
Your backside's elevation
And whatever consolation

Lies in the fact that they can watch our progress.
Yet when I set
Gently your beautiful buttocks down again
And, lifting lip and trunk, reveal your face,
Your smile, your hair in place,
Only a slight
Worry about mucus mingles with your response
To them and their applause.
And when you twist and show on solid ground
Around the ring to all of them the tight
Behind and breasts which I have carried round,
And doing so invite
With effulgent wave and kiss
Them all to re-possess
The high-heeled girl that lately ran such risk—
I am the loser for my tenderness.

PEARSE HUTCHINSON

Pearse Hutchinson was born in 1927 in Glasgow, Scotland. He was educated in Dublin at the Christian Brothers School, and at University College. From 1951 to 1953 Hutchinson worked as a translator for the International Labor Organization in Geneva, Switzerland. He was drama critic for Radio Eireann from 1957 to 1961, and for Telefis Eireann in 1968. Hutchinson lived in Spain for seven years. He was a Gregory Fellow in Poetry at the University of Leeds from 1971 to 1973, and received the Butler Award for Gaelic writing in 1969. He has published two collections of translations: **Josep Carner: 30 Poems** (from Catalan, 1962) and **Friend Songs: Medieval Love-Poems** (from Galaico-Portuguese, 1970). His five collections of poetry are: **Tongue Without Hands** (1963), **Faoistin Bhacach (Imperfect Confession)** (1968), **Expansions** (1969), **Watching the Morning Grow** (1972), and **The Frost Is All Over** (1975).

DISTORTIONS

What a surprise you got—
aging yourself and using
sexagenarians calmly
as mirrors

not really distorting
but merely prophetic
and so much more reliable
than the glass in the bathroom
that gets the sun in the morning
or the one in the hall
that never gets any at all—
What a surprise you got
when one reliable mirror
who knew himself 60 not 40
so could not need you as a mirror,
thought you were flesh not glass
human not mineral
and therefore unbreakable,
and not recognizing
himself as a mirror
in your extravagant sense
proceeded to treat you
like a toy, like a brother,
and though you were flesh not glass
you broke, and bled,
not sand or calcium either
nor dull red lead—
so how surprised you felt
assembling yourself on the pavement
flesh not glass
watching his creased nape
moving away, calmly,
as if it had never seen
itself in a flower, a child,
or another old man.

INTO THEIR TRUE GENTLENESS

For Katherine Kavanagh

If love is the greatest reality,
and I believe it is,
the gentle are more real
than the violent or than
those like me who
hate violence,
long for gentleness,
but never in our own act
achieve true gentleness.
We fall in love with people
we consider gentle,
we love them violently
for their gentleness,
so violently we drive
them to violence,
for our gentleness
is less real
than their breaking patience,
so falsely we accuse
them of being false.

But with any luck,
time half-opens our eyes
to at least a hundredth
part of our absurdity,
and lets them travel back
released from us,
into their true gentleness,
even with us.

COPPER-BEECH AND BUTTER-FINGERS

"en ti como sol"
(Octavio Paz)

You made me feel so young again
that imagining I was over eighty,
basking in a second
but more precocious childhood,
I started climbing trees
to bring you down the moon growing
on every tree-top.

But always a branch broke,
or my butter-fingers lost their hold,
and I fell to the ground
(never mind the bruises),
clutching perhaps a torn leaf—
copper-beech or baobab—
as a peace-offering or ersatz.

So instead of me fetching you the moon
I turn to you to give me back again
the sun: en ti como sol.

But I mustn't feel such
a failure after all:
in certain lights the copper-beech-leaf
looks almost the same color as your hair
and eyes,
     blends
          into your rioting hair.

But I mustn't feel too cocky after all:
no leaf compares to your body's
whitegold slender grace:
on whom how soon
must these butter-fingers lose their
adoring gluttonous contrite grateful
so precarious but miraculous foothold?

RICHARD MURPHY

Richard Murphy was born in 1927 in County Galway, Ireland, and educated in England; he received his B.A. and M.A. degrees in English Language and Literature from Oxford. Before returning to Ireland in 1956, he worked for Lloyds of London, taught at the English School in Crete, and studied at the Sorbonne. In 1951 he won the AE Memorial Award for Poetry. He has toured the United States giving poetry readings and taught at many American universities including the University of Virginia (1965), Colgate University (1971), Bard College (1972), the Writers' Workshop at the University of Iowa (1976), and Syracuse University (1977). He has also held a visiting fellowship at Reading University, England (1968), and the Compton Lectureship in Poetry at the University of Hull, England (1969). In 1961 he settled in Cleggan, County Galway, where he skippered a Galway hooker for seven years during the summer. In 1969 he bought High Island off the west coast of Ireland. His collections of poetry include **Sailing to an Island** (1963), **The Battle of Aughrim** (1968), and **High Island** (1974).

THE PHILOSOPHER AND THE BIRDS

(In memory of Wittgenstein at Rossroe)

A solitary invalid in a fuchsia garden
Where time's rain eroded the root since Eden,
He became for a tenebrous epoch the stone.

Here wisdom surrendered the don's gown
Choosing, for Cambridge, two deck chairs,
A kitchen table, undiluted sun.

He clipped with February shears the dead
Metaphysical foliage. Old, in fieldfares
Fantasies rebelled though annihilated.

He was haunted by gulls beyond omega shade,
His nerve tormented by terrified knots
In pin-feathered flesh. But all folly repeats

Is worth one snared robin his fingers untied.
He broke prisons, beginning with words,
And at last tamed, by talking, wild birds.

Through accident of place, now by belief
I follow his love which bird-handled thoughts
To grasp growth's terror or death's leaf.

He last on this savage promontory shored
His logical weapon. Genius stirred
A soaring intolerance to teach a blackbird.

So before alpha you may still hear sing
In the leaf-dark dusk some descended young
Who exalt the evening to a wordless song.

His wisdom widens: he becomes worlds
Where thoughts are wings. But at Rossroe hordes
Of village cats have massacred his birds.

THE POET ON THE ISLAND

(To Theodore Roethke)

On a wet night, laden with books for luggage,
And stumbling under the burden of himself,
He reached the pier, looking for a refuge.

Darkly he crossed to the island six miles off:
The engine pulsed, the sails invented rhythm,
While the sea expanded and the rain drummed softly.

Safety on water, he rocked with a new theme:
And in the warmth of his mind's greenhouse bloomed
A poem as graceful as a chrysanthemum.

His forehead, a Prussian helmet, moody, domed,
Relaxed in the sun: a lyric was his lance.
To be loved by the people, he, a stranger, hummed

In the herring-store on Sunday crammed with drunks
Ballads of bawdry with a speakeasy stress.
Yet lonely they left him, "one of the Yanks."

The children understood. This was not madness.
How many orphans had he fathered in words
Robust and cunning, but never heartless.

He watched the harbour scouted by sea-birds:
His fate was like fish under poetry's beaks:
Words began weirdly to take off inwards.

Time that they calendar in seasons not in clocks,
In gardens dug over and houses roofed,
Was to him a see-saw of joys and shocks,

Where his body withered but his style improved.
A storm shot up, his glass cracked in a gale:
An abstract thunder of darkness deafened

The listeners he'd once given roses, now hail.
He'd burst the lyric barrier: logic ended.
Doctors were called, and he agreed to sail.

from THE BATTLE OF AUGHRIM

Deep red bogs divided
Aughrim, the horse's ridge
Of garland hedgerows and the summer dance,
Ireland's defence
From the colonists' advance:
Twenty thousand soldiers on each side,
Between them a morass
Of godly bigotry and pride of race,
With a causeway two abreast could cross.

In opposite camps our ancestors
Ten marriages ago,
Caught in a feud of absent kings
Who used war like a basset table
Gambling to settle verbal things,
Decide if bread be God
Or God a parable,
Lit matches, foddered horses, thirsted, marched,
Halted, and marched to battle.

*　　　　*　　　　*

"They pick us for our looks
To line up with matchlocks,
Face shot like sandbags,
Fall, and manure the grass
Where we wouldn't be let trespass
Alive, but to do their work
Till we dropped in muck.

Who cares which foreign king
Governs, we'll still fork dung,
No one lets *us* grab soil:
Roman or English school
Insists it is God
Who must lighten our burden
Digging someone else's garden."

          *   *   *

God was eaten in secret places among the rocks
His mother stood in a cleft with roses at her feet
And the priests were whipped or hunted like stags.

God was spoken to at table with wine and bread
The soul needed no heavenly guide to intercede
And heretics were burnt at stakes for what they said.

God was fallen into ruins on the shores of lakes
Peasants went on milking cows or delving dikes
And landlords corresponded with landlords across bogs.

SEALS AT HIGH ISLAND

The calamity of seals begins with jaws.
Born in caverns that reverberate
With endless malice of the sea's tongue

Clacking on shingle, they learn to bark back
In fear and sadness and celebration.
The ocean's mouth opens forty feet wide
And closes on a morsel of their rock.

Swayed by the thrust and backfall of the tide,
A dappled grey bull and a brindled cow
Copulate in the green water of a cove.
I watch from a cliff-top, trying not to move.
Sometimes they sink and merge into black shoals;
Then rise for air, his muzzle on her neck,
Their winged feet intertwined as a fish-tail.

She opens her fierce mouth like a scarlet flower
Full of white seeds; she holds it open long
At the sunburst in the music of their loving;
And cries a little. But I must remember
How far their feelings are from mine marooned.
If there are tears at this holy ceremony
Theirs are caused by brine and mine by breeze.

When the great bull withdraws his rod, it glows
Like a carnelian candle set in jade.
The cow ripples ashore to feed her calf;
While an old rival, eyeing the deed with hate,
Swims to attack the tired triumphant god.
They rear their heads above the boiling surf,
Their terrible jaws open, jetting blood.

At nightfall they haul out, and mourn the drowned,
Playing to the sea sadly their last quartet,
An improvised requiem that ravishes
Reason, while ripping scale up like a net:
Brings pity trembling down the rocky spine
Of headlands, till the bitter ocean's tongue
Swells in their cove, and smothers their sweet song.

HIGH ISLAND

A shoulder of rock
Sticks high up out of the sea,
A fisherman's mark
For lobster and blue-shark.

Fissile and stark
The crust is flaking off,
Seal-rock, gull-rock,
Cove and cliff.

Dark mounds of mica schist,
A lake, mill and chapel,
Roofless, one gable smashed,
Lie ringed with rubble.

An older calm,
The kiss of rock and grass,
Pink thrift and white sea-campion,
Flowers in the dead place.

Day keeps lit a flare
Round the north pole all night.
Like brushing long wavy hair
Petrels quiver in flight.

Quietly as the rustle
Of an arm entering a sleeve,
They slip down to nest
Under altar-stone or grave.

Round the wrecked laura
Needles flicker
Tacking air, quicker and quicker
To rock, sea and star.

ENIGMA

Her hair has a sweet smell of girlhood under his face
    Darkening the moon on her pillow.

Tenderly her fingertips probe the furrows of his temple
    And find the questionmark of an ear.

How can she play in the rubble of his pleasure ground
    Paths overgrown with laurel and briar?

How can he pick the fruit she will bear in time to come
    On her lips' not yet flowering bud?

Her future is an apple tree, his past a dark old yew
    Growing together in this orchard now.

TROUVAILLE

This root of bog-oak the sea dug up she found
Poking about, in old age, and put to stand
Between a snarling griffin and a half-nude man
Moulded of lead on my chimney-piece.
It looks like a heron rising from a pond,
Feet dipped in brown-trout water,
Head shooting arrow-sharp into blue sky.

"What does it remind you of?" she wanted to know.
I thought of trees in her father's demesne
Levelled by chainsaws;
Bunches of primroses I used to pick
Before breakfast, hunting along a limestone lane,
To put at her bedside before she woke;
And all my childhood's broken promises.

No, no! It precedes alphabets,
Planted woods, or gods.
Twisted and honed as a mind that never forgets
It lay dead in bog acids, undecayable:
Secretively hardening in a womb of moss, until
The peat burnt off, a freak tide raised
The feathered stick she took to lure me home.

RICHARD KELL

Richard Kell was born in 1927, in Youghal, County Cork. After being educated at Methodist College, Belfast, and at Wesley College in Dublin, Kell attended Trinity College, Dublin, where he received his B.A. in English and French literature. He is married and has four children. Kell has been a senior lecturer in English at Newcastle upon Tyne Polytechnic since 1970. He has contributed to many Irish and British periodicals. His poems are collected in **Poems** (1957), **Control Tower** (1962), **Differences** (1969), and **Humours** (1978).

FISHING HARBOUR TOWARDS EVENING

Slashed clouds leak gold. Along the slurping wharf
The snugged boats creak and seesaw. Round the masts

Abrasive squalls flake seagulls off the sky:
Choppy with wings the rapids of shrill sound.

Wrapt in spliced airs of fish and tar,
Light wincing on their knives, the clockwork men

Incise and scoop the oily pouches, flip
The soft guts overboard with blood-wet fingers.

Among three rhythms the slapping silver turns
To polished icy marble upon the deck.

THE MAKERS

The artisan didn't collect his gear and say
"What beautiful object shall I make today?"

The poet didn't fondle a phrase and gape,
And think, "What elegant structure can I shape?"

The artisan made a gatepost
So that a certain gate could be opened and closed.

The poet started a poem
So that a meaning could reveal a form.

The gatepost is itself, sturdy and straight:
Precisely this gatepost for this gate.

The poem is itself, the form-in-content:
Exactly these words for what was meant.

The gatepost is rough, distinct and lovable,
Untouched by the purpose that made it possible.

The poem is plain, final, able to please,
Clear of the hungers that made it what it is.

CALYPSO

Crazed by the suck and roar
of spinning water—nine days
clear of the drowned—tugged from a lurching spar,

flopped like a seal where waves elide and glaze
warm sand, I came ashore.
The sailor found his woman standing there.

Firelight on hair and skin: a scent
of smoke from cedar logs and pepperwood.
She called me and I went,
making no choice of bad or good:
whatever choosing meant,
only the girl, half goddess, understood.

The coiled sea takes us in.
Freeing ourselves we bind ourselves:
doing what we need, we do what must be done.
The cone of darkness fills as it revolves,
lifts us out into the foaming sun.
Climactic water swills the jagged shelves.

The crusts of fire flake down: a red spark
dissolves in moonlight . . . Dawn, the slow
focusing of rock where four streams play
beneath a vine; deep woods for owl and crow,
clear of the filtered dark.
A trance of distance sublimates the bay

to a thin sift of thunder . . .
After such nights, such days. At first,
leaving her there asleep, I used to wander
back to the crude source, where combers burst
spilling white grains of water,
and squealing gulls—touched nerves in the wind—

were twinges of sharp lust.
Both day and night, it seemed, were provident,
reciprocal as host and guest.
And yet the idyll faltered, the enchantment
left something over, grit of discontent:
the innocence of dawn became a cyst.

Hunched in the cool dark one afternoon,
I heard Calypso singing while she wove—
her body, in the opening of the cave,
edged with a down of light. Perhaps the tune,
the blonde hair brimming over in the sun,
a movement, or some old domestic flavour

tricked me—or indeed
I solved an absence by telepathy,
from the deep shafts of truth a slighted need
drew substance: but I saw Penelope
there, in an arched radiance, and she made
from whispering spools a web of loyalty.

The dour eroding pain
grown harsh, I left the cave,
clambered through wind that sawed against the grain
of gnarled blue water: in the grumbling cove
loitered all afternoon,
hearing the shingle rasp, the gulls complain.

Perhaps desire and guilt
grinding together, or the lie
that strikes through self-fulfilment, a rock's fault.
On jagged shelves the leaping foam gives way
in slack pools, finally in grains, a dry
precipitate, the irony of salt.

THOMAS KINSELLA

Thomas Kinsella was born in 1928 in Dublin. He was educated at University College, Dublin, and worked from 1948 to 1965 in the Irish civil service. In 1965 he moved to the United States, where he became first writer-in-residence and then professor of English at Southern Illinois University. He has been professor of English at Temple University in Philadelphia since 1970, and now divides his time between living in Ireland, where he has his own press (Peppercanister), and the United States. Kinsella is one of the most widely acclaimed of modern Irish poets. He has received numerous awards, including the Guinness Award (1958), the Irish Arts Council Triennial Book Award (1961), the Denis Devlin Memorial Award (1967 and 1970), and Guggenheim Fellowships (1968 and 1971). In 1965 he became a member of the Irish Academy of Letters. He is married and has three children. Kinsella has translated a substantial amount of material from the Irish, including the epic of the Ulster cycle, **The Tain** (1969). Kinsella's major collections of poetry include **Poems** (1956), **Another September** (1958), **Moralities** (1960), **Poems and Translations** (1961), **Downstream** (1962), **Nightwalker and Other Poems** (1967), **Notes From the Land of the Dead and Other Poems** (1972), **New Poems, 1973** (1973), **Selected Poems 1956–1968** (1973), and **A Technical Supplement** (1977).

BAGGOT STREET DESERTA

Lulled, at silence, the spent attack.
The will to work is laid aside.
The breaking-cry, the strain of the rack,
Yield, are at peace. The window is wide
On a crawling arch of stars, and the night
Reacts faintly to the mathematic
Passion of a cello suite
Plotting the quiet of my attic.
A mile away the river toils
Its buttressed fathoms out to sea;
Tucked in the mountains, many miles
Away from its roaring outcome, a shy
Gasp of waters in the gorse
Is sonnetting origins. Dreamers' heads
Lie mesmerised in Dublin's beds
Flashing with images, Adam's morse.

A cigarette, the moon, a sigh
Of educated boredom, greet
A curlew's lingering threadbare cry
Of common loss. Compassionate,
I add my call of exile, half-
Buried longing, half-serious
Anger and the rueful laugh.
We fly into our risk, the spurious.

Versing, like an exile, makes
A virtuoso of the heart,
Interpreting the old mistakes
And discords in a work of Art
For the One, a private masterpiece
Of doctored recollections. Truth
Concedes, before the dew, its place
In the spray of dried forgettings Youth

Collected when they were a single
Furious undissected bloom.
A voice clarifies when the tingle
Dies out of the nerves of time:
Endure and let the present punish.
Looking backward, all is lost;
The Past becomes a fairy bog
Alive with fancies, double crossed
By pad of owl and hoot of dog,
Where shaven, serious-minded men
Appear with lucid theses, after
Which they don the mists again
With trackless, cotton-silly laughter;
Secretly a swollen Burke
Assists a decomposing Hare
To cart a body of good work
With midnight mutterings off somewhere;
The goddess who had light for thighs
Grows feet of dung and takes to bed,
Affronting horror-stricken eyes,
The marsh bird that children dread.

I nonetheless inflict, endure,
Tedium, intracordal hurt,
The sting of memory's quick, the drear
Uprooting, burying, prising apart
Of loves a strident adolescent
Spent in doubt and vanity.
All feed a single stream, impassioned
Now with obsessed honesty,
A tugging scruple that can keep
Clear eyes staring down the mile,
The thousand fathoms, into sleep.

Fingers cold against the sill
Feel, below the stress of flight,
The slow implosion of my pulse
In a wrist with poet's cramp, a tight
Beat tapping out endless calls
Into the dark, as the alien
Garrison in my own blood
Keeps constant contact with the main
Mystery, not to be understood.
Out where imagination arches
Chilly points of light transact
The business of the border-marches
Of the Real, and I—a fact
That may be countered or may not—
Find their privacy complete.

My quarter-inch of cigarette
Goes flaring down to Baggot Street.

ANOTHER SEPTEMBER

Dreams fled away, this country bedroom, raw
With the touch of the dawn, wrapped in a minor peace,
Hears through an open window the garden draw
Long pitch black breaths, lay bare its apple trees,
Ripe pear trees, brambles, windfall-sweetened soil,
Exhale rough sweetness against the starry slates.
Nearer the river sleeps St. John's, all toil
Locked fast inside a dream with iron gates.

Domestic Autumn, like an animal
Long used to handling by those countrymen,
Rubs her kind hide against the bedroom wall
Sensing a fragrant child come back again
—Not this half-tolerated consciousness,
Its own cold season never done,
But that unspeaking daughter, growing less
Familiar where we fell asleep as one.

Wakeful moth-wings blunder near a chair,
Toss their light shell at the glass, and go
To inhabit the living starlight. Stranded hair
Stirs on the still linen. It is as though
The black breathing that billows her sleep, her name,
Drugged under judgment, waned and—bearing daggers
And balances—down the lampless darkness they came,
Moving like women: Justice, Truth, such figures.

CLARENCE MANGAN

Sometimes, childishly watching a beetle, thrush or trout,
Or charting the heroes and animals of night-time, sudden
    unhappiness
Would bewilder me, strayed in the long void of youth
Where nothing is understood.

Later, locked in a frantic pose, all mankind calling,
I, being anxious, eager to please, shouted my fear
That something was wrong.

Back to a wall, facing tumultuous talking faces,
Once I lost the reason for speech. My heart was taken,
Stretched with terror by only a word a mouth had
    uttered,
Clipped to a different, faceless destroyer.

Long I waited to know what naked meeting would come
With what was moving behind my eyes and desolating
What I touched.

Over a glass, or caught in lamplight, caught on the edge
Of act, my hand is suddenly stopped and fills with waiting.
Out of the shadows behind my laughter surgical fingers
Come and I am strapped to a table.

Ultimate, pitiless, again I ply the knife.

COVER HER FACE

She has died suddenly, aged twenty-nine years, in Dublin.
Some of her family travel from the country to bring her body
home. Having driven all morning through a storm

I

They dither softly at her bedroom door
In soaking overcoats, and words forsake
Even their comforters. The bass of prayer
Haunts the chilly landing while they take
Their places in a murmur of heartbreak.

Shabby with sudden tears, they know their part,
Mother and brother, resigning all that ends
At these drab walls. For here, with panicked heart,
A virgin broke the seal; who understands
The sheet pulled white and Maura's locked blue hands?

Later her frown will melt, when by degrees
They flinch from grief; a girl they have never seen,
Sunk now in love and horror to her knees,
The black official giving discipline
To shapeless sorrow, these are more their kin,

By grace of breath, than that grave derelict
Whose blood and feature, like a sleepy host,
Agreed a while with theirs. Her body's tact
Swapped child for woman, woman for a ghost,
Until its buried sleep lay uppermost;

And Maura, come to terms at last with pain,
Rests in her ruptured mind, her temples tight,
Patiently weightless as her time burns down.
Soon her few glories will be shut from sight:
Her slightness, the fine metal of her hair spread out,

Her cracked, sweet laugh. Such gossamers as hold
Friends, family—all fortuitous conjunction—
Sever with bitter whispers; with untold
Peace shrivel to their anchors in extinction.
There, newly trembling, others grope for function.

II

Standing by the door, effaced in self,
I cannot deny her death, protest, nor grieve,
Dogged by a scrap of memory: some tossed shelf
Holds, a secret shared, that photograph,
Her arm tucked tiredly into mine; her laugh,

As though she also knew a single day
Would serve to bleed us to a diagram,
Sighs and confides; she waived validity
The night she drank the furnace of the Lamb,
Draining one image of its faint *I am*.

I watch her drift, in doubt whether dead or born
—Not with Ophelia's strewn virginity
But with a pale unmarriage—out of the worn
Bulk of day, under its sightless eye,
And close her dream in hunger. So we die.

Monday, without regret, darkens the pane
And sheds on the shaded living, the crystal soul,
A gloomy lustre of the pouring rain.
Nuns have prepared her for the holy soil
And round her bed the faded roses peel

That the fruit of justice may be sown in peace
To them that make peace, and bite its ashen bread.
Mother, brother, when our questions cease
Such peace may come, consenting to the good,
Chaste, biddable, out of all likelihood.

A COUNTRY WALK

Sick of the piercing company of women
I swung the gate shut with a furious sigh,
Rammed trembling hands in pockets and drew in
A breath of river air. A rook's wet wing
Cuffed abruptly upward through the drizzle.

On either hand dead trunks in drapes of creeper,
Strangled softly by horse-mushroom, writhed
In vanished passion, broken down like sponge.
I walked their hushed stations, passion dying,
Each slow footfall a drop of peace returning.

I clapped my gloves. Three cattle turned aside
Their fragrant bodies from a corner gate
And down the sucking chaos of a hedge
Churned land to liquid in their dreamy passage.
Briefly through the beaded grass a path
Led to the holy stillness of a well
And there in the smell of water, stone and leaf
I knelt, baring my hand, and scooped and drank,
Shivering, and inch by inch rejoiced:
Ferocity became intensity.

Or so it seemed as with a lighter step
I turned an ivied corner to confront
The littered fields where summer broke and fled.
Below me, right and left, the valley floor
Tilted, in a silence full of storms;
A ruined aqueduct in delicate rigor
Clenched cat-backed, rooted to one horizon;
A vast asylum reared its potent calm
Up from the other through the sodden air,
Tall towers ochre where the gutters dripped;
A steeple; the long yielding of a railway turn
Through thorn and willow; a town endured its place . . .

Joining the two slopes, blocking an ancient way
With crumbled barracks, castle and brewery
It took the running river, wrinkling and pouring,
Into its blunt embrace. A line of roofs
Fused in veils of rain and steely light
As the dying sun struck it huge glancing blows.
A strand of idle smoke mounted until
An idler current combed it slowly west,
A hook of shadow dividing the still sky . . .
Mated, like a fall of rock, with time,
The place endured its burden: as a froth
Locked in a swirl of turbulence, a shape
That forms and fructifies and dies, a wisp
That hugs the bridge, an omphalos of scraps.

I moved, my glove-backs glistening, over flesh-
And forest-fed earth; till, skirting a marshy field
Where melancholy brambles scored the mud
By the gapped glitter of a speckled ford,
I shuddered with a visual sweet excitement.

Those murmuring shallows made a trampling place
Apt for death-combat, as the tales agree:
There, the day that Christ hung dying, twin
Brothers armed in hate on either side;
The day darkened but they moved to meet
With crossed swords under a dread eclipse
And mingled their bowels at the saga's end.
There the first Normans massacred my fathers,
Then stroked their armoured horses' necks, disposed
In ceremony, sable on green sward.
Twice more the reeds grew red, the stones obscured:
When knot-necked Cromwell and his fervent sword
Dispatched a convent shrieking to their Lover;
And when in peasant fear a rebel host,
Through long retreat grown half hysterical
—Methodical, ludicrous—piked in groups of three
Cromwell's puritan brood, their harmless neighbours,
Forked them half living to the sharp water
And melted into the martyred countryside,
Root eaters, strange as badgers. Pulses calmed;
The racked heroic nerved itself for peace;
Then came harsh winters, motionless waterbirds,
And generations that let welcome fail.

Road and river parted. Now my path
Lay gleaming through the greasy dusk, uphill
Into the final turn. A concrete cross
Low in the ditch grew to the memory
Of one who answered latest the phantom hag,
Tireless Rebellion, when with mouth awry
She hammered at the door, disrupting harvest.
There he bled to death, his line of sight
Blocked by the corner-stone, and did not see
His town ablaze with joy, the grinning foe
Driven in heavy lorries from the field;

And he lay cold in the Hill Cemetery
When freedom burned his comrades' itchy palms,
Too much for flesh and blood, and—armed in hate—
Brother met brother in a modern light.
They turned the bloody corner, knelt and killed,
Who gather still at Easter round his grave,
Our watchful elders. Deep in his crumbled heart
He takes their soil, and chatting they return
To take their town again, that have exchanged
A trenchcoat playground for a gombeen jungle.

Around the corner, in an open square,
I came upon the sombre monuments
That bear their names: MacDonagh & McBride,
Merchants; Connolly's Commercial Arms . . .
Their windows gave me back my stolid self
In attitudes of staring as I paced
Their otherworldly gloom, reflected light
Playing on lens and raincoat stonily.
I turned away. Down the sloping square
A lamp switched on above the urinal;
Across the silent handball alley, eyes
That never looked on lover measured mine
Over the Christian Brothers' frosted glass
And turned away. Out of the neighbouring shades
A car plunged soundlessly and disappeared
Pitching downward steeply to the bridge.
I too descended. Naked sycamores,
Gathered dripping near the quay, stood still
And dropped from their combining arms a single
Word upon my upturned face. I trod
The river underfoot; the parapet
Above the central arch received my hands.

Under a darkening and clearing heaven
The hastening river streamed in a slate sheen,
Its face a-swarm. Across the swollen water
(Delicate myriads vanishing in a breath)
Faint ripples winked; a thousand currents broke,
Kissing, dismembering, in threads of foam
Or poured intact over the stony bed
Glass-green and chill; their shallow, shifting world
Slid on in troubled union, forging together
Surfaces that gave and swallowed light;
And grimly the flood divided where it swept
An endless debris through the failing dusk
Under the thudding span beneath my feet.

Venit Hesperus;
In green and golden light; bringing sweet trade.
The inert stirred. Heart and tongue were loosed:
"The waters hurtle through the flooded night . . ."

MIRROR IN FEBRUARY

The day dawns, with scent of must and rain,
Of opened soil, dark trees, dry bedroom air.
Under the fading lamp, half dressed—my brain
Idling on some compulsive fantasy—
I towel my shaven jaw and stop, and stare,
Riveted by a dark exhausted eye,
A dry downturning mouth.

It seems again that it is time to learn,
In this untiring, crumbling place of growth
To which, for the time being, I return.
Now plainly in the mirror of my soul
I read that I have looked my last on youth
And little more; for they are not made whole
That reach the age of Christ.

Below my window the wakening trees,
Hacked clean for better bearing, stand defaced
Suffering their brute necessities;
And how should the flesh not quail, that span for span
Is mutilated more? In slow distaste
I fold my towel with what grace I can,
Not young, and not renewable, but man.

WORMWOOD

I have dreamt it again: standing suddenly still
In a thicket, among wet trees, stunned, minutely
Shuddering, hearing a wooden echo escape.

A mossy floor, almost colourless, disappears
In depths of rain among the tree shapes.
I am straining, tasting that echo a second longer.

If I can hold it . . . familiar if I can hold it . . .
A black tree with a double trunk—two trees
Grown into one—throws up its blurred branches.

The two trunks in their infinitesimal dance of growth
Have turned completely about one another, their join
A slowly twisted scar, that I recognise . . .

A quick arc flashes sidewise in the air,
A heavy blade in flight. A wooden stroke:
Iron sinks in the gasping core.

I will dream it again.

RITUAL OF DEPARTURE

A man at the moment of departure, turning
To leave, treasures some stick of furniture
With slowly blazing eyes, or the very door
Broodingly with his hand as it falls shut.

*

Open the soft string that clasps in series
A dozen silver spoons, and spread them out,
Matched perfectly, one maker and to the year:
                                 brilliance in use that fell
Open before the first inheritor.

A stag crest stares from the soft solid silver
And grimaces, with fat cud-lips but jaws
That could crack bones.
                            The stag heart stumbles.
He rears at bay, slavering silver; rattles
A trophied head among my gothic rocks.

*

Stones of a century and a half ago.
The same city distinct in the same air,
More open in an earlier evening light.
Dublin under the Georges . . .
                           stripped of Parliament,
Lying powerless in sweet-breathing death-ease
                           after forced Union.

Under a theatre of swift-moving cloud
Domes, pillared, in the afterglow—
A portico, beggars moving on the steps—

A horserider locked in soundless greeting,
Bowed among dogs and dung; the panelled vista
Closing on pleasant smoke-blue far-off hills.

*

The ground opens. Pale wet potatoes
Break into light. The black soil falls from their flesh,
From the hands that tear them up and spread them out
In fresh disorder, perishable roots to eat.
                                    The fields vanish in rain
Among white rock and red bog—saturated
High places traversed by spring sleet
Or thrust up in summer through the thin wind
Into pounding silence. Farther south: cattle,
Wheat, salmon glistening, the sea.
Landscape with ancestral figures . . . names
Settling and intermixing on the earth,
The seed in slow retreat, through time and blood,
Into bestial silence.
                    Faces sharpen and grow blank,
With eyes for nothing.
                        And their children's children
Venturing to disperse, some came to Dublin
To vanish in the city lanes.
                        I saw the light
Enter from the laneway, through the scullery
To the foot of the stairs, creep across grey floorboards,
Sink in plush in the staleness of an inner room.

I scoop at the earth, and sense famine, a first
Sourness in the clay. The roots tear softly.

HEN WOMAN

The noon heat in the yard
smelled of stillness and coming thunder.
A hen scratched and picked at the shore.
It stopped, its body crouched and puffed out.
The brooding silence seemed to say "Hush . . ."

The cottage door opened,
a black hole
in a whitewashed wall so bright
the eyes narrowed.
Inside, a clock murmured "Gong . . ."

(I had felt all this before . . .)

She hurried out in her slippers
muttering, her face dark with anger,
and gathered the hen up jerking
languidly. Her hand fumbled.
Too late. Too late.

It fixed me with its pebble eyes
(seeing what mad blur?).
A white egg showed in the sphincter;
mouth and beak opened together;
and time stood still.

Nothing moved: bird or woman,
fumbled or fumbling—locked there
(as I must have been) gaping.

*

There was a tiny movement at my feet,
tiny and mechanical; I looked down.
A beetle like a bronze leaf
was inching across the cement,
clasping with small tarsi
a ball of dung bigger than its body.
The serrated brow pressed the ground humbly,
lifted in a short stare, bowed again;
the dung-ball advanced minutely,
losing a few fragments,
specks of staleness and freshness.

*

A mutter of thunder far off
—time not quite stopped.
I saw the egg had moved a fraction:
a tender blank brain
under torsion, a clean new world.

As I watched, the mystery completed.
The black zero of the orifice
closed to a point
and the white zero of the egg hung free,
flecked with greenish brown oils.

It slowly turned and fell.
Dreamlike, fussed by her splayed fingers,
it floated outward, moon-white,
leaving no trace in the air,
and began its drop to the shore.

*

I feed upon it still as you see;
there is no end to that which,
not understood, may yet be noted
and hoarded in the imagination,
in the yolk of one's being, so to speak,
there to undergo its (quite animal) growth,
dividing blindly,
twitching, packed with will,
searching in its own tissue
for the structure
in which it may wake.
Something that had—clenched
in its cave—not been
now was: an egg of being.
Through what seemed a whole year it fell
—as it still falls, for me,
solid and light, the red gold beating
in its silvery womb,
alive as the yolk and white
of my eye; as it will continue
to fall, probably, until I die,
through the vast indifferent spaces
with which I am empty.

*

It smashed against the grating
and slipped down quickly out of sight.
It was over in a comical flash.
The soft mucous shell clung a little longer,
then drained down.

She stood staring, in blank anger.
Then her eyes came to life, and she laughed
and let the bird flap away.
"It's all the one.
There's plenty more where that came from!"

Hen to pan!
It was a simple world.

DEATH BED

Motionless—his sons—
we watched his brows draw together with strain.
The wind tore at the leather walls of our tent;
two grease lamps fluttered
at the head and foot of the bed.
Our shadows sprang here and there.

At that moment our sign might
have coursed across the heavens,
and we had spared no one to watch.

*

Our people are most vulnerable to loss
when we gather like this to one side,
around some death,

and try to weave it into our lives
—who can weave nothing but our ragged
routes across the desert.

And it is those among us
who most make the heavens their business
who go most deeply into this death-weaving.

As if the star might
spring from the dying mouth
or shoot from the agony of the eyes.

"We must not miss it,
however it comes."
—If it comes.

He stretched out his feet
and seemed to sink deeper in the bed,
and was still.
                    Sons no longer,
we pulled down his eyelids
and pushed the chin up gently to close his mouth,
and stood under the flapping roof.
Our shelter sheltered under the night.

*

Hides, furs and skins,
are our shelter and our garments.

We can weave nothing.

from A TECHNICAL SUPPLEMENT

XIX

It is hard to beat a good meal
and a turn on the terrace,
or a picnic on the beach at evening,
watching the breakers blur and gleam
as the brain skews softly.
Or an enjoyable rest, with a whodunit
under a flowering chestnut, an essay or two
on a park bench, a romance devoured
at one stroke on a grassy slope.

But for real pleasure there is nothing to equal
sitting down to a *serious* read,
getting settled down comfortably for the night
with a demanding book on your knee
and your head intent over it,
eyes bridging the gap, closing a circuit.

Except that it is not a closed circuit,
more a mingling of lives, worlds simmering
in the entranced interval: all that you are
and have come to be
—or as much as can be brought to bear—
"putting on" the fixed outcome of another's
encounter with what he was
and had come to be
impelled him to stop in flux, living,
and hold that encounter out from
the streaming away of lifeblood, timeblood,
a nexus a nexus a nexus
wriggling with life not of our kind.

Until one day as I was . . .

I met a fair maid all shining
with hair all over her cheeks
and pearly tongue
who spoke to me and sighed
as if my own nervous nakedness
spoke to me and said:

My *heart is a black fruit.*
It is a piece of black coal.
When I laugh a black thing hovers.

XXIII

That day when I woke
a great private blade
was planted in me from bowels to brain.
I lay there alive round it. When I moved
it moved with me, and there was no hurt.
I knew it was not going to go away.
I got up carefully, transfixed.

From that day forth I knew
what it was to taste reality
and not to; to suffer tedium or pain
and not to; to eat, swallowing with pleasure,
and not to; to yield and fail,
to note this or that withering in me,
and not to; to anticipate
the Breath, the Bite, with cowering arms,
and not to . . .

(Tiny delicate dawn-antelope that go without water
getting all they need in vegetation and the dew.
Night-staring jerboa.
The snapping of their slender bones,
rosy flesh bursting in small sweet screams
against the palate fine. Just a quick
note. Lest we forget.)

Meanwhile, with enormous care,
to the split id—delicate
as a flintflake—the knifed nous . . .

JOHN MONTAGUE

John Montague was born in Brooklyn, New York, in 1929, but his family returned to County Tyrone, Northern Ireland, a few years later. He was educated at University College, Dublin, where he received his B.A. and M.A. degrees. In 1955 he received a M.F.A. degree from the University of Iowa. From 1956 to 1959 he worked for Bord Failte, the Irish tourist agency, and then as Paris correspondent for the **Irish Times**. He was visiting lecturer at the University of California, Berkeley, in 1961 and has taught since then at universities in France, Ireland, Canada, and the United States. In 1976 Montague received the award for Irish writers from the Irish-American Cultural Institute, and in 1977 the Martin Toonder Award for Literature. He is presently a member of the English department at University College, Cork, and serves as a contributing editor for the Toronto quarterly, **Exile**. He is married and lives with his wife and daughter in Cork. In addition to his translations, critical articles, and short stories, he has edited **The Faber Book of Irish Verse** (1974) and published six major collections of poetry, **Poisoned Lands** (1961—reissued 1976), **A Chosen Light** (1967), **Tides** (1970), **The Rough Field** (1972), **A Slow Dance** (1975), and **The Great Cloak** (1978).

WILD SPORTS OF THE WEST

The landlord's coat is tulip red,
A beacon on the wine-dark moor;
He turns his well-bred foreign devil's face,
While his bailiff trots before.

His furious hooves drum fire from stone,
A beautiful sight when gone;
Contemplation holds the noble horseman
In his high mould of bone.

Not so beautiful the bandy bailiff,
Churlish servant of an alien will:
Behind the hedge a maddened peasant
Poises his shotgun for the kill.

Evening brings the huntsman home,
Blood of pheasants in a bag:
Beside a turfrick the cackling peasant
Cleanses his ancient weapon with a rag.

The fox, evicted from the thicket,
Evades with grace the snuffling hounds:
But a transplanted bailiff, in a feudal paradise,
Patrols for God His private grounds.

ALL LEGENDARY OBSTACLES

All legendary obstacles lay between
Us, the long imaginary plain,
The monstrous ruck of mountains
And, swinging across the night,
Flooding the Sacramento, San Joaquin,
The hissing drift of winter rain.

All day I waited, shifting
Nervously from station to bar
As I saw another train sail
By, the San Francisco Chief or
Golden Gate, water dripping
From great flanged wheels.

At midnight you came, pale
Above the negro porter's lamp.
I was too blind with rain
And doubt to speak, but
Reached from the platform
Until our chilled hands met.

You had been travelling for days
With an old lady, who marked
A neat circle on the glass
With her glove, to watch us
Move into the wet darkness
Kissing, still unable to speak.

THAT ROOM

Side by side on the narrow bed
We lay, like chained giants,
Tasting each other's tears, in terror
Of the news which left little to hide
But our two faces that stared
To ritual masks, absurd and flayed.

Rarely in a lifetime comes such news
Shafting knowledge straight to the heart
Making shameless sorrow start—
Not childish tears, querulously vain—
But adult tears that hurt and harm,
Seeping like acid to the bone.

Sound of hooves on the midnight road
Raised a romantic image to mind:
Someone riding late to Marley?
But we must suffer the facts of self;
No one endures a similar fate
And no one will ever know

What happened in that room
But that when we came to leave
We scrubbed each other's tears
Prepared the usual show. That day
Love's claims made chains of time and place
To bind us together more: equal in adversity.

SPECIAL DELIVERY

The spider's web
of your handwriting
on a blue envelope

brings up too much
to bear, old sea-sick-
ness of love, retch

of sentiment, night
& day devoured by
the worm of delight

which turns to
feed upon itself;
emotion running so

wildly to seed
between us that
it assumes a third,

a ghost or child's
face, the soft skull
pale as an eggshell

& the life-cord
of the emerging body—
fish, reptile, bird—

which trails
like the cable
of an astronaut

as we whirl & turn
in our bubble of
blood & sperm

before the gravities
of earth claim us
from limitless space.

*

Now, light years later
your nostalgic letter
admitting failure,

claiming forgiveness.
When fire pales to
so faint an ash

so frail a design
why measure guilt
your fault or mine:

but blood seeps where
I sign before tearing
down the perforated line.

THE HAG OF BEARE

Ebb tide has come for me:
My life drifts downwards
Like a retreating sea
With no tidal turn.

I am the Hag of Beare,
Fine petticoats I used to wear,
Today, gaunt with poverty,
I hunt for rags to cover me.

Girls nowadays
Dream only of money—
When we were young
We cared more for our men.

Riding over their lands
We remember how, like nobles,
They treated us well;
Courted, but didn't tell.

Today every upstart
Is a master of graft;
Skinflint, yet sure to boast
Of being a lavish host.

But I bless my King who gave—
Balanced briefly on time's wave—
Largesse of speedy chariots
And champion thoroughbreds.

These arms, now bony, thin
And useless to younger men,
Once caressed with skill
The limbs of princes!

Sadly my body seeks to join
Them soon in their dark home—
When God wishes to claim it,
He can have back his deposit.

No more gamy teasing
For me, no wedding feast:
Scant grey hair is best
Shadowed by a veil.

Why should I care?
Many's the bright scarf
Adorned my hair in the days
When I drank with the gentry.

So God be praised
That I mis-spent my days!
Whether the plunge be bold
Or timid, the blood runs cold.

After spring and autumn
Come age's frost and body's chill:
Even in bright sunlight
I carry my shawl.

Lovely the mantle of green
Our Lord spreads on the hillside!
Every spring the divine craftsman
Plumps its worn fleece.

But my cloak is mottled with age—
No, I'm beginning to dote—
It's only grey hair straggling
Over my skin like a lichened oak.

And my right eye has been taken away
As down-payment on heaven's estate;
Likewise the ray in the left
That I may grope to heaven's gate.

No storm has overthrown
The royal standing stone.
Every year the fertile plain
Bears its crop of yellow grain.

But I, who feasted royally
By candlelight, now pray
In this darkened oratory.
Instead of heady mead

And wine, high on the bench
With kings, I sup whey
In a nest of hags:
God pity me!

Yet may this cup of whey
O! Lord, serve as my ale-feast—
Fathoming its bitterness
I'll learn that you know best.

Alas, I cannot
Again sail youth's sea;
The days of my beauty
Are departed, and desire spent.

I hear the fierce cry of the wave
Whipped by the wintry wind.
No one will visit me today
Neither nobleman nor slave.

I hear their phantom oars
As ceaselessly they row
And row to the chill ford,
Or fall asleep by its side.

Flood tide
And the ebb dwindling on the sand!
What the flood rides ashore
The ebb snatches from your hand.

Flood tide
And the sucking ebb to follow!
Both I have come to know
Pouring down my body.

Flood tide
Has not yet rifled my pantry
But a chill hand has been laid
On many who in darkness visited me.

Well might the Son of Mary
Take their place under my roof-tree
For if I lack other hospitality
I never say "No" to anybody—

Man being of all
Creatures the most miserable—
His flooding pride always seen
But never his tidal turn.

Happy the island in mid-ocean
Washed by the returning flood
But my ageing blood
Slows to final ebb.

I have hardly a dwelling
Today, upon this earth.
Where once was life's flood
All is ebb.

(translation from the Irish)

THE WILD DOG ROSE

I

I go to say goodbye to the *Cailleach*
that terrible figure who haunted my childhood
but no longer harsh, a human being
merely, hurt by event.
                    The cottage,
circled by trees, weathered to admonitory
shapes of desolation by the mountain winds,
straggles into view. The rank thistles
and leathery bracken of untilled fields
stretch behind with—a final outcrop—
the hooped figure by the roadside,
its retinue of dogs
                    which give tongue
as I approach, with savage, whinging cries
so that she slowly turns, a moving nest
of shawls and rags, to view, to stare
the stranger down.
                    And I feel again
that ancient awe, the terror of a child
before the great hooked nose, the cheeks
dewlapped with dirt, the staring blue
of the sunken eyes, the mottled claws
clutching a stick

         but now hold
and return her gaze, to greet her,
as she greets me, in friendliness.
Memories have wrought reconciliation
between us, we talk in ease at last,
like old friends, lovers almost,
sharing secrets.
         Of neighbours
she quarreled with, who now lie
in Garvaghey graveyard, beyond all hatred;
of my family and hers, how she never married,
though a man came asking in her youth.
"You would be loath to leave your own"
she sighs, "and go among strangers"—
his parish ten miles off.
         For sixty years
since she has lived alone, in one place.
Obscurely honoured by such confidences,
I idle by the summer roadside, listening,
while the monologue falters, continues,
rehearsing the small events of her life.
The only true madness is loneliness,
the monotonous voice in the skull
that never stops
         because never heard.

II

And there
where the dog rose shines in the hedge
she tells me a story so terrible
that I try to push it away,
my bones melting.
         Late at night
a drunk came, beating at her door

to break it in, the bolt snapping
from the soft wood, the thin mongrels
rushing to cut, but yelping as
he whirls with his farm boots
to crush their skulls.
                        In the darkness
they wrestle, two creatures crazed
with loneliness, the smell of the
decaying cottage in his nostrils
like a drug, his body heavy on hers,
the tasteless trunk of a seventy year
old virgin, which he rummages while
she battles for life
                        bony fingers
reaching desperately to push
against his bull neck. "I prayed
to the Blessed Virgin herself
for help and after a time
I broke his grip."
                    He rolls
to the floor, snores asleep,
while she cowers until dawn
and the dogs' whimpering starts
him awake, to lurch back across
the wet bog.

III

                    And still
the dog rose shines in the hedge.
Petals beaten wide by rain, it
sways slightly, at the tip of a
slender, tangled, arching branch
which, with her stick, she gathers
into us.

"The wild rose
is the only rose without thorns,"
she says, holding a wet blossom
for a second, in a hand knotted
as the knob of her stick.
"Whenever I see it, I remember
the Holy Mother of God and
all she suffered."
                    Briefly
the air is strong with the smell
of that weak flower, offering
its crumbling yellow cup
and pale bleeding lips
fading to white
                    at the rim
of each bruised and heart-
shaped petal.

THE CAGE

My father, the least happy
man I have known. His face
retained the pallor
of those who work underground:
the lost years in Brooklyn
listening to a subway
shudder the earth.

But a traditional Irishman
who (released from his grille
in the Clark Street I.R.T.)
drank neat whiskey until
he reached the only element
he felt at home in
any longer: brute oblivion.

And yet picked himself
up, most mornings,
to march down the street
extending his smile
to all sides of the good
(non negro) neighbourhood
belled by St Teresa's church.

When he came back
we walked together
across fields of Garvaghey
to see hawthorn on the summer
hedges, as though
he had never left;
a bend of the road

which still sheltered
primroses. But we
did not smile in
the shared complicity
of a dream, for when
weary Odysseus returns
Telemachus must leave.

Often as I descend
into subway or underground
I see his bald head behind
the bars of the small booth;
the mark of an old car
accident beating on his
ghostly forehead.

LAMENT FOR THE O'NEILLS

> This was a distinguished crew for one
> ship; for it is indeed certain that the
> sea had not supported, and the winds
> had not wafted from Ireland, in
> modern times, a party of one ship
> who would have been more illustrious,
> or noble in point of genealogy, or
> more renowned for deeds, valour or
> high achievements. . . .
> *Annals of the Four Masters*

The fiddler settles in
to his playing so easily;
rosewood box tucked under chin,
saw of rosined bow
& angle of elbow

that the mind elides
for a while what he plays:
hornpipe or reel to warm
us up well, heel to toecap
twitching in tune

till the sound expands
in the slow climb of a lament.
As by some forest campfire
listeners draw near, to honour
a communal loss

& a shattered procession
of anonymous suffering
files through the brain:
burnt houses, pillaged farms,
a province in flames.

> We have killed, burnt and despoiled
> all along the Lough to within four
> miles of Dungannon . . . in which
> journeys we have killed above a
> hundred of all sorts, besides such as
> we have burned, how many I know
> not. We spare none, of what quality or
> sex soever, and it had bred much
> terror in the people who heard not a
> drum nor saw not a fire of long time.
> *Chichester to Mountjoy, Spring 1601*

With an intricate
& mournful mastery
the thin bow glides & slides,
assuaging like a bardic poem,
our tribal pain—

          Is uaigneach Eire

Disappearance & death
of a world, as down Lough Swilly
the great ship, encumbered with nobles,
swells its sails for Europe:

The Flight of the Earls.

A GRAFTED TONGUE

 (Dumb,
bloodied, the severed
head now chokes to
speak another tongue:—

As in
a long suppressed dream,
some stuttering garb-
led ordeal of my own)

An Irish
child weeps at school
repeating its English.
After each mistake

The master
gouges another mark
on the tally stick
hung about its neck

Like a bell
on a cow, a hobble
on a straying goat.
To slur and stumble

In shame
the altered syllables
of your own name;
to stray sadly home

and find
the turf cured width
of your parents' hearth
growing slowly alien:

In cabin
and field, they still
speak the old tongue.
You may greet no one.

To grow
a second tongue, as
harsh a humiliation
as twice to be born.

Decades later
that child's grandchild's
speech stumbles over lost
syllables of an old order.

from A NEW SIEGE: AN HISTORICAL MEDITATION

for Bernadette Devlin

Lines of history
    lines of power
the long sweep
    of the Bogside
under the walls
    up to Creggan
the black muzzle
    of Roaring Meg
staring dead on
    cramped houses
the jackal shapes
    of James's army
watching the city
    stiffen in siege

Lines of defiance
    lines of discord
under Walker's arm
    brisk with guns
British soldiers
    patrol the walls
the gates between
    Ulster Catholic
Ulster Protestant
    a Saracen slides
past the Guildhall
    a black Cuchulain
bellowing against
    the Scarlet Whore
twin races petrified
    the volcanic ash
of religious hatred

SMALL SHOT HATH
   POURED LIKE HAIL
THE GREAT GUNS
   SHAKEN OUR WALLS
a spectral garrison
   no children left
sick from eating
   horseflesh, vermin
curs fattened on
   the slain Irish
still flaunting
   the bloody flag
of "No Surrender"
   GOD HAS MADE US
AN IRON PILLAR
   AND BRAZEN WALLS
AGAINST THIS LAND.

     *   *   *

Lines of action
   lines of reaction
the white elephant
   of Stormont, Carson's
raised right claw
   a Protestant parliament
a Protestant people
   major this and
captain that and
   general nothing
the bland, pleasant
   face of mediocrity
confronting in horror
   its mirror image
bull-voiced bigotry

symbol of Ulster
   these sloping streets
blackened walls
   sick at heart and
seeking a sign
   the flaghung gloom
of St. Columb's
   the brass eagle of
the lectern bearing
   the Sermon on the Mount
in its shoulders
   "A city that is
set on a hill
   cannot be hid."

Lines of loss
   lines of energy
always changing
   always returning
A TIDE LIFTS
   THE RELIEF SHIP
OFF THE MUD
   OVER THE BOOM
the rough field
   of the universe
growing, changing
   a net of energies
crossing patterns
   weaving towards
a new order
   a new anarchy
always different
   always the same

the emerging order
   of the poem invaded
by cries, protestations
   a people's pain
the defiant face
   of a young girl
campaigning against
   memory's mortmain
a blue banner
   lifting over a
broken province
   DRIVE YOUR PLOUGH
a yellow bulldozer
   raising the rubble
a humming factory
   a housing estate
hatreds sealed into
   a hygienic honeycomb

Across the border
   a dead man
drives to school
   past the fort
at Green Castle
   a fury of love
for North, South
   eats his heart
on the far side
   a rocky promontory
his family name
   O'Cahan, O'Kane
my uncle watches
   sails upon Foyle
(a flock of swans)
   drives forward

WINDHARP

for Patrick Collins

The sounds of Ireland,
that restless whispering
you never get away
from, seeping out of
low bushes and grass,
heatherbells and fern,
wrinkling bog pools,
scraping tree branches,
light hunting cloud,
sound hounding sight,
a hand ceaselessly
combing and stroking

the landscape, till
the valley gleams
like the pile upon
a mountain pony's coat.

from THE CAVE OF NIGHT

for Sean Lucy

> Men *who believe in absurdities*
> *will commit atrocities.*
> Voltaire

CAVE

The rifled honeycomb
of the high-rise hotel
where a wind tunnel moans.
While jungleclad troops
ransack the Falls, race
through huddled streets,
we lie awake, the wide
window washed with rain,
your oval face, and tide
of yellow hair luminous
as you turn to me again
seeking refuge as the
cave of night blooms
with fresh explosions.

ALL NIGHT

All night spider webs
of nothing. Condemned to
that treadmill of helplessness.
Distended, drowning fish,
frogs with lions' jaws.
A woman breasted butterfly
copulates with a dying bat.
A pomegranate bursts slowly
between her ladyship's legs.
Her young peep out
with bared teeth:
the eggs of hell
fertilizing the abyss.

> Frail skyscrapers incline
> together like stilts.
> Grain elevators melt.
> Cities subside as liners
> leave by themselves
> all radios playing.
> A friendly hand places
> a warm bomb under
> the community centre
> where the last evacuees
> are trying a hymn.
> Still singing, they
> part for limbo, still
> tucking their blankets
> over separating limbs.

A land I did not seek
to enter. Pure terror.
Ice floes sail past

grandly as battleships.
Blue gashed arctic distances
ache the retina and
the silence grows to
a sparkle of starlight—
sharpened knives.
Lift up your telescope,
old colonel, and learn
to lurch with the penguins!
In the final place
a solitary being begins
its slow dance. . . .

FALLS FUNERAL

Unmarked faces
fierce with grief

a line of children
led by a small coffin

the young
mourning the young

a sight beyond tears
beyond pious belief

David's brethren
in the Land of Goliath.

WALKING LATE

Walking late
we share night sounds
so delicate the heart misses
a beat to hear them:

shapes in the half-dark
where the deer feed or
rest, the radar of small
ears & horns still alert
under the glooming boles
of the great oaks

         to unfold
their knees from the wet grass
with a single thrust & leap away
stiff-legged, in short, jagged
bursts as we approach

           stars lining
our path through the woods
with a low coiling mist
over the nocturnal meadows
so that we seem to wade
through the filaments
of a giant silver web
the brain crevices of a cloud.

      *

Bleached and white
as a fish's belly,
a road curves towards the city
which, with the paling dawn,

will surge towards activity again,
the bubble of the Four Courts
overruling the stagnant quays,
their ghostly Viking prows,

and the echoing archways,
tenebrous walls of the Liberties
where we briefly share a life
to which we must return

as we circle uncertainly
towards a home, your
small, damp hand in mine,
no heavier than a leaf.

HERBERT STREET REVISITED

for Madeleine

I

A light is burning late
in this Georgian Dublin street:
someone is leading our old lives!

And our black cat scampers again
through the wet grass of the convent garden
upon his masculine errands.

The pubs shut: a released bull,
Behan shoulders up the street,
topples into our basement, roaring "John!"

A pony and donkey cropped flank
by flank under the trees opposite;
short neck up, long neck down,

as Nurse Mullen knelt by her bedside
to pray for her lost Mayo hills,
the bruised bodies of Easter Volunteers.

Animals, neighbours, treading the pattern
of one time and place into history,
like our early marriage, while

tall windows looked down upon us
from walls flushed light pink or salmon
watching and enduring succession.

II

As I leave, you whisper,
"don't betray our truth"
and like a ghost dancer,
invoking a lost tribal strength
I halt in tree-fed darkness

to summon back our past,
and celebrate a love that eased
so kindly, the dying bone,
enabling the spirit to sing
of old happiness, when alone.

III

So put the leaves back on the tree,
put the tree back in the ground,
let Brendan trundle his corpse down
the street singing, like Molly Malone.

Let the black cat, tiny emissary
of our happiness, streak again
through the darkness, to fall soft
clawed into a landlord's dustbin.

Let Nurse Mullen take the last
train to Westport, and die upright
in her chair, facing a window
warm with the blue slopes of Nephin.

And let the pony and donkey come—
look, someone has left the gate open—
like hobbyhorses linked in
the slow motion of a dream

parading side by side, down
the length of Herbert Street,
rising and falling, lifting
their hooves through the moonlight.

SEAN LUCY

Born in Bombay, India, in 1931, Sean Lucy was brought home to Ireland in 1935. He was educated at University College, Cork, where he received a B.A. degree in History and an M.A. degree in English. After teaching for eight years in England, he became a lecturer in English at University College, Cork, where he has taught since 1962. Presently he is professor of Modern English and head of the department. He is married and has five children. He has lectured on English and Anglo-Irish literature in Ireland, the United States, Canada, and France and he is the recipient of the Kavanagh Poetry Award. His publications include a critical study, **T. S. Eliot and the Idea of Tradition** (1960); a collection of critical essays, **Irish Poets in English** (1973); and two anthologies of Irish poetry, **Love Poems of the Irish** (1967), and **Five Irish Poets** (1970) (which includes a selection of his own work). Most recently, his poetry has been featured in **Etudes Irlandaises** (1977). A collection of poems, **Thunder and After**, is forthcoming.

SENIOR MEMBERS

Tadhg sat up on his hills
Sniping at passing Tommies from the barracks,
Growling in Gaelic,
Plowtilth on his boots.

Vincent was just a boy
Kept in at curfew by a careful Da
In a soft suburb
Of the cautious city.

Tadhg was two-and-three with Fionn the Hero
(Meaning his cousin)
And helped to shoot him
After the treaty split them.

Vincent is solid stock:
His uncle was Home Rule M.P.:
His face is sleek with merchant generation;
"Liberal plumbing makes a cultured nation."

Tadhg is a bully on the committees
As full of malice as intelligence;
His language is as hairy as his ears;
He has a drover's voice.

Vincent works mainly for the money men.
Deep in his heart he fears the tinker's shout,
The eyes of mountain goats,
The gunman's shot.

Save us Saint Patrick! Is it gin and plush,
Or the grey ash-plant that shall master us?
The bourgeois coma or the bully's push?
This is a dilemma, not a choice.

Footnote
The new politico answers my sad voice:

Vincent and Tadhg, though sadly out of date,
Each taught me in his way to rule the state,
Ruthless as mountain rocks, slick as the city street
I am the inheritor. Kneel at my feet.

SUPERVISING EXAMINATIONS

Stuffy chill of clouded Summer, crowdsmell, booksmell;
Grey light in the tall college hall.
Hammerbeams. Dark crosswired bookshelves of dim titles.
Portraits of former presidents. Peeling walls.

Pace slowly down the rows of little tables,
Down the long rows of bowed figures from whom rise
Gentle and continuous noises:
Scribbling-scratch, shifting, clittering, rustling, sighs.

On ranked brownsquares heraldic with hands and elbows
A hundred long white papers catch the light.
Among the clumps of dark thick mensuits
The scattering of girls looks strangely bright.

Jiggling pens trail out long rows of writing—
Loose, cramped, untidy, neat—line after line.
In the westwall stainedglass windows grouped allegorical
     figures
(The Arts and Sciences) enrich slightly the dull dayshine.

The peace of boredom holds the supervisors:
He swings his legs from the high table. She wonders.
     Another goes up and down.
They hear, unhearing, the clicking silence,
Backed by the far traffic rumour of the town.

With faint benevolence they move among the candidates,
Handing out ink and paper; going the old rounds.
Below those heavy trees which can be seen through the
     south windows
The river creeps, choked with weeds, through the lower
     grounds.

LONGSHORE INTELLECTUAL

After all, Charlie, we shall see them go,
And feel renewal with the buff sails stirring,
After this bad weather the tall fleets will embark
Leaving the women on the quayside staring.

The dark pubs at night will become old men's places
Where the wind rattles the bar-room shutters:
Knowing only in retrospect the loud voices and beery
        faces,
Dim as the inarticulate story the senile drinker stutters.

And after all, Charlie, they are the men of action:
We chose the shore life of the seedy dreamer,
Deliberately abandoning the ships then weighing anchor,
Deliberately ignoring the bravado recruiting drummer.

It only needles us when they come home in glory
In camaraderie and the glow of doing,
Making their memory into a mutual and lovely story,
Leaving us wordless with our book contentment dying;

They steal our women and deride our wisdom,
They drink our whiskey and borrow our possessions,
This is their ancient and abiding custom,
With uncultured voices and unbridled passions.

But after all, Charlie, we know how they end:
Their bodies washing on the beaches of far nations,
Their eye sockets empty, their mouths full of sand,
And their girl-friends lonely—we have our consolations.

RICHARD WEBER

Richard Weber was born in 1932 in Dublin, and educated in Dublin public schools, then at the National College of Art in Dublin. He is presently librarian in the National College of Art and Design and occasionally lecturer in English at this institution. He has held a variety of jobs, including that of librarian at the Chester Beatty Library in Dublin. Weber was poet-in-residence at the University of Massachusetts at Amherst in 1967 and from 1967 to 1970 he was a visiting lecturer at Mount Holyoke College in Massachusetts. He is married and has one daughter. Weber has been advisory editor for **Icarus** (produced at Trinity College, Dublin) and poetry editor for **Poetry Ireland**. He has contributed to many Irish, English, and American journals. His major collections are **Lady and Gentleman** (1963) and **Stephen's Green Revisited: Poems** (1968).

ENVYING THE PELICAN

Why cannot we eat enough for a week
In one day and make do with that?
Why must the daily stomach ache
For new nourishment when a thought
Of any value can hold itself off

For a week or a month or a year?
Certainly food is very good stuff,
And essential, but I could desire
That the large, handsome, special meal
Resulted in larger thoughts, better still
Profounder poems, without the usual
Word-changing, fuss, weakness of will
That come when even this kind of thing
Follows a meal and the simple urge to sing.

A PRIMER FOR SCHOOLCHILDREN

And what is life?
It is mainly strife
And the struggle for power
And the need to pair,
From the earliest breath
To the day of death.

And what is man?
With him life began
Its consciousness of itself
And awareness of the gulf
Between the animals and him,
Though all animals look like him.

And sexual desire?
It is the demanding fire
That roars in the loins,
Melts the mind's chains
And presses down the head
To the level of a jerking bed.

And what is love?
O love is above
All these, sharpening the mind,
Moving free as the wind,
Though the end seems the same:
A bed for two with one name.

And what is death?
An end to the fear of death
And life; that is,
It is what it always was
For the fully conscious man;
Who still must ask why it all began.

THE POET'S DAY

Morning, and the poet up again and out and about
His job of collecting the day's correct and sacred phrases,
A way of saying by singing out life's praises,
What without words would be an undistinguished shout.

Among a crowd of crimes and offscene evil noises
He records the cries and crises of a life-loving heart,
Reveals the fate and faith of that actor looking for a part
Already over-played and plagiarized by old and new voices.

Afternoon, and the poet begins to re-space his praises,
Like a boy with a stamp collection beautiful as butterflies.
The reverse being also true for the one who versifies,
Life is a collection as well as a collecting of phrases.

Slowly he works to escape the merely temporary
    contemporary,
Enters his hope in words on the white page of eternity,
Attempts to check and change his drift away from
    humanity
And hopes his example will prove more than exemplary.

Night, and the poet proposes the marriage of Heaven and
    Hell
And at once celebrates it till late in the small hours,
Whether in suburban houses or in rented ivory towers;
Despite his modernity, angels and devils still symbolize
    well.

So, eternal life for the poet who knows and shows he
    knows it,
Mystery of the world and mastery of the word;
Though his songs must eventually enter the night unheard
When his language dies and our atom of Earth is finally
    split.

TOM MacINTYRE

Tom MacIntyre was born in 1933 in County Cavan, and educated at University College, Dublin. He subsequently taught at Clongowes Wood College. Presently he lives and works on Inishbofin (an island off County Galway), occasionally teaching creative writing at American universities. He has published a volume of poems (translations from the Irish) entitled **Blood Relations** (1971).

CHILD

Often
he wears my son's face,
seizes me
as of right,

takes me
the unused path
to the high gate
almost hidden
under a mat of ivy;
the leaves are smooth,
my fingers touch vines,
the vines grip iron.

Naked in the field,
shoulders like a bull-calf,
he pucks the ball
ten times the length
within my compass.

I have tried
to kill him.

I have seen
the digger,
dripping mud and stones,
hold up
his broken shape

and, months later,
met him on the road,
untouched, unchanged,

my breath,
my clay,
my open hand.

ON SWEET KILLEN HILL

Flower of the flock,
Any time, any land,
Plenty your ringlets,
Plenty your hand,
Sunlight your window,
Laughter your sill,
And I must be with you
On sweet Killen Hill.

Let sleep renegue me,
Skin lap my bones,
Love and tomorrow
Can handle the reins,
You my companion
I'd never breathe ill,
And I guarantee bounty
On sweet Killen Hill.

You'll hear the pack yell
As puss devil-dances,
Hear cuckoo and thrush
Pluck song from the branches,
See fish in the pool
Doing their thing,
And the bay as God made it
From sweet Killen Hill.

Pulse of my life,
We come back to—*Mise.*
Why slave for McArdle,
That bumbailiff's issue?
I've a harp in a thousand,
Love songs at will,
And the air is cadenza
On sweet Killen Hill.

Gentle one, lovely one,
Come to me,
Now sleep the clergy,
Now sleep their care,
Sunrise will find us
But sunrise won't tell
That love lacks surveillance
On sweet Killen Hill.

(translation from the Irish)

THE YELLOW BITTERN

Sickens my gut, Yellow Bittern,
To see you stretched there,
Whipped—not by starvation
But the want of a jar;
Troy's fall was skittles to this,
You flattened on bare stones,
You harmed no one, pillaged no crop,
Your preference always—the wee drop.

Sours my spit, Yellow Bittern
Thought of you done for,
Heard your shout many's the night,
You mudlarkin'—and no want of a jar;
At that game I'll shape a coffin,
So all claim—but look at this,
A darlin' bird downed like a thistle,
Causa mortis: couldn't wet his whistle.

Sands my bones, Yellow Bittern, that's fact,
Your last earthlies under a bush,
Rats next—rats for the waking,
Pipes in their mouths, and them all smoking;
Christ's sake, if you'd only sent word,
Tipped me the wink you were in a bind,
Dunt of a crow-bar, the ice splitter-splatter,
Nothing to stop another week on the batter.

Heron, blackbird, thrush—they've had it too,
Sorry friends, I'm occupied,
I'm blinds down for the Yellow Bittern,
A blood relation—on the mother's side;
Whole-hog merchants, we lived it up,
Carpe'd our *diem*, hung out our sign,
Collared life's bottle, disregarding the label,
Angled our elbows, met under the table

While the wife moaned with the rest,
'Give it up—you're finished—a year'—
I told her she lied,
My staple and staff for the regular jar.
Now—naked proof—this lad with a gullet
Who, forced on the dry, surely prayed for a bullet.
No, men, drink it up—and piss it down,
Warm them worms waitin' undergroun'.

(translation from the Irish)

THE CORRS

Miserable shower those Corrs.
Miserable women, miserable men,
Give them gold, give them wine,
They'd help no one.

No one,
Not for the world—
Up, down, East, West,
Their game is Badger's game.

Badger's game is burrowing
Darkness—night and day,
He'll help no one.
Not for the world.

Far from the gay life Buck Badger was reared,
Far from The Muses they were reared,
Far from me, far from my kind,
But burrow seed, you're root and rind.

(translation from the Irish)

JAMES SIMMONS

James Simmons was born in Derry, Northern Ireland, in 1933 and received a B.A. degree from Leeds University, England, in 1958. He has published widely in England and Ireland and received the Eric Gregory Award for poetry in 1962. He taught for five years at the Friends School, Northern Ireland, and for three years at Ahmadu Bello University in Nigeria. Since 1968 he has been lecturing in drama and Anglo-Irish literature at the New University of Ulster where he started the **Honest Ulsterman**, an influential new literary magazine; Ulsterman Press also publishes pamphlets by the younger poets in the North. Simmons is also a songwriter and performer; recently he founded the Poor Genius record company. He is married and has five children. His collections of poetry include **Late But in Earnest** (1967), **In the Wilderness and Other Poems** (1969), **Energy to Burn** (1971), **The Long Summer Still to Come** (1973), **West Strand Visions** (1974), and **Judy Garland and the Cold War** (1976). He has also edited the anthology **Ten Irish Poets** (1974). A **Selected Simmons**, edited by Edna Longley, is forthcoming.

FEAR TEST: INTEGRITY OF HEROES

Of those rebellions that we start in jest
some must be fought out in the open street
with barricades and possible defeat.
I shake with fear, but those days are my best.

Each time a chance of love is here
it seems her kids sleep in the room below,
neighbours are going to let her husband know.
Those are my best nights when I shake with fear.

Waiting backstage to sing, hating displays
of self, yet filled with songs
that no one knows but me . . . well, pain belongs
to birth, all births. I shake on my best days.

At last asking my silly boss to take
my resignation, getting off the fence
and telling him why. Who needs a reference!
I know my best days, but I always shake.

Good risks are those you hardly dare to take.
Who has a faculty for turbulence
and storm is sick; the healthy have more sense.
They have a use for courage when they shake.

That shock of horror when the way is clear!
I wish I had more stomach for a fight.
I wish I had panache—but I'm alright.
Those are my best days when I shake with fear.

LETTER TO A JEALOUS FRIEND

You could not say, "What now?" you said, "Too late!"
What energies bad principles have spilt.
Old friend, you hate me and you aggravate
Me, for I will not feel regret or guilt

When your white face stares at me from the door
With wizard eyes that change the three of us
Into a cuckold, a roué, a whore—
A stupid, ugly metamorphosis.

Acquaintances are mocking my belief
That we could still be friends when it was known.
I tremble when you treat me like a thief;
But I touched nothing you can call your own.

A child might own the doll it sleeps beside
And men own money and what money buys;
But no one earns a friend or owns his bride
However much he needs or hard he tries.

You try to run me over with your bus
And call me out of restaurants to fight.
I smile weakly and wait for all the fuss
To fade. I need to get my sleep at night.

I hear in some domestic tiff she tossed
Our love at you and scored. Each time I try
To fit that in my creed I lose my place.
There's more in animals than meets the eye.

Sweet fun and freedom didn't last for long
With you out shouting we'd betrayed your trust.
We said it was our business. We were wrong.
Your jealousy's as natural as our lust.

Our thoughts of other people paralyse
Our minds and make us act the silly parts
We think they cast us in. Feeling their eyes
On us, we seem to lose touch with our hearts.

Crippled by hate you have to crouch in dude
Levis and dark glasses, glaring at us.
We have to lie unnaturally nude
And vulnerable, trapped, ridiculous.

EXPERIENCE

"I want to fight you," he said in a Belfast accent.
Amazed and scared, with hurried words I resisted.
"Fighting solves nothing. Tell me how I've annoyed you,"
I said. But more insulted the man persisted.

In the lavatory he squared his fists and approached me:
"Now you can talk." I backed over cold stone in
A room that contained us and joined us. "It's all so silly."
I pleaded, searching for spaces to be alone in.

I shrank from his strangeness, not only afraid.
But at last of course I suffered what could not be delayed,
The innocuous struggle, the fighting words, "bastard" and
    "fuck,"
A torn shirt and my lip numb and bloody,
My anger and—strange—the feel of my own body
New to me, as I struck, as he struck.

ART AND REALITY

for James Boyce

From twenty yards I saw my old love
Locking up her car.
She smiled and waved, as lovely still
As girls of twenty are.

That cloud of auburn hair that bursts
Like sunrise round her head,
The smile that made me smile
At ordinary things she said.

But twenty years have gone and flesh
Is perishable stuff;
Can art and exercise and diet
Ever be enough

To save the tiny facial muscles
And keep taut the skin,
And have the waist, in middle-age,
Still curving firmly in?

Beauty invites me to approach,
And lies make truth seem hard
As my old love assumes her age,
A year for every yard.

JOHN DONNE

"There's more to style than honesty."

When you lost touch with lovers' bare skin
how could the textures not get thin

in your verse. The real blood the fleas sucked
that sang through your and her veins when you fucked
was lost for God's magic bargain drops,
and life was teasing torture, nice when it stops.
Genius is tempted to ingenious lying,
to brazening out betrayal, justifying
such acts as that old interfering king
forced you toward. *You* could do anything!

After a brave attempt to marry free,
gaoled and neglected, you chose piety,
turned an encrusted back on sweet enjoyment
and—fuck you, John—made love to your employment
improvising belief after the fact,
acting in bad faith, living the act,
faking a hot lust for the Holy Ghost!
I dare dispute because I loved you most.
They'll say I want you to write more like me,
with truly liberal consistency:

but your young self, your verse, condemns defection
from the erection to the resurrection,
bullying congregations like a bawd
for Him, then grovelling. Gawd!
It was a difficult position,
like Galileo's with the Inquisition;
but he at least had grace to stay indoors
and not make weapons for the torturers.
You, having once made such a lovely fuss
on Love's behalf, betrayed her, worse than us.

JAMES LIDDY

James Liddy was born in 1934 in Dublin. He was educated at University College, Dublin, where he received his B.A. and M.A., and at King's Inns, Dublin where he was barrister-at-law. From 1961 to 1966 Liddy was in practice at the Irish Bar. He has since held positions at several American and Irish universities as lecturer in English and poet-in-residence. Liddy served on the editorial board of **Poetry Ireland**, and was founder/editor of the Dublin magazine **Arena**. His published collections include **In a Blue Smoke** (1964), **Blue Mountain** (1968), **A Life of Stephen Dedalus** (1968), **A Munster Song of Love and War** (1969), the pamphlet **Orpheus in the Ice Cream Parlour** (1975), **Baudelaire's Bar Flowers** (a translation of **Les Fleurs de Mal**, 1975), and **Corca Bascinn** (1977).

THE VOICE OF AMERICA 1961

My hour switched on the cameras take.
The flash white of their advertisement roll:
beside the click faces in the colours
of the universe gaze upwards for my word.
I leave obscurity, stacking my symbols
on the shelf, Dollar, Steak, Mother (furies

of my springtime, a century and a half).
I was born in liberty and I cherish all,
so help me God, for the idealism of Lincoln,
Eisenhower, Kennedy, the kids on Main St.
At the cross bombs of history and ideology
I have prepared, the speeches typed,
and intercontinental missiles on alert;
the great heat presses: the buttons sweat.
I mount the stage to swear nuclear love,
for ever, even unto my ashes and dust.
The minute before I walk on I hesitate.
Between the wings with a book open on
his knees I catch sight of the old pioneer,
dove-eyed and his beard streaming in love.
Daddy Whitman, deployer of democracy,
serene in your chair of founder's timber,
let me steer close to touch YOUR BIG WHISKERS.

THE REPUBLIC 1939

In the last village before the frontier
The refugees squatted down
To scrape a handful of earth of the Republic
Then, with that amulet, crossed.
The soil held more dearly than any baggage
Did not tend grey olive trees
Nor rose-coloured almonds nor green pines almost blue
But dried among the bric-a-brac
On mantlepieces of Peru and Mexico.

THINKING OF BOOKSHOPS

I have been introduced to death in bookshops
a cultivated personality no pedlar of patent clichés
who explained to me we should read for interest
or for knowledge if the intellectual type
while all around young people were buying blue penguins
and second hand hard covers such as *The Imagination of
    Reason*
unpocketing five bob to the mortician
cutting the white pages to eat in their silent rooms
heaven and hell distant from the things we know are better
the uncounted wisdoms and graces towards happiness
with a girl on the beach under a crown jewel sky
grey acres away from the most real thing the whisper
"I love you" "I love you" again (never often enough)
    "I love you"

PAEAN TO EVE'S APPLE

for Allen Ginsberg

Bud fantasies, dreams of an ear of corn,
Comas where we reduce to leaves . . .
In an orchard heady as Eden
We eat out of the way of the official keeper
Our senses exotically mutated
By transplanting and the rich hybrids,
We drop like butterflies
To the smells from psychotic flowers and grasses.

And, as the new needs words of welcome,
Pausing in our earthwatch
We pick from the windfalls under the boughs
A litany of forbidden fruit
And rechart the stars and the sins.

HISTORY

"Tell us, streaming lady,
The cause of your wave travel
Have you left your man
You're certainly in a bad state."

"I have no husband I have
Not touched a man, Fenian
King of character, I have
The fondness only for your son."

"To which of my sons, sexual
Blossoming flower, are you giving
Passion—the opportunity
Tell us the whole story, girl."

"I'll tell you, Finn, it's that
Witty blonde son of yours
Oisin with his beautiful
Bright arms that are so long."

"You're strong for him I see,
Virgin of the unstroked hair,
Why him—there are many
Youths with wealth of skin."

"The cause is, Fenian father
I came all that distance
Because his soul's a mansion
His body has a bedroom in

Many a king's chit and courtling
Offered their brownness to get
My love—I never gave my lips
I warmly dreamed of Oisin's."

Laying my hand on you, Patrick,
It's no shame to a sensual pagan
Every inch of me was panting
For the tresses none had rifled

I clasped her soft sweating hand
Gasped in trembling sweet talk:
"I thank you for saying all that
About me, lovely little lady

You are the nicest girl I've met—
I would prefer to be marched off
By you in chains than by any
Others I've danced with."

"I have my spell on you, Oisin,
You are a hero and now my husband
Get up on my nag and we'll ride
To the cosmetic suburbs of rejuvenation."

*　　　　　*　　　　　*

On the horse's back I was put
The untouched feminine in front:
"Let us steal softly out of town,
Oisin, until we reach my place."

(translation from the Irish)

DESMOND O'GRADY

Desmond O'Grady was born in 1935 in Limerick, and was educated in Catholic schools in Limerick and at University College, Dublin. In 1964 he received an M.A. degree in Celtic Studies from Harvard University, where he studied with Professor John Kelleher. Since then, he has taught in Rome and Cairo. He has a permanent residence in Paros, Greece. Over the past ten years, he has given many poetry readings and public lectures both in the United States and Europe. In addition to his own poetry, which has appeared in numerous magazines and anthologies, he has translated many poems from Irish, Italian, French, German, Armenian, Rumanian, Greek, Yugoslavian, and Russian. His major collections include **Reilly and Other Poems** (1961), **The Dark Edge of Europe** (1967), **Off License** (1968), **The Dying Gaul** (1968), **Separations** (1973), **Sing Me Creation** (1974), and **The Headgear of the Tribe** (1977). His version of the Welsh epic, **The Gododdin**, was also published in 1977.

PROFESSOR KELLEHER AND THE CHARLES RIVER

The Charles river reaps here like a sickle. April
Light sweeps flat as ice on the inner curve
Of the living water. Overhead, far from the wave, a dove

White gull heads inland. The spring air, still
Lean from winter, thaws. Walking, John
Kelleher and I talk on the civic lawn.

West, to our left, past some trees, over the ivy walls,
The clock towers, pinnacles, the pillared university yard,
The Protestant past of Cambridge New England
    selfconsciously dead
In the thawing clay of the Old Burying Ground. Miles
East, over the godless Atlantic, our common brother,
Ploughing his myth-muddy fields, embodies our order.

But here, while the students row by eights and fours on
    the river—
As my father used to row on the Shannon when, still a
    child,
I'd cross Thomond Bridge every Sunday, my back to the
    walled
And turreted castle, listening to that uncle Mykie deliver
His version of history—I listen now to John Kelleher
Unravel the past a short generation later.

Down at the green bank's nerve ends, its roots half in the
    river,
A leafing tree gathers refuse. The secret force
Of the water worries away the live earth's under-surface.
But his words, for the moment, hold back time's being's
    destroyer,
While the falling wave on both thighs of the ocean
Erodes the coasts, at its dying conceptual motion.

Two men, one young, one old, stand stopped acrobats in
    the blue
Day, their bitch river to heel. Beyond,
Some scraper, tower or ancestral house's gable end.
Then, helplessly, as in some ancient dance, the two
Begin their ageless struggle, while the tree's shadow
With all its arms, crawls on the offal-strewn meadow.

Locked in their mute struggle there by the blood-loosed
    tide
The two abjure all innocence, tear down past order—
The one calm, dispassionate, clearsighted, the other
Wild with ecstasy, intoxicated, world mad.
Surely some new order is at hand;
Some new form emerging where they stand.

Dusk. The great dim tide of shadows from the past
Gathers for the end—the living and the dead.
All force is fruitful. All opposing powers combine.
Aristocratic privilege, divine sanction, anarchy at last
Yield the new order. The saffron sun sets.
All shadows procession in an acropolis of lights.

IF I WENT AWAY

If I went away I should never come back
but hike the hills, sound each hollow,
tramp the stony goatherd track
and my own wild will happily follow.

My heart is as black as a burned door,
or the burnt out coal in a kitchen range,
or the stamp of a boot on a whitewashed floor
and memory makes my smile turn strange.

My heart in a thousand bits lies shattered
like broken ice on the water's face,
like a heap of stones you've knocked and scattered
or a virgin fallen in disgrace.

I shall leave this town as soon as I can
for sharp is the stone here, deep the dung;
there's nothing of value here for a man
but the heavy word from everyone's tongue.

(translation from the Irish)

THE POET IN OLD AGE FISHING AT EVENING

for Ezra Pound

Comes a time
When even the old and familiar ideas
Float out of reach of the mind's hooks,
And the soul's prime
Has slipped like a fish through the once high weirs
Of an ailing confidence. O where are the books
On this kind of death?

Upright as love
Out on the tip of a tail of rock,
The sea ravelling off from the eye,
The line like the nerve
Straining the evening back from the clock,
He merges awhile into the lie
Of his own silhouette.

THE DAY CONCLUDES BURNING

The day concludes burning.
The north breathes like a dragon.

Held upright by a tree-stump
he fights what cannot die
but must replace him:
sun, sea, river,
moon and marketplace.

What's forceful beyond man
mounts up in one black-crested wave
and sweeps the sod between them.

Disevaluation of all value
bartered reputation,
disdained endeavour
flood forward for the kill
upon him.

Bulls of land and sea
lock in final combat.
Black confronts white.

Over his hanging head
his seacrow circles thrice
and settling on his shoulder
folds her wings,
caws.

THE PITCH PILES UP IN PART

The pitch piles up in part
on part of the heart's abyss.
Unbalanced from exaggeration
I career towards crisis.

Blood gangs up in the groin.
Nerves knot at the temples.
In one flush fury thrusts
and the wall of reason tumbles.

The eye rolls out of orbit.
The body bucks like a beast's.
Driven daft by his dream
the whole man bursts.

Spannered, the works
fly all over the shop:
wardrobes, women, babies,
bedrooms, kitchens—scrap.

In bits
things mean more
terribly themselves—
undone for.

I pick, prefer,
accept, adopt
just like a feather sorter
in his feather loft.

The blindness over,
bleakness stretches out
empty as an ocean
round one small boat.

But something's always had it,
burnt out, destroyed;
for whatever new comes from it
something old died.

BRENDAN KENNELLY

Brendan Kennelly was born in 1936 in County Kerry. He was educated at St. Ita's College in Kerry, and at Trinity College, Dublin, where he received his Ph.D. in 1969. Kennelly is now professor of Modern Literature at Trinity. In 1971–72 he was visiting professor of English Literature at Swarthmore College in Pennsylvania. Kennelly is the editor of the **Penguin Book of Irish Verse** (1970). His numerous collections of poetry include: **Collection One: Getting Up Early** (1966), **Selected Poems** (1969), **A Drinking Cup: Poems from the Irish** (1970), **Bread** (1971), **Love-Cry** (1972), **A Kind of Trust** (1975), and **New and Selected Poems** (1976).

MY DARK FATHERS

My dark fathers lived the intolerable day
Committed always to the night of wrong,
Stiffened at the hearthstone, the woman lay,
Perished feet nailed to her man's breastbone.
Grim houses beckoned in the swelling gloom
Of Munster fields where the Atlantic night
Fettered the child within the pit of doom,
And everywhere a going down of light.

And yet upon the sandy Kerry shore
The woman once had danced at ebbing tide
Because she loved flute music—and still more
Because a lady wondered at the pride
Of one so humble. That was long before
The green plant withered by an evil chance;
When winds of hunger howled at every door
She heard the music dwindle and forgot the dance.

Such mercy as the wolf receives was hers
Whose dance became a rhythm in a grave,
Achieved beneath the thorny savage furze
That yellowed fiercely in a mountain cave.
Immune to pity, she, whose crime was love,
Crouched, shivered, searched the threatening sky,
Discovered ready signs, compelled to move
Her to her innocent appalling cry.

Skeletoned in darkness, my dark fathers lay
Unknown, and could not understand
The giant grief that trampled night and day,
The awful absence moping through the land.
Upon the headland, the encroaching sea
Left sand that hardened after tides of Spring,
No dancing feet disturbed its symmetry
And those who loved good music ceased to sing.

Since every moment of the clock
Accumulates to form a final name,
Since I am come of Kerry clay and rock,
I celebrate the darkness and the shame
That could compell a man to turn his face
Against the wall, withdrawn from light so strong
And undeceiving, spancelled in a place
Of unapplauding hands and broken song.

THE THATCHER

He whittled scallops for a hardy thatch,
His palm and fingers hard as the bog oak.
You'd see him of an evening, crouched
Under a tree, testing a branch. If it broke
He grunted in contempt and flung it away,
But if it stood the stretch, his sunken blue
Eyes briefly smiled. Then with his long knife he
Chipped, slashed, pointed. The pile of scallops grew.

Astride a house on a promised day,
He rammed and patted scallops into place
Though wind cut his eyes till he seemed to weep.
Like a god after making a world, his face
Grave with the secret, he'd stare and say—
"Let the wind rip and the rain pelt. This'll keep."

THE GRIP

In Moynihan's meadow
The badger turned on the hound
And gripped.

The hound bit and tore
At the badger's body.
Harder, harder
The badger gripped.

The men ran up.
O'Carroll shouted "Quick! Quick! Crack a stick."

The stick cracked.
Deceived,
The iron jaws relaxed.

The hurt hound bit in fury.
Again the badger
Gripped.
The neck, this time.

No loosening now.
Fangs tightened in a fierce embrace
Of vein and sinew.
No complex expertise, no difficult method,
No subtle undermining, no lying guile,
Only the simple savage style

As the hound weakened, slumped, died.
The white teeth parted
Red with the fresh blood.

The men watched him turn,
Head for a hedge,
Low grey killer,
Skin ripped from sides, back, head, neck.

O'Carroll prodded the dead hound
With a blackthorn stick,
Said, more to himself than to others
Standing there—

"A hundred hurts are bad
But a good grip
Will break the heart
Of the best hound in the land."

PROOF

I would like all things to be free of me,
Never to murder the days with presupposition.
Never to feel they suffer the imposition
Of having to be this or that. How easy
It is to maim the moment
With expectation, to force it to define
Itself. Beyond all that I am, the sun
Scatters its light as though by accident.

The fox eats its own leg in the trap
To go free. As it limps through the grass
The earth itself appears to bleed.
When the morning light comes up
Who knows what suffering midnight was?
Proof is what I do not need.

SEAMUS HEANEY

Seamus Heaney was born in 1939 in County Derry, Northern Ireland, where he was educated at local schools and at St. Columb's College. He received a B.A. in English from Queen's University, Belfast, and lectured there from 1966 to 1972, spending an academic year as visiting professor at the University of California, Berkeley. After moving to County Wicklow in 1972, he made his living for a time as a free-lance writer, doing work for radio and television and for various journals. He has been the recipient of numerous awards and prizes including the Somerset Maugham Award (1968), the Denis Devlin Award (1973), the Duff Cooper Award (1975), and the W. H. Smith Literary Award (1976). Since 1975, he has been teaching at Carysfort College, Dublin, where he is now head of the English Department. He is married and has three children. Heaney has edited the Ulster literary journals **Threshold** and **Soundings 2**. His four major collections of poetry are **Death of a Naturalist** (1966), **Door Into the Dark** (1969), **Wintering Out** (1972), and **North** (1975); a fifth collection, **Field Work**, is forthcoming.

DIGGING

Between my finger and my thumb
The squat pen rests; snug as a gun.

Under my window, a clean rasping sound
When the spade sinks into gravelly ground:
My father, digging. I look down

Till his straining rump among the flowerbeds
Bends low, comes up twenty years away
Stooping in rhythm through potato drills
Where he was digging.

The coarse boot nestled on the lug, the shaft
Against the inside knee was levered firmly.
He rooted out tall tops, buried the bright edge deep
To scatter new potatoes that we picked
Loving their cool hardness in our hands.

By God, the old man could handle a spade.
Just like his old man.

My grandfather cut more turf in a day
Than any other man on Toner's bog.
Once I carried him milk in a bottle
Corked sloppily with paper. He straightened up
To drink it, then fell to right away

Nicking and slicing neatly, heaving sods
Over his shoulder, going down and down
For the good turf. Digging.

The cold smell of potato mould, the squelch and slap
Of soggy peat, the curt cuts of an edge
Through living roots awaken in my head.
But I've no spade to follow men like them.

Between my finger and my thumb
The squat pen rests.
I'll dig with it.

TROUT

Hangs, a fat gun-barrel,
deep under arched bridges
or slips like butter down
the throat of the river.

From depths smooth-skinned as plums
his muzzle gets bull's eye;
picks off grass-seed and moths
that vanish, torpedoed.

Where water unravels
over gravel-beds he
is fired from the shallows
white belly reporting

flat; darts like a tracer-
bullet back between stones
and is never burnt out.
A volley of cold blood

ramrodding the current.

IN SMALL TOWNLANDS

For Colin Middleton

In small townlands his hogshair wedge
Will split the granite from the clay
Till crystal in the rock is bared:
Loaded brushes hone an edge
On mountain blue and heather grey.
Outcrops of stone contract, outstared

The spectrum bursts, a bright grenade,
When he unlocks the safety catch
On morning dew, on cloud, on rain.
The splintered lights slice like a spade
That strips the land of fuzz and blotch,
Pares clean as bone, cruel as the pain

That strikes in a wild heart attack.
His eyes, thick, greedy lenses, fire
This bare bald earth with white and red,
Incinerate it till it's black
And brilliant as a funeral pyre:
A new world cools out of his head.

LIMBO

Fishermen at Ballyshannon
Netted an infant last night
Along with the salmon.
An illegitimate spawning,

A small one thrown back
To the waters. But I'm sure
As she stood in the shallows
Ducking him tenderly

Till the frozen knobs of her wrists
Were dead as the gravel,
He was a minnow with hooks
Tearing her open.

She waded in under
The sign of her cross.
He was hauled in with the fish.
Now limbo will be

A cold glitter of souls
Through some far briny zone.
Even Christ's palms, unhealed,
Smart and cannot fish there.

REQUIEM FOR THE CROPPIES

The pockets of our great coats full of barley—
No kitchens on the run, no striking camp—
We moved quick and sudden in our own country.
The priest lay behind ditches with the tramp.
A people, hardly marching—on the hike—
We found new tactics happening each day:
We'd cut through reins and rider with the pike
And stampede cattle into infantry,
Then retreat through hedges where cavalry must be
    thrown.
Until, on Vinegar Hill, the fatal conclave.
Terraced thousands died, shaking scythes at cannon.
The hillside blushed, soaked in our broken wave.
They buried us without shroud or coffin
And in August the barley grew up out of the grave.

LINEN TOWN

High Street, Belfast, 1786

It's twenty to four
By the public clock. A cloaked rider
Clops off into an entry

Coming perhaps from the Linen Hall
Or Cornmarket
Where, the civic print unfrozen,

In twelve years' time
They hanged young McCracken—
This lownecked belle and tricorned fop

Still flourish undisturbed
By the swinging tongue of his body.
Pen and ink, water tint

Fence and fetch us in
Under bracketed tavern signs,
The edged gloom of arcades.

It's twenty to four
On one of the last afternoons
Of reasonable light.

Smell the tidal Lagan:
Take a last turn
In the tang of possibility.

from A NORTHERN HOARD

And some in dreams assured were
Of the Spirit that plagued us so

ROOTS

Leaf membranes lid the window.
In the streetlamp's glow
Your body's moonstruck
To drifted barrow, sunk glacial rock.

And all shifts dreamily as you keen
Far off, turning from the din
Of gunshot, siren and clucking gas
Out there beyond each curtained terrace

Where the fault is opening. The touch of love,
Your warmth heaving to the first move,
Grows helpless in our old Gomorrah.
We petrify or uproot now.

I'll dream it for us before dawn
When the pale sniper steps down
And I approach the shrub.
I've soaked by moonlight in tidal blood

A mandrake, lodged human fork,
Earth sac, limb of the dark;
And I wound its damp smelly loam
And stop my ears against the scream.

NO MAN'S LAND

I deserted, shut out
their wounds' fierce awning,
those palms like streaming webs.

Must I crawl back now,
spirochete, abroad between
shred-hung wire and thorn,
to confront my smeared doorstep
and what lumpy dead?
Why do I unceasingly
arrive late to condone
infected sutures
and ill-knit bone?

MOSSBAWN: TWO POEMS IN DEDICATION

For Mary Heaney

1. Sunlight

There was a sunlit absence.
The helmeted pump in the yard
heated its iron,
water honeyed

in the slung bucket
and the sun stood
like a griddle cooling
against the wall

of each long afternoon.
So, her hands scuffled
over the bakeboard,
the reddening stove

sent its plaque of heat
against her where she stood
in a floury apron
by the window.

Now she dusts the board
with a goose's wing,
now sits, broad-lapped,
with whitened nails

and measling shins:
here is a space
again, the scone rising
to the tick of two clocks.

And here is love
like a tinsmith's scoop
sunk past its gleam
in the meal-bin.

2. The Seed Cutters

They seem hundreds of years away. Breughel,
You'll know them if I can get them true.
They kneel under the hedge in a half-circle
Behind a windbreak wind is breaking through.
They are the seed cutters. The tuck and frill
Of leaf-sprout is on the seed potatoes
Buried under that straw. With time to kill
They are taking their time. Each sharp knife goes
Lazily halving each root that falls apart
In the palm of the hand: a milky gleam,
And, at the centre, a dark watermark.
O calendar customs! Under the broom
Yellowing over them, compose the frieze
With all of us there, our anonymities.

THE GRAUBALLE MAN

As if he had been poured
in tar, he lies
on a pillow of turf
and seems to weep

the black river of himself.
The grain of his wrists
is like bog oak,
the ball of his heel

like a basalt egg.
His instep has shrunk
cold as a swan's foot
or a wet swamp root.

His hips are the ridge
and purse of a mussel,
his spine an eel arrested
under a glisten of mud.

The head lifts,
the chin is a visor
raised above the vent
of his slashed throat

that has tanned and toughened.
The cured wound
opens inwards to a dark
elderberry place.

Who will say "corpse"
to his vivid cast?
Who will say "body"
to his opaque repose?

And his rusted hair,
a mat unlikely
as a foetus's.
I first saw his twisted face

in a photograph
a head and shoulder
out of the peat,
bruised like a forceps baby,

but now he lies
perfected in my memory,
down to the red horn
of his nails,

hung in the scales
with beauty and atrocity:
with the Dying Gaul
too strictly compassed

on his shield,
with the actual weight
of each hooded victim,
slashed and dumped.

THE BADGERS

When the badger glimmered away
into another garden
you stood, half-lit with whiskey,
sensing you had disturbed
some soft returning.

The murdered dead,
you thought.
But could it not have been
some violent shattered boy
nosing out what got mislaid
between the cradle and the explosion,
evenings when windows stood open
and the compost smoked down the backs?

Visitations are taken for signs.
At a second house I listened
for duntings under the laurels
and heard intimations whispered
about being vaguely honoured.

And to read even by carcasses
the badgers have come back.
One that grew notorious
lay untouched in the roadside.
Last night one had me braking
but more in fear than in honour.

Cool from the sett and redolent
of his runs under the night,
the bogey of fern country
broke cover in me
for what he is:
pig family
and not at all what he's painted

How perilous is it to choose
not to love the life we're shown?
His sturdy dirty body
and interloping grovel.
The intelligence in his bone.
The unquestionable houseboy's shoulders
that could have been my own.

TRIPTYCH

I

There they were, as if our memory hatched them,
As if the unquiet founders walked again:
Two young men with rifles on the hill,
Profane and bracing as their instruments.

Who's sorry for our trouble?
Who dreamt that we might dwell among ourselves
In rain and scoured light and wind-dried stones?
Basalt, blood, water, headstones, leeches.

In that neuter original loneliness
From Brandon to Dunseverick
I think of small-eyed survivor flowers,
The pined-for, unmolested orchid.

I see a stone house by a pier.
Elbow room. Broad window light.
The heart lifts. You walk twenty yards
To the boats and buy mackerel.

And to-day a girl walks in home to us
Carrying a basket full of new potatoes,
Three tight green cabbages, and carrots
With the tops and mould still fresh on them.

II

My tongue moved, a swung relaxing hinge.
I said to her, "What will become of us?"
And as forgotten water in a well might shake
At an explosion under morning

Or a crack run up a gable,
She began to speak.
"I think our very form is bound to change.
Dogs in a siege. Saurian relapses. Pismires.

Unless forgiveness finds its nerve and voice,
Unless the helmeted and bleeding tree
Can green and open buds like infants' fists
And the creeping fundament incubate

Bright nymphs. . . . My people think money
And talk weather. Oil-rigs lull their future
On single acquisitive stems. Silence
Has shoaled into the trawlers' echo-sounders.

The ground we kept our ear to for so long
Is flayed or calloused, and its entrails
Tented by an impious augury.
Our island is full of comfortless noises."

III

On Devenish I heard a snipe
And the keeper's recital of elegies
Under the tower. Carved monastic heads
Were crumbling like bread on water.

On Boa the god-eyed, sec-mouthed stone
Socketed between graves, two-faced, trepanned,
Answered my silence with silence.
A stoup for rain water. Anathema.

From a cold hearthstone on Horse Island
I watched the sky beyond the open chimney
And listened to the thick rotations
Of an army helicopter patrolling.

A hammer and a cracked jug full of cobwebs
Lay on the windowsill. Everything in me
Wanted to bow down, to offer up,
To go barefoot, foetal and penitential,

And pray at the water's edge.
How we crept before we walked! I remembered
The helicopter shadowing our march at Newry,
The scared, irrevocable steps.

A DREAM OF JEALOUSY

Walking with you and another lady
In wooded parkland, the whispering grass
Ran its fingers through our guessing silence
And the trees opened into a shady
Unexpected clearing where we sat down.
I think the candour of the light dismayed us.
We talked about desire and being jealous,
Our conversation a loose single gown
Or a white picnic tablecloth spread out
Like a book of manners in the wilderness.
"Show me," I said to our companion, "what
I have much coveted, your breast's mauve star."
And she consented. O neither these verses
Nor my prudence, love, can heal your wounded stare.

THE SINGER'S HOUSE

When they said Carrickfergus I could hear
the frosty echo of saltminers' picks.
I imagined it, chambered and glinting,
a township built of light.

What do we say any more
to conjure the salt of our earth?
So much comes and is gone
that should be crystal and kept

and amicable weathers
that bring up the grain of things,
their tang of season and store,
are all the packing we'll get.

So I say to myself *Gweebarra*
and its music hits off the place
like water hitting off granite.
I see the glittering sound

framed in your window,
knives and forks set on oilcloth,
and the seals' heads,
suddenly outlined, dark and intelligent.

People here used to believe
that drowned souls lived in the seals.
At spring tides they might change shape.
They loved music and swam in for a singer

who stood at the end of summer
in the mouth of a whitewashed turf-shed,
his shoulder to the jamb, his song
a rowboat far out in evening.

When you came here first you were always singing,
a hint of the clip of the pick
in your winnowing climb and attack.
Raise it again, man. We still believe what we hear.

THE WANDERER

In a semi-circle we toed the line chalked round the master's
desk and on a day when the sun was incubating milktops
and warming the side of the jamjar where the bean had
split its stitches, he called me forward and crossed my
palm with silver. "At the end of the holidays this man's
going away to Derry, so this is for him winning the
scholarship. . . . We all wish him good luck. Now, back to
your places."

I have wandered far from that ring-giver and would not renege on this migrant solitude. I have seen halls in flames, hearts in cinders, the benches filled and emptied, the circles of companions called and broken. That day I was a rich young man, who could tell you now of flittings, night-vigils, let-downs, women's cried-out eyes.

ENGLAND'S DIFFICULTY

I moved like a double agent among the big concepts.

The word "enemy" had the toothed efficiency of a mowing machine. It was a mechanical and distant noise beyond that opaque security, that autonomous ignorance.

"When the Germans bombed Belfast it was the bitter Orange parts were hit the worst."

I was on somebody's shoulder, conveyed through the starlit yard to see the sky glowing over Anahorish. Grown-ups lowered their voices and resettled in the kitchen as if tired-out after an excursion.

Behind the blackout, Germany called to lamplit kitchens through fretted baize, dry battery, wet battery, capillary wires, domed valves that squeaked and burbled as the dial-hand absolved Stuttgart and Leipzig.

"He's an artist, this Haw Haw. He can fairly leave it into them."

I lodged with "the enemies of Ulster," the scullions outside the walls. Squires of the cockpit, barkers of auction notices, arbitrators of the burial grounds. An adept at banter, I crossed the lines with carefully enunciated passwords, manned every speech with check-points and reported back to nobody.

EXPOSURE

It is December in Wicklow:
Alders dripping, birches
Inheriting the last light,
The ash tree cold to look at.

A comet that was lost
Should be visible at sunset,
Those million tons of light
Like a glimmer of haws and rose-hips,

And I sometimes see a falling star.
If I could come on meteorite!
Instead I walk through damp leaves,
Husks, the spent flukes of autumn,

Imagining a hero
On some muddy compound,
His gift like a slingstone
Whirled for the desperate.

How did I end up like this?
I often think of my friends'
Beautiful prismatic counselling
And the anvil brains of some who hate me

As I sit weighing and weighing
My responsible *tristia.*
For what? For the ear? For the people?
For what is said behind-backs?

Rain comes down through the alders,
Its low conducive voices
Mutter about let-downs and erosions
And yet each drop recalls

The diamond absolutes.
I am neither internee nor informer;
An inner émigré, grown long-haired
And thoughtful; a wood-kerne

Escaped from the massacre,
Taking protective colouring
From bole and bark, feeling
Every wind that blows;

Who, blowing up these sparks
For their meagre heat, have missed
The once-in-a-lifetime portent,
The comet's pulsing rose.

MICHAEL LONGLEY

Born in Belfast in 1939, Michael Longley was educated at the Royal Belfast Academical Institute and Trinity College, Dublin, where he read classics. After teaching for several years, he was appointed Director for Literature and the Traditional Arts on the Arts Council of Northern Ireland. He is married to the critic Edna Longley and has three children. He has edited **Causeway: The Arts in Ulster**, and **Under the Moon: Over the Stars**, an anthology of children's poetry. Three collections of his poetry have been published: **No Continuing City** (1969), **An Exploded View** (1973), and **Man Lying on a Wall** (1976). A fourth collection, **The Hunters' Circle**, is forthcoming. His work has also been included in **Penguin Modern Poets 26**.

EPITHALAMION

These are the small hours when
Moths by their fatal appetite
That brings them tapping to get in,
　　Are steered along the night
To where our window catches light.

Who hazard all to be
Where we, the only two it seems,
Inhabit so delightfully
    A room it bursts its seams
And spills on to the lawn in beams,

    Such visitors as these
Reflect with eyes like frantic stars
This garden's brightest properties,
    Cruising its corridors
Of light above the folded flowers,

    Till our vicinity
Is rendered royal by their flight
Towards us, till more silently
    The silent stars ignite,
Their aeons dwindling by a night,

    And everything seems bent
On robing in this evening you
And me, all dark the element
    Our light is earnest to,
All quiet gathered round us who,

    When over the embankments
A train that's loudly reprobate
Shoots from silence into silence,
    With ease accommodate
Its pandemonium, its freight.

    I hold you close because
We have decided dark will be
For ever like this and because,
    My love, already
The dark is growing elderly.

With dawn upon its way,
Punctually and as a rule,
The small hours widening into day,
 Our room its vestibule
Before it fills all houses full,

 We too must hazard all,
Switch off the lamp without a word
For the last of night assembled
 Over it and unperturbed
By the moth that lies there littered,

 And notice how the trees
Which took on anonymity
Are again in their huge histories
 Displayed, that wherever we
Attempt, and as far as we can see,

 The flowers everywhere
Are withering, the stars dissolved,
Amalgamated in a glare,
 Which last night were revolved
Discreetly round us—and, involved,

 The two of us, in these
Which early morning has deformed,
Must hope that in new properties
 We'll find a uniform
To know each other truly by, or,

 At the least, that these will,
When we rise, be seen with dawn
As remnant yet part raiment still,
 Like flags that linger on
The sky when king and queen are gone.

CHRISTOPHER AT BIRTH

Your uncle, totem and curator bends
Above your cot. It is you I want to see.
Your cry comes out like an eleison.
Only the name tag round your wrist extends
My surprised compassion to loyalty.
Your mother tells me you are my godson.

The previous room still moulds your shape
Which lies unwashed, out of its element,
Smelling like rain on soil. I stoop to lift
You out of bed and into my landscape,
Last arrival, obvious immigrant
Wearing the fashions of the place you left.

As winds are balanced in a swaying tree
I cradle your cries. And in my arms reside,
Till you fall asleep, your uncontended
Demands that the world be your nursery.
And I, a spokesman of that world outside,
Creation's sponsor, stand dumbfounded,

Although there is such a story to unfold
—Whether as forecast or reminder—
Of cattle steaming in their byres, and sheep
Beneath a hedge, arranged against the cold,
Our cat at home blinking by the fender,
The wolf treading its circuits towards sleep.

EMILY DICKINSON

Emily Dickinson, I think of you
Wakening early each morning to write,
Dressing with care for the act of poetry.

Yours is always a perfect progress through
Such cluttered rooms to eloquence, delight,
To words—your window on the mystery.

By christening the world you live and pray—
Within those lovely titles is contained
The large philosophy you tend towards:
Within your lexicon the birds that play
Beside your life, the wind that holds your hand
Are recognised. Your poems are full of words.

In your house in Amherst Massachusetts,
Though like love letters you lock them away,
The poems are ubiquitous as dust.
You sit there writing while the light permits—
While you grow older they increase each day,
Gradual as flowers, gradual as rust.

KINDERTOTENLIEDER

There can be no songs for dead children
Near the crazy circle of explosions,
The splintering tangent of the ricochet,

No songs for the children who have become
My unrestricted tenants, fingerprints
Everywhere, teethmarks on this and that.

IRISH POETRY

Impasto or washes as a rule:
Tuberous clottings, a muddy
Accumulation, internal rhyme—
Fuchsia's droop towards the ground,
The potato and its flower:

Or a continuing drizzle,
Specialisations of light,
Bog-water stretched over sand
In small waves, elisions—
The dialects of silence:

Or, sometimes, in combination
Outlining the bent spines,
The angular limbs of creatures—
Lost minerals colouring
The initial letter, the stance.

DESERT WARFARE

Though there are distances between us
I lean across and with my finger
Pick sleep from the corners of her eyes,
Two grains of sand. Could any soldier
Conscripted to such desert warfare
Discern more accurately than I do
The manifold hazards—a high sun,
Repetitive dunes, compasses jamming,
Delirium, death—or dare with me
During the lulls in each bombardment
To address her presence, her absence?
She might be a mirage, and my long
Soliloquies part of the action.

FLEADH

for Brian O'Donnell

Fiddle

Stained with blood from a hare,
Then polished with beeswax
It suggests the vibration
Of diaphanous wings
Or—bow, elbow dancing—
Follows the melted spoors
Where fast heels have spun
Dewdrops in catherine-wheels.

Flute

Its ebony and silver
Mirror a living room
Where disembodied fingers
Betray to the darkness
Crevices, every knothole—
Hearth and chimney-corner
For breezes igniting
The last stick of winter.

Bodhran

We have eaten the goat:
Now his discarded horns
From some farflung midden
Call to his skin, and echo
All weathers that rattle
The windows, bang the door:
A storm contained, hailstones
Melting on this diaphragm.

Whistle

Cupped hands unfolding
A flutter of small wings
And fingers a diamond
Would be too heavy for,
Like ice that snares the feet
Of such dawn choruses
And prevents the robin
Ripening on its branch.

Pipes

One stool for the fireside
And the field, for windbag
And udder: milk and rain
Singing into a bucket
At the same angle: cries
Of water birds homing:
Ripples and undertow—
The chanter, the drones.

MAN LYING ON A WALL

Homage to L. S. Lowry

You could draw a straight line from the heels,
Through calves, buttocks and shoulderblades
To the back of the head: pressure points
That bear the enormous weight of the sky.
Should you take away the supporting structure
The result would be a miracle or
An extremely clever conjuring trick.
As it is, the man lying on the wall
Is wearing the serious expression

Of popes and kings in their final slumber,
His deportment not dissimilar to
Their stiff, reluctant exits from this world
Above the shoulders of the multitude.

It is difficult to judge whether or not
He is sleeping or merely disinclined
To arrive punctually at the office
Or to return home in time for his tea.
He is wearing a pinstripe suit, black shoes
And a bowler hat: on the pavement
Below him, like a relic or something
He is trying to forget, his briefcase
With everybody's initials on it.

PEACE

after Tibullus

Who was responsible for the very first arms deal—
The man of iron who thought of marketing the sword?
Or did he intend us to use it against wild animals
Rather than ourselves? Even if he's not guilty
Murder got into the bloodstream as gene or virus
So that now we give birth to wars, short cuts to death.
Blame the affluent society: no killings when
The cup on the dinner table was made of beechwood,
And no barricades or ghettoes when the shepherd
Snoozed among sheep that weren't even thoroughbreds.

I would like to have been alive in the good old days
Before the horrors of modern warfare and warcries
Stepping up my pulse rate. Alas, as things turn out
I've been press-ganged into service, and for all I know
Someone's polishing a spear with my number on it.
God of my Fathers, look after me like a child!

And don't be embarrassed by this handmade statue
Carved out of bog oak by my great-great-grandfather
Before the mass-production of religious art
When a wooden god stood simply in a narrow shrine.

A man could worship there with bunches of early grapes,
A wreath of whiskery wheat-ears, and then say Thank you
With a wholemeal loaf delivered by him in person,
His daughter carrying the unbroken honeycomb.
Lord, if you will keep me out of the firing line
I'll pick a porker from the steamy sty and dress
In my Sunday best, a country cousin's sacrifice.
Someone else can slaughter enemy commanders
And, over a drink, rehearse with me his memoirs,
Mapping the camp in wine upon the table top.

It's crazy to beg black death to join the ranks
Who dogs our footsteps anyhow with silent feet—
No cornfields in Hell, nor cultivated vineyards,
Only yapping Cerberus and the unattractive
Oarsman of the Styx: there an anaemic crew
Sleepwalks with smoky hair and empty eye-sockets.
How much nicer to have a family and let
Lazy old age catch up on you in your retirement,
You keeping track of the sheep, your son of the lambs,
While the woman of the house puts on the kettle.

I want to live until the white hairs shine above
A pensioner's memories of better days. Meanwhile
I would like peace to be my partner on the farm,
Peace personified: oxen under the curved yoke;
Compost for the vines, grape-juice turning into wine,
Vintage years handed down from father to son;
Hoe and ploughshare gleaming, while in some dark corner
Rust keeps the soldier's grisly weapons in their place;
The labourer steering his wife and children home
In a hay cart from the fields, a trifle sozzled.

Then, if there are skirmishes, guerilla tactics,
It's only lovers quarrelling, the bedroom door
Wrenched off its hinges, a woman in hysterics,
Hair torn out, cheeks swollen with bruises and tears—
Until the bully-boy starts snivelling as well
In a pang of conscience for his battered wife:
Then sexual neurosis works them up again
And the row escalates into a war of words.
He's hard as nails, made of sticks and stones, the chap
Who beats his girlfriend up. A crime against nature.

Enough, surely, to rip from her skin the flimsiest
Of negligees, ruffle that elaborate hair-do,
Enough to be the involuntary cause of tears—
Though upsetting a sensitive girl when you sulk
Is a peculiar satisfaction. But punch-ups,
Physical violence, are out: you might as well
Pack your kit-bag, goose-step a thousand miles away
From the female sex. As for me, I want a woman
To come and fondle my ears of wheat and let apples
Overflow between her breasts. I shall call her Peace.

THE SMALL HOTEL

The back of the mind is a small hotel
And when the residents go on picnics
Or take buckets and spades down to the sea
The betrayals begin: each crumpled sheet
Its own story; and the dressing table
And the chest-of-drawers open like books,
So that no one escapes the chamber-maid
Who becomes a waitress at dinner time,
Or the night-porter's knowledgeable smile.

SEAMUS DEANE

Seamus Deane was born in Derry, Northern Ireland, in 1940. He received B.A. and M.A. degrees from Queen's University, Belfast, and a Ph.D. from Cambridge University, England. He has taught at the University of California, Berkeley, from 1966 to 1968 and was Woodrow Wilson Fellow at Reed College, Oregon; in 1977–1978 he taught at Notre Dame and again at the University of California, Berkeley. He is senior lecturer in the English Department at University College, Dublin. His essays and poetry have been published in many Irish, English, and American journals, and he won the AE Award for Literature in 1973. His first collection, **Gradual Wars**, was published in 1972 and a second collection, **Rumours**, was published in 1977.

NORTHERN IRELAND: TWO COMMENTS

ONE: A HUSBAND
History, the angel, was stirred
To turn her face upon us. Bird
Or beast, as she turned,
The streets split and burned.
Homeward she glanced and we cried

At the feathery rush of her wide
And spreadeagling wings
Which the wind has split and flings
So severely back that it seems
She cannot fly. In her face the wind screams.

TWO: A WIFE
We see them kill as they have always done,
Imperialists in their khaki slum;
Men who hold a watching brief
For the permanence of grief.
See the street consumed by wind,
Blurred by fire and thinned
To those cadaverous bones
Which the Norwich Union owns?
There is the gaunt power
That sucks men for their marrow.

DERRY

I

The unemployment in our bones
Erupting on our hands in stones;

The thought of violence a relief,
The act of violence a grief;

Our bitterness and love
Hand in glove.

II

At the very most
The mind's eye
Perceives the ghost
Of the hands try
To timidly knock
On the walled rock
But nothing will come
And the hands become
As they insist
Mailed fists.

III

The Scots and English
Settling for the best.
The unfriendly natives
Ready for the worst.
It has been like this for years
Someone says,
It might be so forever, someone fears,
Or for days.

ELEGY: THREE

Whatever you call it,
It comes as a second thought,
Almost an aftermath
Routine as water in the bath
Beginning to detonate,
Or as spray in a raised lace
Flung like blood across the face.

Nothing prohibits the sense of death
When we are so exposed.
The bulb darkens and after
We hear the explosion,
Guerilla laughter.
The window savours the shock,
And the red startled sopranos

Of the sirens settle
To a blue yap. Whatever you call it,
Night after night we consume
The noise as an alcoholic
Drinks glass after glass until his voice
Is hurled like a flaw
Into his numbed palate.

FORDING THE RIVER

Sunday afternoon and the water
Black among the stones, the forest
Ash-grey in its permanent dusk
Of unquivering pine. That day
You unexpectedly crossed the river.

It was cold and you quickly shouted
As your feet felt the wet white stones
Knocking together. I had bent
To examine a strand of barbed wire
Looping up from a buried fence

When I heard you shout. And,
There you were, on the other side,
Running away. In a slow puncturing
Of anticipation I shivered
As if you had, unpermitted, gone for ever.

Gone, although you were already in the middle
Coming back; I picked up
Your shoes with a sense that years
Had suddenly decided to pass.
I remembered your riddle

On the way up here. " 'Brother or sister
I have none, but that man's father
Is my father's son.' Who am I
Talking about?" About my son,
Who crossed cold Lethe, thought it Rubicon.

SCHOLAR II

I remember at times
How irresponsible I have
Become. No ruling passion
Obsesses me, although passions
Are what I play among.
I'll know the library in a city
Before I know there is a slum.
I could wish the weight of
Learning would bring me down
To where things are done.

I remember the thief who fell
Half way down the wall
Of the Houghton Library because
His rope broke under the extra
Weight of the Gutenberg Bible.
Perhaps he came from a slum,
Hired to rifle the mint of published
Knowledge too. I could have told him
The difference a book would have made.

Saved him perhaps his broken leg.
Told him the new Faust stories
Of a thousand men who made
The same error and now lie
Under the weight of that beautiful,
Intransitive print. He had to fail.
And now he lies, perhaps for years,
With other slum-children in a jail,
The university of the third degree,
While in other circles move the frail
Inquirers, trailing printed liberty.

MICHAEL HARTNETT

Born in County Limerick in 1941, Michael Hartnett studied at University College, Dublin, and lived for some years in London. He has contributed to numerous Irish journals and newspapers, as well as to British and Irish radio. From 1963 to 1965 he co-edited **Arena** magazine. He was the recipient of the Irish-American Cultural Institute's Award for Irish writing in 1975, and the Arts Council of Ireland Award in the same year. For several years he worked for the Dublin Telephone Company, but has recently returned to Limerick where he teaches creative writing. He is married and has two children. A talented translator, he has published versions of the Old Irish **Hag of Beare** (1969), Lorca's **Gypsy Ballads** (1976), and the ancient Chinese classic, **Tao** (1971). His other publications include **Anatomy of a Cliché** (1968), **Selected Poems** (1970), **Cúlú Íde / The Retreat of Ita Cagney**—a bilingual poem (1975), **A Farewell to English** (1975), and **Poems in English 1958–1974** (1977). At present he is working on a collection of poems in Irish to be entitled **Adharce Broic**.

I HAVE EXHAUSTED THE DELIGHTED RANGE . . .

I have exhausted the delighted range
of small birds, and now, a new end to pain

makes a mirage of what I wished my life.
torture, immediate to me, is strange:
all that is left of the organs remain
in an anaesthetic of unbelief.

coerced by trivia, nothing to gain
but now, or to be pleased through one long night

and forsake instead something immortal?
and the graceless heron is killed in flight
and falls like a lopped flower into the stalks.

small birds, small poems are not immortal;
nor, however passed, is one intense night.
there is no time now for my dream of hawks.

ALL THE DEATH-ROOM NEEDS . . .

all the death-room needs,
long hair in silver
spiralled and unbright:
shadows of the eyes,
finest lace: finest
wax and candles and
finest wax the face,
the gnarled horn beads
about the lax hand.
the priest in passion
for the dead, his soft
hands and quiet sounds
deathbed linen kept.
and the ritual
of prayer: and cries:
and Christ's chrism.

A SMALL FARM

All the perversions of the soul
I learnt on a small farm.
How to do the neighbours harm
by magic, how to hate.
I was abandoned to their tragedies,
minor but unhealing:
bitterness over boggy land,
casual stealing of crops,
venomous cardgames
across swearing tables,
a little music on the road,
a little peace in decrepit stables.
Here were rosarybeads,
a bleeding face,
the glinting doors
that did encase
their cutler needs,
their plates, their knives,
the cracked calendars
of their lives.

I was abandoned to their tragedies
and began to count the birds,
to deduce secrets in the kitchen cold
and to avoid among my nameless weeds
the civil war of that household.

I THINK SOMETIMES . . .

I think sometimes
    of the fingernail slotted
    to most sensitive red flesh.
I think of it
    ripped out, broken and made raw
    with a bone-contracting pain.

naked, bleeding,
    white concave of hard dermis
    and its red, moist groove of pain.
        death or going
away of you is all this,
the break of a fingernail
    from a finger,
your mooncapped fingers lucid
to blood beneath, my own blood,
      O my sweet wife!

FOR MY GRANDMOTHER, BRIDGET HALPIN

maybe morning lightens over
the coldest time in all the day,
but not for you: a bird's hover,
seabird, blackbird, or bird of prey
was rain, or death, or lost cattle:
the day's warning, like red plovers
so etched and small the clouded sky,
was book to you, and true bible.
you died in utter loneliness,
your acres left to the childless.
you never saw the animals
of God, and the flower under
your feet: and the trees change a leaf:
and the red fur of a fox on
a quiet evening: and the long
birches falling down the hillside.

from A FAREWELL TO ENGLISH

for Brendan Kennelly

Gaelic is the conscience of our leaders,
the memory of a mother-rape they will
not face, the heap of bloody rags they see
and scream at in their boardrooms of mock oak.
They push us towards the world of total work,
our politicians with their seedy minds
and dubious labels, Communist or
Capitalist, none wanting freedom—
only power. All that reminds us
we are human and therefore not a herd
must be concealed or killed or slowly left
to die, or microfilmed to waste no space.
For Gaelic is our final sign that
we are human, therefore not a herd.

I saw our governments the other night—
I think the scene was Leopardstown—
horribly deformed dwarfs rode the racetrack
each mounted on a horribly deformed dwarf:
greenfaced, screaming, yellow-toothed, prodding
each other with electric prods, thrashing
each others' skinny arses, dribbling snot
and smeared with their own dung, they galloped
towards the prize, a glass and concrete anus.

I think the result was a dead heat.

DEATH OF AN IRISHWOMAN

Ignorant, in the sense
she ate monotonous food
and thought the world was flat,

and pagan, in the sense
she knew the things that moved
at night were neither dogs nor cats
but púcas and darkfaced men
she nevertheless had fierce pride.
But sentenced in the end
to eat thin diminishing porridge
in a stone-cold kitchen
she clenched her brittle hands
around a world
she could not understand.
I loved her from the day she died.
She was a summer dance at the crossroads.
She was a cardgame where a nose was broken.
She was a song that nobody sings.
She was a house ransacked by soldiers.
She was a language seldom spoken.
She was a child's purse, full of useless things.

THE RETREAT OF ITA CAGNEY

for Liam Brady

I

Their barbarism did not assuage the grief:
their polished boots, their sunday clothes,
the drone of hoarse melodeons.
The smoke was like the edge of blue scythes.
The downpour smell of overcoats
made the kitchen cry for air:
snuff lashed the nose like nettles
and the toothless praising of the dead
spun on like unoiled bellows.

She could not understand her grief:
the women who had washed his corpse
were now more intimate with him
than she had ever been.
She put a square of silk upon her head
and hidden in the collars of her coat
she felt her way along the white-washed walls.
The road became a dim knife.
She had no plan
but instinct neighed around her
like a pulling horse.

II

Moulded to a wedge of jet
by the wet night, her black hair
showed one grey rib, like a fine
steel filing on a forge floor.
One deep line, cut by silent
days of hate in the expanse
of sallow skin above her brows,
dipped down to a tragic slant.
Her eyebrows were thin penlines
finely drawn on parchment sheets,
hair after miniscule hair
a linear masterpiece.
Triangles of minute gold
broke her open blue of eyes
that had looked on bespoke love,
seeing only to despise.
Her long nose was almost bone
making her face too severe:
the tight and rose-edged nostrils
never belled into a flare.
A fine gold down above the

upper lip did not maintain
its prettiness nor lower's swell
make it less a graph of pain.
Chin and jawline delicate,
neither weak nor skeletal:
bone in definite stern mould,
small and strong like a fox-skull.
Her throat showed no signs of age.
No sinews reinforced flesh
or gathered in clenched fistfuls
to pull skin in lined mesh.

The rest was shapeless, in black woollen dress.

III

Door opened halving darkness bronze
and half an outlined man
filled half the bronze.
Lamplight whipped upright into gold
the hairs along his nose,
flowed coils of honey
around his head.
In the centre of his throat
clipped on his blue-striped shirt
a stud briefly pierced a thorn of light.
The male smell of the kitchen
engulfed her face,
odours of lost gristle
and grease along the wall:
her headscarf laughed a challenge
its crimson wrinkles crackling.
He knuckled up the wooden latch
and closed the door for many years.

IV

Great ceremony later causes pain:
next year in hatred and in grief, the vain
white dress, the bulging priest, the frantic dance,
the vowing and the sickening wishes, land
like careful hammers on a broken hand.
But in this house no sacred text was read.
He offered her some food: they went to bed,
his arm and side a helmet for her head.
This was no furtive country coupling: this
was the ultimate hello, kiss and kiss
exchanged and bodies introduced: their sin—
to choose so late a moment to begin
while shamefaced chalice, pyx, ciborium
clanged their giltwrapped anger in the room.

V

The swollen leather creaks
like lost birds
and the edges of her shawl
fringe down into the dark
while glaciers of oilskins drip around her
and musical traces and chafing of harness
and tedious drumming of hooves on the gravel
make her labour pains become
the direct rebuke and pummel of the town.
Withdrawing from her pain
to the nightmare warmth
beneath her shawl
the secret meeting in the dark
becomes a public spectacle

and baleful sextons turn their heads
and sullen shadows mutter hate
and snarl and debate
and shout vague threats of hell.

The crossroads blink their headlamp warning
and break into a rainbow on the shining tar:
the new skull turns in its warm pain,
the new skull pushes towards its morning.

VI

O my small and warm creature
with your gold hair and your skin
that smells of milk and apples,
I must always lock you in
where nothing can happen.
But you will hate these few rooms,
for a dove is bound to come
with leaves and outdoor perfumes.
Already the talons drum
a beckoning through the slates
bringing from the people words
and messages of hate.
Soon the wingbeats of this bird
will whisper down in their dive:
I dread the coming of this dove
for its beak will be a knife
and if you leave armed with my love
they will tell you what you lack:
they will make you wear my life
like a hump upon your back.

VII

. . . each footprint being green in the wet grass
in search of mushrooms like white moons of lime,
each hazel ooze of cowdung through the toes,
being warm, and slipping like a floor of silk . . .
but all the windows are in mourning here:
the giant eye gleams like a mucous hill.
She pictured cowslips, then his farmer's face,
and waited in a patient discontent.
A heel of mud fell from his garden boots
embossed with nails and white-hilt shoots of grass:
a hive of hayseeds in the woollen grooves
of meadow coats fell golden on the floor,
and apples with medallions of rust
englobed a thickening cider on the shelf:
and holly on the varnished frames bent in
and curved its catsharp fingernails of green.
The rooms became resplendent with these signs.

VIII

I will put purple crepe and crimson crepe
and white crepe on the shelf
and watch the candles cry
o *salutaris hostia.*
I will light the oil lamp till it burns
like a scarlet apple
and watch the candlegrease
upon the ledges interweave
to ropes of ivory.
I have not insulted God:
I have insulted
crombie coats and lace mantillas
sunday best and church collections

and they declare my life a sinful act:
not because it hurts
the God they say they love—
not because their sins are less—
but because my happiness
is not a public fact.

IX

In rhythmic dance the neighbours move
outside the door: become dumb dolls
as venom breaks in strident fragments
on the glass: broken insults clatter
on the slates: the pack retreats,
the instruments of siege withdraw
and skulk into the foothills to regroup.
The houses nudge and mutter through the night
and wait intently for the keep to fall.
She guards her sleeping citizen
and paces the exhausting floor:
on the speaking avenue of stones
she hears the infantry of eyes advance.

MARBAN, A HERMIT, SPEAKS

For I inhabit a wood
        unknown but to my God
my house of hazel and ash
        as an old hut in a rath.

And my house small, not too small,
        is always accessible:
women disguised as blackbirds
        talk their words from its gable.

The stags erupt from rivers,
    brown mountains tell the distance:
I am glad as poor as this
    even in men's absence.

Death-green of yew,
huge green of oak
    sanctify,
and apples grow
close by new nuts:
    water hides.

        Young of all things,
        bring faith to me,
            guard my door:
        the rough, unloved
        wild dogs, tall deer,
            quiet does.

In small tame bands
the badgers are,
    grey, outside:
and foxes dance
before my door
    all the night.

        All at evening
        the day's first meal
            since dawn's bread:
        trapped trout, sweet sloes
        and honey, haws,
            beer and herbs.

Moans, movements of
silver-breasted
    birds rouse me:
pigeons perhaps.
And a thrush sings
    constantly.

Black winged beetles
boom, and small bees:
　　November
through the lone geese
a wild winter
　　music stirs.

Come fine white gulls
all sea-singing,
　　and less sad,
lost in heather,
the grouses' song,
　　little sad.

For music I
have pines, my tall
　　music-pines:
so who can I
envy here, my
　　gentle Christ?

(translation from the Irish)

DEREK MAHON

Derek Mahon was born in 1941 in Belfast. He received his education at the Royal Belfast Academical Institution and at Trinity College, Dublin, where he took his B.A. in 1965. In the same year he received the Eric Gregory Award for poetry. He spent two years in the United States and Canada, where he held a variety of jobs. Since then he has worked on the staff of **Vogue** in London and taught at the New University of Ulster. Mahon is editor of the anthology **The Sphere Book of Modern Irish Poetry** (1972), and a frequent contributor to Irish and British literary journals. His poems are collected in **Night Crossing** (1968), **Lives** (1972), and **The Snow Party** (1975). A pamphlet entitled **Light Music** was published in 1977. A fourth collection, **Poems: 1962–1978**, is expected shortly.

GLENGORMLEY

for Padraic Fiacc

Wonders are many and none is more wonderful than man
Who has tamed the terrier, trimmed the hedge
And grasped the principle of the watering can.
Clothes-pegs litter the window-ledge
And the long ships lie in clover. Washing lines
Shake out white linen over the chalk thanes.

Now we are safe from monsters, and the giants
Who tore up sods twelve miles by six
And hurled them out to sea to become islands
Can worry us no more. The sticks
And stones that once broke bones will not now harm
A generation of such sense and charm.

Only words hurt us now. No saint or hero,
Landing at night from the conspiring seas,
Brings dangerous tokens to the new era—
Their sad names linger in the histories.
The unreconciled, in their metaphysical pain,
Strangle on lamp-posts in the dawn rain

And much dies with them. I should rather praise
A worldly time under this worldly sky—
The terrier-taming, garden-watering days
Those heroes pictured as they struggled through
The quick noose of their finite being. By
Necessity, if not choice, I live here too.

IN CARROWDORE CHURCHYARD

(at the grave of Louis MacNeice)

Your ashes will not stir, even on this high ground,
However the wind tugs, the headstones shake—
This plot is consecrated, for your sake,
To what lies in the future tense. You lie
Past tension now, and spring is coming round
Igniting flowers on the peninsula.

Your ashes will not fly, however the rough winds burst
Through the wild brambles and the reverend trees.
All we may ask of you we have. The rest
Is not for publication, will not be heard.
Maguire, I believe, suggested a blackbird
And over your grave a phrase from Euripides.

Which suits you down to the ground, like this churchyard
With its play of shadow, its humane perspective.
Locked in the winter's fist, these hills are hard
As nail, yet soft and feminine in their turn
When fingers open and the hedges burn.
This you implied, is how we ought to live—

The ironical, loving crush of roses against snow,
Each fragile, solving ambiguity. So
From the pneumonia of the ditch, from the ague
Of the blind poet and the bombed-out town you bring
The all-clear to the empty holes of spring,
Rinsing the choked mud, keeping the colours new.

I AM RAFTERY

I am Raftery, hesitant and confused among the
cold-voiced graduate students and inter-
changeable instructors. Were it not for the
nice wives who do the talking I would have
run out of hope some time ago, and of love.
I have traded in the simplistic maunderings
that made me famous for a wry dissimulation,
an imagery of adventitious ambiguity dredged
from God knows what polluted underground spring.
Death is near, I have come of age, I doubt if
I shall survive another East Anglian winter.
Scotch please, plenty of water. I am reading
Joyce in braille and it's killing me. Is it
empty pockets I play to? Not on your life,
they ring with a bright inflationary music—
two seminars a week and my own place reserved
in the record library. Look at me now,
my back to the wall, taking my cue from a
grinning disc-jockey between commercials.

DEREK MAHON

AN IMAGE FROM BECKETT

for Doreen Douglas

In that instant
There was a sea, far off,
As bright as lettuce,

A northern landscape
(Danish?) and a huddle of
Houses along the shore.

Also, I think,
A white flicker of gulls and
Washing hung to dry—

The poignancy of those
Back yards—and the gravedigger
Putting aside his forceps.

Then the hard boards
And darkness once again.
Oh, I might have proved

So many heroes!
Sorel, perhaps, or
Kröger, given the time.

For in that instant
I was struck by the sweetness and light,
The sweetness and light,

Imagining what grave
Cities, what lasting monuments,
Given the time.

But even my poor house
I left unfinished;
And my one marriage

Was over as soon as it started,
Its immanence so brief as to be
Immeasurable.

They will have buried
My great-grandchildren, and theirs,
Beside me by now

With a subliminal
Batsqueak of reflex lamentation.
Our hair and excrement

Litter the rich earth
Changing, second by second,
To civilizations.

It was good while it lasted;
And if it only lasted
The Biblical span

Required to drop six feet
Through a glitter of wintry light,
There is No-one to blame.

Still, I am haunted
By that landscape,
The soft rush of its winds,

The uprightness of its
Utilities and schoolchildren—
To whom in my will,

This, I have left my will.
I hope they had time, and light
Enough to read it.

AFTERLIVES

for James Simmons

I

I wake in a dark flat
To the soft roar of the world.
Pigeons neck on the white
Roofs as I draw the curtains
And look out over London
Rain-fresh in the morning light.

This is our element, the bright
Reason on which we rely
For the long-term solutions.
The orators yap, and guns
Go off in a back street;
But the faith does not die

That in our time these things
Will amaze the literate children
In their non-sectarian schools
And the dark places be
Ablaze with love and poetry
When the power of good prevails.

What middle-class cunts we are
To imagine for one second
That our privileged ideals

Are divine wisdom, and the dim
Forms that kneel at noon
In the city not ourselves.

II

I am going home by sea
For the first time in years.
Somebody thumbs a guitar
On the dark deck, while a gull
Dreams at the masthead,
The moon-splashed waves exult.

At dawn the ship trembles, turns
In a wide arc to back
Shuddering up the grey lough
Past lightship and buoy,
Slipway and dry dock
Where a naked bulb burns;

And I step ashore in a fine rain
To a city so changed
By five years of war
I scarcely recognise
The places I grew up in,
The faces that try to explain.

But the hills are still the same
Grey-blue above Belfast.
Perhaps if I'd stayed behind
And lived it bomb by bomb
I might have grown up at last
And learnt what is meant by home.

DEREK MAHON

THE SNOW PARTY

for Louis Asekoff

Basho, coming
To the city of Nagoya,
Is asked to a snow party.

There is a tinkling of china
And tea into china,
There are introductions.

Then everyone
Crowds to the window
To watch the falling snow.

Snow is falling on Nagoya
And farther south
On the tiles of Kyoto.

Eastward, beyond Irago,
It is falling
Like leaves on the cold sea.

Elsewhere they are burning
Witches and heretics
In the boiling squares,

Thousands have died since dawn
In the service
Of barbarous kings—

But there is silence
In the houses of Nagoya
And the hills of Ise.

MATTHEW V.29–30

Lord, mine eye offended
So I plucked it out.
Imagine my chagrin

When the offence continued.
So I plucked out
The other but

The offence continued.
In the dark now and
Working by touch, I shaved

My head, the offence continued.
Removed an ear,
Another, dispatched the nose,

The offence continued.
Imagine my chagrin.
Next, in long strips, the skin—

Razored the tongue, the toes,
The personal nitty-gritty.
The offence continued.

But now, the thing
Finding its own momentum,
The more so since

The offence continued,
I entered upon
A prolonged course

Of lobotomy and vivisection,
Reducing the self
To a rubble of organs,

A wreckage of bones
In the midst of which, somewhere,
The offence continued.

Quicklime, then, for the
Calcium, paraquat
For the unregenerate offal,

A spreading of topsoil,
A ploughing of this
And a sowing of it with barley.

Paraffin for the records
Of birth, flu
And abortive scholarship,

For the whimsical postcards,
The cheques
Dancing like hail,

The surviving copies
Of poems published
And unpublished. A scalpel

For the casual turns
Of phrase engraved
On the minds of others,

A chemical spray
For the stray
Thoughts hanging in air,

For the people
Who breathed them in.
Sadly, therefore, deletion

Of the many people
From their desks, beds,
Breakfasts, buses,

Pick-ups and catamarans.
Deletion of their
Machinery and architecture,

All evidence whatever
Of civility and reflection,
Of laughter and tears.

Destruction of all things on which
That reflection fed,
Of vegetable and bird,

Erosion of all rocks
From the holiest mountain
To the least stone,

Evaporation of all seas,
The extinction of heavenly bodies—
Until, at last, offence

Was not to be found
In that silence without bound.
Only then was I fit for human society.

A DISUSED SHED IN CO. WEXFORD

Let them not forget us, the weak souls among the asphodels.
                              Seferis, *Mythistorema*

for J. G. Farrell

Even now there are places where a thought might grow—
Peruvian mines, worked out and abandoned
To a slow clock of condensation,
An echo trapped for ever, and a flutter of

Wildflowers in the lift-shaft,
Indian compounds where the wind dances
And a door bangs with diminished confidence,
Lime crevices behind rippling rainbarrels,
Dog corners for shit burials;
And in a disused shed in Co. Wexford,

Deep in the grounds of a burnt-out hotel,
Among the bathtubs and the washbasins
A thousand mushrooms crowd to a keyhole.
This is the one star in their firmament
Or frames a star within a star.
What should they do there but desire?
So many days beyond the rhododendrons
With the world waltzing in its bowl of cloud,
They have learnt patience and silence
Listening to the crows querulous in the high wood.

They have been waiting for us in a foetor of
Vegetable sweat since civil war days,
Since the gravel-crunching, interminable departure
Of the expropriated mycologist.
He never came back, and light since then
Is a keyhole rusting gently after rain.
Spiders have spun, flies dusted to mildew,
And once a day, perhaps, they have heard something—
A trickle of masonry, a shout from the blue
Or a lorry changing gear at the end of the lane.

There have been deaths, the pale flesh flaking
Into the earth that nourished it;
And nightmares, born of these and the grim
Dominion of stale air and rank moisture.
Those nearest the door grow strong—
Elbow room! Elbow room!
The rest, dim in a twilight of crumbling
Utensils and broken pitchers, groaning

For their deliverance, have been so long
Expectant that there is left only the posture.

A half century, without visitors, in the dark—
Poor preparation for the cracking lock
And creak of hinges. Magi, moonmen,
Powdery prisoners of the old regime,
Web-throated, stalked like triffids, racked by drouth
And insomnia, only the ghost of a scream
At the flash-bulb firing squad we wake them with
Shows there is life yet in their feverish forms.
Grown beyond nature now, soft food for worms,
They lift frail heads in gravity and good faith.

They are begging us, you see, in their wordless way,
To do something, to speak on their behalf
Or at least not to close the door again.
Lost people of Treblinka and Pompeii!
Save us, save us, they seem to say,
Let the god not abandon us
Who have come so far in darkness and in pain.
We too had our lives to live.
You with your light meter and relaxed itinerary,
Let not our naive labours have been in vain!

CONSOLATIONS OF PHILOSOPHY

(For Eugene Lambe)

When we start breaking up in the wet darkness
And the rotten boards fall from us, and the ribs
Crack under the constriction of tree-roots
And the seasons slip from the fields unknown to us

Oh, then there will be the querulous complaining
From citizens who had never dreamed of this—
Who, shaken to the bone in their stout boxes
By the latest bright cars, will not inspect them

And, kept awake by the tremors of new building,
Will not be there to comment. When the broken
Wreath bowls are speckled with rain water
And the grass grows wild for want of a caretaker

Oh, then a few will remember with affection
Dry bread, mousetrap cheese, and the satisfaction
Of picking long butts from a wet gutter
Like daisies from a clover field in summer.

ECCLESIASTES

God, you could grow to love it, God-fearing, God-
    chosen purist little puritan that,
for all your wiles and smiles, you are (the
    dank churches, the empty streets,
the shipyard silence, the tied-up swings) and
    shelter your cold heart from the heat
of the world, from woman-inquisition, from the
    bright eyes of children. Yes you could
wear black, drink water, nourish a fierce zeal
    with locusts and wild honey, and not
feel called upon to understand and forgive
    but only to speak with a bleak
afflatus, and love the January rains when they
    darken the dark doors and sink hard
into the Antrim hills, the bog meadows, the heaped
    graves of your fathers. Bury that red
bandana and stick, that banjo, this is your
    country, close one eye and be king.
Your people await you, their heavy washing
    flaps for you in the housing estates—
a credulous people. God, you could do it, God
    help you, stand on a corner stiff
with rhetoric, promising nothing under the sun.

A DEPARTURE

(for John Hewitt)

I am saying goodbye to the trees,
The beech, the cedar, the elm,
The mild woods of these parts
Misted with car exhaust,
And sawdust, and the last
Gasps of the poisoned nymphs.

I have watched girls walking
And children playing under
Lilac and rhododendron,
And me flicking my ash
Into the rose bushes
As if I owned the place;

As if the trees responded
To my ignorant admiration
Before dawn when the branches
Glitter at first light,
Or later on when the finches
Disappear for the night;

And often thought if I lived
Long enough in this house
I would turn into a tree
Like somebody in Ovid
—A small tree certainly
But a tree nonetheless—

Perhaps befriend the oak,
The chestnut and the yew,
Become a home for birds,
A shelter for the nymphs,
And gaze out over the downs
As if I belonged here too.

But where I am going the trees
Are few and far between.
No richly forested slopes,
Not for a long time,
And few winking woodlands;
There are no nymphs to be seen.

Out there you would look in vain
For a rose bush: but find,
Rooted in stony ground,
A last stubborn growth
Battered by constant rain
And twisted by the sea-wind

With nothing to recommend it
But its harsh tenacity
Between the blinding windows
And the forests of the sea,
As if its very existence
Were a reason to continue

Crone crow, scarecrow,
Its worn fingers scrabbling
At a torn sky, it stands
On the edge of everything
Like a burnt-out angel
Raising petitionary hands.

Grotesque by day, at twilight
An almost tragic figure
Of anguish and despair,
It merges into the funeral
Cloud-continent of night
As if it belongs there.

EILÉAN NI CHUILLEANÁIN

Eiléan Ni Chuilleanáin was born in 1942 in Cork city, and educated at University College, Cork, and at Oxford. She is presently a lecturer at Trinity College, Dublin. Ni Chuilleanáin has been the recipient of various awards, including the **Irish Times** Award for Poetry (1966) and the Patrick Kavanagh Award (1973). Gallery Press received the Irish Publishers Award in 1976 for her second book, **Site of Ambush**. Her major collections of poetry are: **Acts and Monuments** (1972), **Site of Ambush** (1975), and **The Second Voyage** (1977).

SWINEHERD

"When all this is over," said the swineherd,
"I mean to retire, where
Nobody will have heard about my special skills
And conversation is mainly about the weather.

I intend to learn how to make coffee at least as well
As the Portuguese lay-sister in the kitchen
And polish the brass fenders every day.
I want to lie awake at night
Listening to cream crawling to the top of the jug
And the water lying soft in the cistern.

I want to see an orchard where the trees grow in straight
    lines
And the yellow fox finds shelter between the navy-blue
    trunks,
Where it gets dark early in summer
And the apple-blossom is allowed to wither on the bough."

DEAD FLY

Sparafucile fought his peasant war
Although his grey crudely-slung chassis lacked
The jet lines of midge or mosquito,
The wasp's armour, the spider's intellectual speed;
Still the rough guerilla survived my stalking,
Until by mistake I closed a bible
And cramped his limbs to soak in his scarce blood.

A monk that read this book and lived alone
Domesticated an insect of your kind,
Taught him to stand and mark the words on the page
And live in peace inside the same stone house
With a mouse he kept to bite his ear·
Whenever he winked, and a cock that blasted him
Out of his bed for matins in the dark.

Planting these three companions as watchmen
At the frontiers of his ambition, he forgot
Mortality, till death knocked them off in a row.
He complained to his friend the exile, across the profound
Indelible sea. Roused by the frosty wind
Of a friend's voice, the thought of home stinging
Fresh and sweet as the smell of oranges,

He considered the island, so far away now it shone
Bright as a theory or a stained-glass window,
Coloured and clear in the sun, his austere mind
Half sure he had invented it, and replied:
To possess is to be capable of loss
Which no possible profit can reconcile
As David, his kingdom sure, could not forget Saul.

LUCINA SCHYNNING IN SILENCE OF THE NIGHT . . .

Moon shining in silence of the night
The heaven being all full of stars
I was reading my book in a ruin
By a sour candle, without roast meat or music
Strong drink or a shield from the air
Blowing in the crazed window, and I felt
Moonlight on my head, clear after three days' rain.

I washed in cold water; it was orange, channelled down
    bogs
Dipped between cresses.
The bats flew through my room where I slept safely;
Sheep stared at me when I woke.

Behind me the waves of darkness lay, the plague
Of mice, plague of beetles
Crawling out of the spines of books,
Plague shadowing pale faces with clay
The disease of the moon gone astray.

In the desert I relaxed, amazed
As the mosaic beasts on the chapel floor
When Cromwell had departed and they saw
The sky growing through the hole in the roof.

Sheepdogs embraced me; the grasshopper
Returned with a lark and bee.
I looked down between hedges of high thorn and saw
The hare, absorbed, sitting still
In the middle of the track; I heard
Again the chirp of the stream running.

OLD ROADS

Missing from the map, the abandoned roads
Reach across the mountain, threading into
Clefts and valleys, shuffle between thick
Hedges of flowery thorn.
The grass flows into tracks of wheels,
Mowed evenly by the careful sheep;
Drenched, it guards the gaps of silence
Only trampled on the pattern day.

And if, an odd time, late
At night, a cart passes
Splashing in a burst stream, crunching bones,
The wavering candle hung by the shaft
Slaps light against a single gable
Catches a flat tombstone
Shaking a nervous beam in a white face

Their arthritic fingers
Their stiffening grasp cannot
Hold long on the hillside—
Slowly the old roads lose their grip.

from SITE OF AMBUSH

Narration

At alarming bell daybreak, before
Scraping of cats or windows creaking over the street,
Eleven miles of road between them,
The enemy commanders synchronised their heartbeats:
Seven forty-five by the sun.
At ten the soldiers were climbing into lorries
Asthmatic engines drawing breath in even shifts.
The others were fretting over guns
Counting up ammunition and money.
At eleven they lay in wait at the cross
With over an hour to go.
The pine trees looked up stiff;
At the angle of the road, polished stones
Forming a stile, a knowing path
Twisting away; the rough grass
Gripped the fragments of the wall.
A small deep stream glassily descended:
Ten minutes to the hour.
The clouds grew grey, the road grey as iron,
The hills dark, the trees deep,
The fields faded; like white mushrooms
Sheep remote under the wind.
The stream ticked and throbbed
Nearer; a boy carried a can to the well
Nearer on the dark road.
The driver saw the child's back,
Nearer; the birds shoaled off the branches in fright.

Deafly rusting in the stream
The lorry now is soft as a last night's dream.
The soldiers and the deaf child

Landed gently in the water
They were light between long weeds
Settled and lay quiet, nobody
To listen to them now.
They all looked the same face down there:
Water too thick and deep to see.
They were separated for good.
It was cold, their teeth shrilling.
They slept like falling hay in waves.
Shells candied their skin; the water
Lay heavy and they could not rise but coiled
By scythefuls limply in ranks.
A long winter stacks their bodies
And words above their stillness hang from hooks
In skeins, like dark nets drying,
Flapping against the stream.
A watch vibrates alone in the filtering light;
Flitters of hair wave at the sun.

STEWART PARKER

Stewart Parker was born in Belfast in 1942, and educated at local schools and Queen's University, Belfast, where he took a B.A. in English in 1963, and an M.A. some years later. He subsequently taught English at Hamilton College and Cornell University in New York. A number of his poems have been anthologized and published in pamphlet form (**The Casualty's Meditation** and **Maw**), but his work has not yet appeared in a collection. Parker is a regular contributor to the **Irish Times**—he writes a pop music column—and has had many plays produced on radio and television. His most recent stage plays, **Spokesong** and **Catchpenny Twist**, have enjoyed critical successes in Dublin and London. He was named most promising playwright of 1976 by the London theater critics.

HEALTH

Is this God's joke? my father screamed,
Gripped by the fingers that sprouted and waggled
From the raw holes in my shoulders.
Why blame a God you can't believe in?
Is this the sin of a generation,
The work of hands that worked together

To annihilate hands? my mother cried.
But I blame no God or man or nation
For my grim disarmament.
Health is my ambition.

Each day, the tin arms swivel.
I tame them, I labour hard for grace, like a
Good guitarist, when they swing and glide.
I am satisfied when I lift a cup to my face,
Or write my name.
What I fight is pride
In these small, humble conquests.
Who would be proud of a body?
There is only the daily struggle for peace, and the search
      from day to day for shared
Living, for
Life is abundant; life will not be squashed.
There is only the lifting of hands to shake hands
And the lifting of arms to embrace.

CHICAGO ALLEGORY

Beef Sandwich in Randy's on Michigan Ave
in the Loop. Fat cop pauses on sidewalk
to read the bill of fare. His belly
is the map of America. Folds of fat
bulge on the west and east coasts,
a gun rides the Pacific, and
a ready nightstick wags at Europe.

Flick a used scrap of dill pickle
off the formica, swill the rye bread with milk,
tongue out the shreds of beef from crevices.
The black belt scarcely buckles, maw.

THREE FITTS

I

Here's the bus now. All aboard please.
Sore eyes in the convalescent
sun (good morning all) sliding
into the tundra between smiles.
The future is a kind of wide
arid silence, isn't it, ghostlit
neither by moon sun nor neon.
You gaze into it through the window
grime, like stout Cortez, laden
with heavy invisible luggage, yawn.
Travelling on Rapid Sic Transit.

II

It's no country for young men.
The bloodman's at the door again.
Transfusions feeding the curdled veins
of a septic mother. The gutters gorged.
Us think with blood. The land bloodlet.
The honourable members represent
constituencies of blood. And yet
we're all in the one red bus, all
in the same familiar skull, good morning
all. Seated thigh by thigh
and all our faces, held in check,
held tight, fares please,
and gums mumbling the right word
that never comes, ruminating
in our fists the sure caress
that's never offered. Lovely day.

III

Will you look at yon poetry man.
Hey, fatstock. Hopalong.
Give us a snatch of your clownish song.
He wants to shimmy rings round you.
He wants the world to love him to death.
He thinks that he's the man in the street
and that's who the streets belong to. Ask him
what side he's on, he'll tell you
the people's side—that's all the sides.
He wonders whether the next spilt
gutbag might be his own, maybe.
He's frightened his words'll be stubbed out.
But he belly laughs. He's not wise.

MICHAEL SMITH

Michael Smith was born in 1942 in Dublin. He was educated at O'Connell's School and University College, Dublin, where he received his B.A. and diploma in Education. He is married and has one daughter. Smith has been a teacher of Latin and English at St. Paul's College, Dublin, since 1966, and is editor of the magazine **The Lace Curtain** and of New Writers Press. He has published one collection of his own poems, **Times & Locations** (1972), and several pamphlets. He has also translated Neruda, Machado, and Bécquer from the Spanish, and edited the poems of James Clarence Mangan.

THE DESOLATE RHYTHM OF DYING RECURS

The desolate rhythm of dying recurs,
The rhythm of outgoing tides, corrosion of stone,

Fall of petal, of leaf and soft rain on empty squares,
The fading memory of song, say, in an old man's head

That never stops in a moment of time,
A rainbowed vertigo spinning beyond the nurse's cool
    hand,

Subsidence of wind and branches against a settling sky,
And stars fading at dawn, or fall of snow:

Something ordered, yet desperate and violent—
A rose, say, or an old man's humiliation.

BLOND HAIR AT THE EDGE OF THE PAVEMENT

for James Liddy

Blonde hair at the edge of the pavement
caught in the sunlight like a bright leaf:
the dull classroom as far away as the heaven
of angels' white wings that never crumple.

The lorries passing the pigeons, the gulls;
the smells from the factories, soap, chocolate, timber;
and the bandy drover's shouts that rise forever
over the thousand brindled backs of the cattle . . .

How infinitely important all that was
to the wide eyes under the blonde hair.

A big stick poised to beat their backs
when the drovers turned theirs . . .

What sense of importance swelled at the smack
of the stick on the dung-caked dumb flesh.

AT THE APPOINTED HOUR THEY CAME

At the appointed hour they came
from who knows where, or who knew then;
from the farthest reaches of the city,
from park bench and slobland and river's edge;
from hostelries and distant places beyond time.

I can remember no details to speak of.
A queue of greasy men against the railings
moving to their own slow tempo
or the whiskered nun's brisk propriety.
I can recall the hour from the tolling of bells.

In the bushes the caterpillars ate voraciously
at the sooty leaves.
The cakeman came with trays of cakes
caught in their last act of decay,
dessert and industrial refuse.

I remember the summer as hot pavements.
The time is imprecise, but the place is there,
and the wailing of factory sirens,
and the workers' clean sweep on foot or bicycle.
In the evening the air sank with the weight of darkness.

HERE IS THE ABATTOIR WHERE

Here is the abattoir where, in the old days, were heard
The ultimate cries of table beasts.

Here is the home for unfortunate women
Who launder a twelve hour day and are never cleansed.

Here is the Union, picturesque on a sunny Sunday,
In fact, stables of appalling decrepitude.

Here are the slums where life swings back and forth
With a thud like a heavy pendulum.

Here is, partly, love's ecology: occasional blue skies
And, more often, thunderous falls of black stars.

AUGUSTUS YOUNG

Augustus Young, the pseu-
donym of James Hogan,
was born in Cork in 1943.
His work has appeared in various Irish and British
magazines. He has published two collections of his
own poetry, **Survival** (1969), and **On Loaning Hill**
(1970); two pamphlets, **Rosemaries** (1976), and
Tapestry Animals (1977); and one collection of transla-
tions, **Dánta Grádha: Love Poems from the Irish (A.D.
1350-1750)** (1975). He has also had two of his plays
performed in Ireland, **Invoices** (1972) and **The Bone in
the Heart** (1976). At present Young lives and works in
London.

THE ADVICE OF AN EFFICIENCY EXPERT

Tie your own noose if you want to be
the perfect executioner. Before the event
it's important to check the scaffold
for woodworm. What would happen if
it fell through: a flop would be fatal.

Always open the tunic at the top button:
'twould never do if you had to apply
an oxygen mask to bring it off.

Just as a matter of interest, women
are preferable to men. They break
easier and beards are an inconvenience.
But don't permit cosmetics. Don't forget,
tears are the essence. But
there must be no messing
with make-up.

No drink for a week before.
A good night's rest and you are ready
as a bride to come down to mother-
earth, ring in hand, rattling the keys.

It is in your hands. Consider.
But it mustn't show. And when
the wall blood-clots, "Freedom
is the last whiff of the rose
before death," spit on it and reply,
"The only freedom that you know
is the moment when the board
goes."

Tie your own noose. Be brave. Remember,
death is on your side: you can't lose.

HERITAGE

(the verb 'to have' does not exist in Gaelic)

One cannot possess
the house until the death
of a father, until the old man,
cutting a twist by the fire,
fails to fill the bowl,
lays down the pipe
or sometimes luckily enough
shovels himself into the earth.

One must not appear to own the place
until the first grass covers the grave.

Then you have it
and the land—one acre in ten
of arable bog. But you cannot possess
a wife until your mother
accepts the death and, in many a case,
accepts her own. There is no choice.

This is being a true son.
Allow the country die for you.

WOMAN, DON'T BE TROUBLESOME

Woman, don't be troublesome,
though your husband I may be;
our two minds were once at one,
why withdraw your hand from me.

Put your mouth of strawberry
on my mouth, cream is your cheek;
wind round white arms about me,
and do not go back to sleep.

Stay with me my flighty maid,
and be done with betrayal;
tonight this bed is wellmade,
let us toss it without fail.

Shut your eyes to other men,
no more women will I see:
the milkwhite tooth of passion
is between us—or should be.

(translation from the Irish)

SHE'S MY LOVE

She's my love,
who only gives me trouble;
    although she has made me ill,
no woman serves me as well.

She's my dear,
who breaks me and doesn't care;
    who yawns when I take my leave,
O she won't grieve on my grave.

She's my precious,
with eyes as green as grass is,
    who won't touch my bending head,
or take presents for caresses.

She's my secret,
not a word from her I get;
    she's deaf to me as the skies,
and never lets our eyes meet.

She's my problem
(strange, how long death takes to come),
    this woman won't come near me,
still I swear, she's my loved one.

(translation from the Irish)

EAVAN BOLAND

Born in Dublin in 1944, Eavan Boland was educated in London, New York, and Dublin. She received a degree in English literature from Trinity College, Dublin, and taught there from 1967 to 1968. In 1976 she was elected a member of the Irish Academy of Letters and is its honorary secretary. She lives in Dublin with her husband, Irish novelist Kevin Casey, and her daughter, Sarah. Besides contributing to the **Dublin Magazine** and the **Irish Times** and writing, with Michael MacLiammoir, **W. B. Yeats and His World**, she has published two collections of poetry: **New Territory** (1967), which won the Macaulay Fellowship in Poetry in 1968, and **War Horse** (1975), which includes translations from Irish, Russian, and German poetry.

NEW TERRITORY

Several things announced the fact to us:
The captain's Spanish tears
Falling like doubloons in the headstrong light,
And then of course the fuss—
The crew jostling and interspersing cheers
With wagers. Overnight
As we went down to our cabins, nursing the last
Of the grog, talking as usual of conquest,
Land hove into sight.

Frail compasses and trenchant constellations
Brought us as far as this,
And now air and water, fire and earth
Stand at their given stations
Out there, and are ready to replace
This single desperate width
Of ocean. Why do we hesitate? Water and air
And fire and earth and therefore life are here,
And therefore death.

Out of the dark man comes to life and into it
He goes and loves and dies,
(His element being the dark and not the light of day)
So the ambitious wit
Of poets and exploring ships have been his eyes—
Riding the dark for joy—
And so Isaiah of the sacred text is eagle-eyed because
By peering down the unlit centuries
He glimpsed the holy boy.

ATHENE'S SONG

(for my father)

From my father's head I sprung
Goddess of the war, created
Partisan and soldiers' physic—
My symbols boast and brazen gong—
Until I made in Athens wood
Upon my knees a new music.

When I played my pipe of bone,
Robbed and whittled from a stag,
Every bird became a lover
Every lover to its tone
Found the truth of song and brag;
Fish sprung in the full river.

Peace became the toy of power
When other noises broke my sleep.
Like dreams I saw the hot ranks
And heroes in another flower
Than any there; I dropped my pipe
Remembering their shouts, their thanks.

Beside the water, lost and mute,
Lies my pipe and like my mind
Remains unknown, remains unknown
And in some hollow taking part
With my heart against my hand
Holds its peace and holds its own.

SONG

Where in blind files
Bats outsleep the frost
Water slips through stones
Too fast, too fast
For ice; afraid he'd slip
By me I asked him first.

Round as a bracelet
Clasping the wet grass,
An adder drowsed by berries
Which change blood to cess;
Dreading delay's venom
I risked the first kiss.

My skirt in my hand,
Lifting the hem high
I forded the river there;
Drops splashed my thigh.
Ahead of me at last
He turned at my cry:

"Look how the water comes
Boldly to my side;
See the waves attempt
What you have never tried."
He late that night
Followed the leaping tide.

THE WAR HORSE

This dry night, nothing unusual
About the clip, clop, casual

Iron of his shoes as he stamps death
Like a mint on the innocent coinage of earth.

I lift the window, watch the ambling feather
Of hock and fetlock, loosed from its daily tether

In the tinker camp on the Enniskerry Road,
Pass, his breath hissing, his snuffling head

Down. He is gone. No great harm is done.
Only a leaf of our laurel hedge is torn

Of distant interest like a maimed limb,
Only a rose which now will never climb

The stone of our house, expendable, a mere
Line of defence against him, a volunteer

You might say, only a crocus its bulbous head
Blown from growth, one of the screamless dead.

But we, we are safe, our unformed fear
Of fierce commitment gone; why should we care

If a rose, a hedge, a crocus are uprooted
Like corpses, remote, crushed, mutilated?

He stumbles on like a rumour of war, huge,
Threatening; neighbours use the subterfuge

Of curtains; he stumbles down our short street
Thankfully passing us. I pause, wait,

Then to breathe relief lean on the sill
And for a second only my blood is still

With atavism. That rose he smashed frays
Ribboned across our hedge, recalling days

Of burned countryside, illicit braid:
A cause ruined before, a world betrayed.

CHILD OF OUR TIME

(for Aengus)

Yesterday I knew no lullaby
But you have taught me overnight to order
This song, which takes from your final cry
Its tune, from your unreasoned end its reason;
Its rhythm from the discord of your murder
Its motive from the fact you cannot listen.

We who should have known how to instruct
With rhymes for your waking, rhythms for your sleep,
Names for the animals you took to bed,
Tales to distract, legends to protect,
Later an idiom for you to keep
And living, learn, must learn from you, dead.

To make our broken images rebuild
Themselves around your limbs, your broken
Image, find for your sake whose life our idle
Talk has cost, a new language. Child
Of our time, our times have robbed your cradle.
Sleep in a world your final sleep has woken.

RICHARD RYAN

Richard Ryan was born in Dublin in 1946 and educated at University College, Dublin, where he received an M.A. degree in Anglo-Irish literature in 1970. He worked at a variety of jobs in Europe and traveled throughout the United States giving poetry readings and lectures. From 1972 to 1973 he taught in the English Department at University College, Dublin, and completed a study of the Irish novelist, Liam O'Flaherty. He joined the Irish foreign service in 1973 and has been living in Japan for the past three years with his Korean wife, Hyun Heeun. He has two collections of poetry, **Ledges** (1970), and **Ravenswood** (1973), as well as many articles and poems published in American and Irish magazines.

IRELAND

That ragged
leaking raft held
between sea and sea

its long
forgotten cable melting
into deeper darkness where,

at the root
of it, the slow
sea circles and chews.

Nightly the dark-
ness lands like hands
to mine downwards, springing

tiny leaks
till dawn finds
field is bog, bog lake.

KNOCKMANY

(for John Montague)

In slow procession
trees ascend
the hill, enter
the mist-held ring
to crowd, chanting,
around the silent
hive of stones.

Giant tree-priests,
slowly they rock
in prayer; searching
the earth, long root
veins writhe down-
ward, probing
for blood the deep

hill's heart. As
the quick sap stirs,
runnels upward

through trunk and
thigh, filling
with its white life
the glistening loins,

louder the branches,
bone-hard arms
dipping, digging
up air, moan—
mad with certainty—
as the mist,
prised up like a stone,

reveals a monstrous
shadow rising, rising
through the forked, skin-
less fingers—the
swaying trees lean
forward, clutching the twitching
shape, humming . . . humming . . .

FROM MY LAI THE THUNDER WENT WEST

and it all died down
to an underground
tapping and then that,
too, stopped dead.

In cornfield, wheat
field, a black
sheet of earth
was drawn neatly

across the seed
they planted.
And the fields turn
daily to the sun.

Come high Summer
and the first shoots
will appear, puzzling
the sun as, growing

through earth, growing
through grass, the
human crop they have sown—
child bone, wife

bone, man
bone will stand
wavering in the pale fields:
the silent, eye-

less army will
march west through
Autumn and Europe
until, streaked

with December rain
they will stand in
New York and Texas;
as the lights click

out across America
they will fence in
the houses, tapping
on window, tapping

on door. Till
dawn, then rain only:
from sea to sea drifting,
drops of bright ruby.

WULF AND EADWACER

a version from the Old English

This gang who protect me
    can't wait to get at him:
a bright welcome he'll feel
    when their blades bite into him!

    Hope fades for us now

Wulf on one island,
    I stuck on another,
seas swamping the reeds
    where armed men move:
their hooked eyes
    are on the horizons,
their hopes are high.

    Hope fades for us now

By the fire in wet
    weather when I thought
of your touch, the
    storms that broke in me!
My body wept after
    one of these ruffians
forced me, but
    Wulf, at the time
I didn't know the difference.

Wulf, Wulf,
    my bones show, but
it's your absence
    has brought me to this;
I take no heed
    of food I don't need.

Hopeless here, do
    you hear, Eadwacer?
He'll slink to the
    wood, escape us all.

Easily stopped what
    had hardly started,
our song together.

KOHOUTEK

Light-years in the dark,
Swimming, a sperm of stone.
I am driven by no hunger.

Out of the dark earth came then,
An amazing pod curving
And brightening through far blue zones.

Human millions, tiny and staring,
Fat bulbs of brain swaying
And turning on long stalks

And I warmed to them
They taught me fear, I drew
Near to them and learned death

I grew cold, I knew time.
Nightly I watched the marvellous
Traffic unroll out of their cities,

Long carpets of blood; all the bright choirs
Of bone sweet in their smoke
I saw, amazed, and priests there

In elaborate kits talking
Urgently of forever then stepping
Off into nothing.

And now, as I turn finally
Away I hear voices fading:
They insist I have meaning, I have none,

Some call me god, I am dead, I would
Tell them but have no lungs,
Would show them but have no hands,

I am in the dark again now, it is over,
A faint odour of bone
Withers quickly, my brain is stone.

A WET NIGHT

Panes of light cracking
Over Aran, all
Day along the cliffs
An unseasonal booming,

But the widow
Connemara with her head
In the clouds lay,
Dreaming of salvation.

An Act of God it was
Surely—all night
Splayed, trampled
She was, hair flying

In the branches, the
Brute Atlantic wave
After wave over
Her, bony legs of

Hedges unlocking,
Fields flowing
Through, a black tide
Turf and potatoes

Cows like whales
Sailing, the swaying
Churches rooted in
Bone tugging and

Straining to be
Away, graveyards
Awash, their full
Cargoes of believers

Shifting and sliding,
Crates spilling, a mess
No angel will untangle
As delirious crows

Tumbled for tit—
Bits; a last mighty
Thrust just before
Dawn, the exhausted

Ocean sliding back
To show her sleeping
Shores aglow under
Its receding inches.

HUGH MAXTON

Hugh Maxton (the pseudonym of W. J. McCormack) was born in 1947 in Dublin. He attended Wesley College, Dublin, then worked in a city bookshop for several years before entering Trinity College, Dublin, where he read General Studies (English, History, and Philosophy). After graduating from Trinity in 1971, he was appointed to a lectureship in Anglo-Irish literature at the New University of Ulster. In 1974 he moved to England. He teaches Anglo-Irish literature at the University of Leeds in Yorkshire and has written widely on nineteenth- and twentieth-century Irish fiction. He is married and has one son. Maxton's published collections of poetry include **Stones** (1970), and **The Noise of the Fields** (1976), a Poetry Book Society Choice; a third collection, **The Broken Horseman**, is expected in 1979. Maxton has also done translations from the Russian of Joseph Brodsky and from the German of Johannes Bobrowski.

CERNUNNOS

Cernunnos, gymnast or god,
crossed his side at Clonmacnois.
Insidious and slipping
from the girdle he lingers
barely.

Once he was allwhere
when he nurtured animals
from his thighs, a helpful wolf.

Fecund one, no warrior
speared so many. None could call
you a squatter for, always
agile, you peopled the first
dawning of darkness that called
you a devilish helper.
Yet undisputed master
you remained relegated
thus; antlers your emblem.

The world grew wider and slack
and your subtle potency
went out of favour falling
foul between the coarser saints.
Censured, you crept underground.

"Dance your dance now, my little
man," they cried. And you lay down
in a bog to coddle them,
curing your codpiece and ram.
Modest, impeccable you
took your serpents by the neck.
And your feet turned in, your ears
reddened with obituaries.

from MASTRIM: A MEDITATION

A halt in the desert where I have in mind
a garden in Russia, ringed by bright earth.
The air lies thickly in the boughs of trees.
The mole rests below, heartshaped and blind,

in his darker element. The birds walk
through the thorns, unmolested by my noise.
I am nothing now but the seer of
moonlight falling like a stick of chalk.

When Maria came here in June, the roses
were drest in snow, and the one-wheeled phaeton
had not turned on the road to Granard
at flung roadmetal under the willows;
no urchin hedgehog sinned in the gravel.
Westward to the dark sea the diocese
lay waiting for the rootless freedom tree
and the planters' shout again "hang the Devil."

And it was warm and still enough for snow.
We ran like dogs through the generations
tonguing the scent that our own game trailed,
writing on windows and fields one word Now.
Bold John, riding from Shelton to Ticknock
to eat well and to take rents at Mastrim,
rises stiff-faced and hale in the morning,
his excrement smelling of woodcock.

Behind the hedge the ladies play tennis,
a globe passing between two tensions.
The unseen has become their dimension
as they keep within their painted limits.
A buried box in the garden saved us,
an infant buried safely till midnight
during disaffection when we shook
at the promise of our best ambitions.

Then the gate grudged over the humped pathway,
A contralto warning of our encroachment
into a world where the blood crackled
and shivered, weakly rhyming in the clay.

Soon the shadows bloomed in the furniture;
the carpet breathed its own life into ours.
In the evening the house hummed with birdsong
and the empty shelves did not fail to answer.

We said that we were the first born outside
the garden though our eyes were shaped like flowers.
The dressed stone of our facade was foreign
to the coast, silkbeautiful, silkfragile.
After that failure we have never stirred
from the room, stare across the area
at the latticed countryside, raised hands
and neutral voices, seen and never heard.

WAKING

in memory of my father, died November 1960

Someone is breathing in the room
apart from me. It is my father;
I recognise the hiss of his nostrils
closing, closing. . . . It is late;
he is doing Milltown work,
we can use the extra money.
That stub in his hand is a rent book
high as a bible, thin as his widow.
Below it, in the shadow, I imagine
the soft metal of his heart
(a gold cog, slipping) finally burred,
refusing to bite. For my life
I cannot picture him; details
melt into light. The angle
of his nose, the slight furrow
of moustache escape me. All I have
is that sound fathered in darkness
carrying a reek of tobacco-y linen,
the taste of his lip.

He rustles
like a curtain. Outside it is six a.m.
A sudden fleet of cars passes
drowning my breath for about the length
of a funeral. This has gone on ten years.

DIALECTIQUE

(for Elaine)

Sitting at table, or
In flight at dancing
We notice something
To happen minutely,
An event so imperceptible
As not, except for us,
To exist.

Then the world turns
An extra revolution,
A movement
In the brute routine
Lithe as grass.

Had we not seen
A shadow pass
Between balance and wit
—and recover itself!—
Heard a word
Sound as though it were
A word repeated
We were never together
At table, or
Arm on arm.

LANDSCAPE WITH MINUTE WILDFLOWERS

The train moves
Stealthily along the shore
Denying its rails
Between inseparable sand
And stone. An invisible
Path leads under the cliff.

Never was green so close
To black, the waves
Pointless with motion,
Wind cranking itself
Through the sublime windows:
Nature is perpetual, alas.

Intent and purposeless,
Neither here nor there,
The process returns to me.
The wisp of diesel
Scaling the cliffs
Is a phrase of perfect execution.

Everything is discreet, nearly:—
The open church door
Of ten-league parishes
Clipped in the horizon,
Which beyond Downhill is
The straightest line in the world.

Viewed from the Mussenden
The sea was marble in the making;
Distant coasts
Curved into focus
Absorbed by liquid movements
And the cold fury of the place.

I stood high enough
To see the deep pools
Designing themselves,
Once when love seemed
At an end, and was not.
I return lowly, blind, at work too.

FRANK ORMSBY

Frank Ormsby was born in County Fermanagh, Northern Ireland, in 1947 and was graduated from Queen's University, Belfast, with an M.A. degree in English. He is Head Master of the English Department at the Royal Belfast Academical Institution and editor of Ulsterman Publications. In 1974 he won the Eric Gregory Award for Poetry and is represented in the anthology, **Ten Irish Poets** (1974). He lives in Belfast with his wife and two children. He has published his poetry in many Irish journals and has two pamphlet collections, **Ripe for Company** (1971) and **Business as Usual** (1973). His first volume, **A Store of Candles**, was published in 1977.

ORNAMENTS

My mother's Council house is occupied
By ornaments. On all flat surfaces
The delft hens roost. Hunched and malignant-eyed
The red dwarfs squat on the mantelpiece,
And panniered donkeys draw their nostrils wide
On mouths that sparkle. The brass bells increase
In cunning mirrors and glass-backed cases.

This the extravagance she must have known
And hoarded in a house where stretching legs
Was luxury, a plaster dog the lone
Flourish that space allowed her. Now she thrives
On detail. For each dog a plaster bone;
The dwarfs have Snow White sweetening their lives;
And today the delft hens have laid delft eggs.

AMELIA STREET

My feet fall in step with absent whores
Whose crippled legs and sallow faces haunt
The pavements here, whose perfume hangs in doors,
A fading spoor that taunts me, will not let

Me dwell on Siren voices, golden hearts.
Across the main street the railway looms—
Right that this slum of blackened brick should start
Beyond a terminus, unscheduled stop

For randy travellers, right that its boom
Was war time, the brief years of rootless Yanks
Welcomed with open legs in dingy rooms
With stretched palms and loveless pelvic shuttle.

Disease and bastardy, the lurid past,
Still stalk Amelia Street, its pores the sum
Of lasting miseries. The pox outlasts
The glands that bred it, rampant in the drains,

Or nesting, hostile virus, on the air,
The brick its victim. Simply walking here
Cancels immunity, allots a share.
Some taint by proxy prickles on my skin.

INFERNO: A NEW CIRCLE

This is the Landlords' Circle, built by me,
The Perpetual Tenant. Its walls are thick
Rent-books all in arrears, and the need for repairs

Is relentless. Water dries in the taps.
The tiles gape on a climate worse than Sodom's
The day of the rain. There is no fire-escape.

Their special torture here will be the scrape
Of huge keys turning. Thinking someone comes
To serve notice, or evict perhaps,

They must instead resign them to the cares
Of open leases. There are no locks to pick.
This is the Landlords' Circle, built by me.

ON DEVENISH ISLAND

I am no Norseman, come to plunder.
The stone I sit on is half-under
Your skin. The grey wind that brought
Me here, honing the lough, is your familiar.
I am your next-of-kin.

In drowned valleys you have kept your head
Above water. Church, round tower still spread
On the waves' top. Down fourteen centuries
The rapt soul homes to the embryo it never fled.
I am no Norseman, come to plunder.
I keep what you gave.

INTERIM

Five years ago we knew such ecstasies
As who in half-dead countrysides find strong
The least life stirring;
We sang first lines and thought we had learned the song.

Six months of marriage sobered us. We found,
Not disenchantment, more a compromise
Charged with affection.
We settled to the limited surprise

That day-to-day insists on, brought to bear
A tact to manage by, a quiet light
That gave its own warmth,
And knew our walking grown to sudden flight

When least expected. O, I loved those years
Of unforced loving, when the urge to stray
Was lulled to sleeping,
And hearth and kitchen sink were nothing grey.

Now, once again, I notice carefree girls
In streets, on buses. Tied, I can't but see
Their untried promise,
All the lost futures catching up with me.

The nerve to be unfaithful is the lack
That curbs my yearnings. Soon again I'm sure,
And pleased to be,
Of trusting wife, my own furniture.

What binds us, love? I struggle to define
Its shifting substance. What strange seeds are met
Within us, fashion there in our despite
This hybrid, half-contentment, half-regret?

Tonight, uncertain if the dreams have cracked,
Let's seek behind the possible illusions
How much is gone, how much remains intact;
Let's talk of change and come to no conclusions.

CIARAN CARSON

Ciaran Carson was born in 1948 in Belfast. He was educated at Queen's University, Belfast, and he has since worked as a civil servant and as a teacher. Carson is presently employed by the Arts Council of Northern Ireland as a Traditional Arts Officer. His work has been published in numerous poetry magazines and anthologies. **The New Estate** (1976) is his first major collection of poetry.

THE INSULAR CELTS

Having left solid ground behind
In the hardness of their place-names,
They have sailed out for an island:

As along the top of a wood
Their boats have crossed the green ridges,
So has the pale sky overhead

Appeared as a milky surface,
A white plain where the speckled fish
Drift in lamb-white clouds of fleece.

They will come back to the warm earth
And call it by possessive names—
Thorned rose, love, woman and mother;

To hard hills of stone they will give
The words for breast; to meadowland,
The soft gutturals of rivers,

Tongues of water; to firm plains, flesh,
As one day we will discover
Their way of living, in their death.

They entered their cold beds of soil
Not as graves, for this was the land
That they had fought for, loved, and killed

Each other for. They'd arrive again:
Death could be no horizon
But the shoreline of their island,

A coming and going, as flood
Comes after ebb. In the spirals
Of their brooches is seen the flight

Of one thing into the other:
As the wheel-ruts on a battle-
Plain have filled with silver water,

The confused circles of their wars,
Their cattle-raids, have worked themselves
To a laced pattern of old scars.

But their death, since it is no real
Death, will happen over again
And again, their bones will seem still

To fall in the hail beneath hooves
Of horses, their limbs will drift down
As the branches that trees have loosed.

We cannot yet say why or how
They could not take things as they were.
Some day we will learn of how

Their bronze swords took the shape of leaves,
How their gold spears are found in cornfields,
Their arrows are found in trees.

ST CIARAN AND THE BIRDS

For my food,
Water-cress and coarse bread.
Singing branches,
Covering for my head.

For my voice,
The tongueless bell,
For my silence
No tongue can tell.

For silence,
The dead;
White stones on their graves
And not bread.

For whiteness, snow;
For snow, silence,
And still my love
Is not the love of death,

Nor yet the love
Of women, but these white birds
Drifted to my hands.
I cannot move.

They pin me down,
Yet make me live;
They love, and cover me
For the squares of bread I give.

THE CAR CEMETERY

On winter nights
the cars bring in snow from the hills,
their bonnets white
above a wide cold smile of chromium.

From miles away
I see you coming in, a distant star
gone out of line, swaying
down from the road to take the thin lane

towards the house,
till my warm light and your cold are married,
your solitary noise
is lost among the rushing of the wind.

All around the world
there is a graveyard of defunct bodies,
wide smiles curled
in sleep. The cars at every door are hushed

beneath a soft corrosion—
robed in white, these brides of silence
whose heaven
is like ours, a detritus of lights.

THE BOMB DISPOSAL

Is it just like picking a lock
with the slow deliberation of a funeral,
hesitating through a darkened nave
until you find the answer?

Listening to the malevolent tick
of its heart, can you read
the message of the threaded veins
like print, its body's chart?

The city is a map of the city,
its forbidden areas changing daily.
I find myself in a crowded taxi
making deviations from the known route,

ending in a cul-de-sac
where everyone breaks out suddenly
in whispers, noting the boarded windows,
the drawn blinds.

VISITING THE DEAD

When she was found
Her tongue protruded from her gums;
Her face was knuckled,
Her hand clenched on the sheet.

Now her skin has eased out,
New-washed cloth in which the wrinkles fade
Beneath the iron's hiss.
They have laid her in clean linen.

We drink tea from her best china.
A knot of mourners unravels upstairs;
A maiden aunt descends, weeping softly
Into her starched handkerchief.

When they brought down the body,
The coffin stuck in the crooked staircase.
We hesitated, awkward in our best suits,
Then rushed to help, and freed her.

PAUL MULDOON

Paul Muldoon was born in County Armagh, Northern Ireland, in 1951 and was educated at Queen's University, Belfast. He now resides in Belfast where he works for the BBC. His first pamphlet, **Knowing My Place**, was published in 1971; in 1972 he received the Eric Gregory Award for poetry. His work has appeared in many magazines and in Faber's **Introduction 2**. He has published two collections of poetry, **New Weather** (1973) and **Mules** (1977).

CLONFEACLE

It happened not far away
In this meadowland
That Patrick lost a tooth.
I translate the placename

As we walk along
The river where he washed,
That translates stone to silt.
The river would preach

As well as Patrick did.
A tongue of water passing
Between teeth of stones.
Making itself clear,

Living by what it says,
Converting meadowland to marsh.
You turn towards me,
Coming round to my way

Of thinking, holding
Your tongue between your teeth.
I turn my back on the river
And Patrick, their sermons

Ending in the air.

THE INDIANS ON ALCATRAZ

Through time their sharp features
Have softened and blurred,
As if they still inhabited
The middle distances,
As if these people have never
Stopped riding hard

In an opposite direction,
The people of the shattered lances
Who have seemed forever going back.
To have willed this reservation,
It is as if they are decided
To be islanders at heart,

As if this island
Has forever been the destination
Of all those dwindling bands.
After the newspaper and TV reports
I want to be glad that
Young Man Afraid Of His Horses lives

As a brilliant guerrilla fighter,
The weight of his torque
Worn like the moon's last quarter,
Though only if he believes
As I believed of his fathers,
That they would not attack after dark.

THE FIELD HOSPITAL

Taking, giving back their lives
By the strength of our bare hands,
By the silence of our knives,
We answer to no grey South

Nor blue North, not self defence,
The lie of just wars, neither
Cold nor hot blood's difference
In their discharging of guns,

But that hillside of fresh graves.
Would this girl brought to our tents
From whose flesh we have removed
Shot that George, on his day off,

Will use to weight fishing lines,
Who died screaming for ether,
Yet protest our innocence?
George lit the lanterns, in danced

Those gigantic, yellow moths
That brushed right over her wounds,
Pinning themselves to our sleeves
Like medals given the brave.

MULES

Should they not have the best of both worlds?

Her feet of clay gave the lie
To the star burned in our mare's brow.
Would Parsons' jackass not rest more assured
That cross wrenched from his shoulders?

We had loosed them into one field.
I watched Sam Parsons and my quick father
Tense for the punch below their belts,
For what was neither one thing or the other.

It was as though they had shuddered
To think of their gaunt, sexless foal
Dropped tonight in the cowshed.

We might yet claim that it sprang from earth
Were it not for the afterbirth
Trailed like some fine, silk parachute,
That we would know from what heights it fell.

from ARMAGEDDON, ARMAGEDDON

When Oisin came back to Ireland
After three hundred years
On one of those enchanted islands
Somewhere in the Western Seas,

He thought nothing of dismounting
From his enchanted steed
To be one again with the mountains,
The bogs and the little fields.

There and then he began to stoop,
His hair, and all his teeth, fell out,
A mildewed belt, a rusted buckle.
The clays were heavy, black or yellow,
Those were the colours of his boots.
And I know something of how he felt.

NOTES

The notes are intended to provide brief explanations of those references in the poems which may not be located in a standard dictionary, and particularly of those that refer to some aspect of Irish life.

DE CIVITATE HOMINUM

The title may be loosely translated as "concerning the state of man" —probably an allusion to St. Augustine's *De Civitate Dei (The City of God)*.

Zillebeke; Hooge; Gheluvelt: Flemish place-names belonging to the area around Ypres in Belgium, one of the major battlefields of World War I.

nature morte: still life.

AODH RUADH O'DOMHNAILL

The title is Irish for Red Hugh O'Donnell (1571-1602), Ulster chieftain and leader (with his father-in-law, Hugh O'Neill) of the rebellion of 1595-1603. After the defeat of the Irish forces and their Spanish allies at Kinsale in 1601, Red Hugh went to Spain in the hopes of mustering another Spanish force. He was poisoned in 1602 at Simancas by an agent of the English crown. He is buried in the church of San Francisco at Valladolid, though the precise resting place of his remains is no longer known.

RECESSIONAL

The title refers to a musical piece (usually played at the end of a religious service).

Roderick Hudson: the artist hero of Henry James's novel of the same name, who dies climbing in the Swiss Alps near Engelberg.

Mal Bay: a bay on the Atlantic coast of Ireland, in County Clare.

PILGRIMAGE

Ara: the Aran Islands.

by dim wells: a Celtic custom (assimilated by Christianity) of tying rags on bushes near a sacred well, still occasionally observed in Ireland—a veneration of water and fertility.

Clonmacnois: one of the best known of the "holy schools" referred to earlier in the poem. Situated in County Offaly, on the River Shannon, it was founded by St. Ciaran in 548. The "holy schools" were not only monasteries but also seats of learning, the equivalent of modern universities.

Cashel: the Rock of Cashel in County Tipperary, site of the finest Celtic Romanesque church in Ireland.

The holy mountain: Croagh Patrick, the hill where St. Patrick, according to one legend, spent the years of his captivity. It is still a place of annual pilgrimage.

Culdees: anchorites.

TENEBRAE

The title refers to a religious ceremony during Holy Week marking the suffering and death of Christ.

THE STRAYING STUDENT

Inishmore: the largest of the Aran Islands.

Salamanca: site of an Irish seminary in Spain in the eighteenth century, when education in Ireland was forbidden to the native

Irish. Irish youth were educated for the priesthood at this and other Continental seminaries.

THE LAST REPUBLICANS

The title refers to the execution of republicans after the civil war by successive Free State governments, including that led by de Valera. (Pierpont was the English hangman.)

INSCRIPTION FOR A HEADSTONE

Larkin: James Larkin (1876–1947), the famous labor leader; he had the reputation of being a great orator. After the police violence used on 16 August against workers in the general strike of 1913, Larkin's comrade James Connolly organized the Irish Citizen Army, a force of about two hundred men. Connolly was commander of the Irish Citizen Army in the Easter Insurrection.

THE END OF CLONMACNOIS

The poem refers to the destruction by the Danes in the ninth century of this monastic settlement and seat of learning. Clonmacnois and the other monastic centers were sacked repeatedly in the second half of the ninth century.

HOPE

Tara: ancient seat of the high kings of Ireland, County Meath.

SHANCODUFF

The title and the other place names in this poem and "Stony Grey Soil" refer to Kavanagh's native border county of Monaghan; Armagh is the neighboring county to the northeast.

THE GREAT HUNGER

Maguire: the persona of the poem.

EPIC

the Munich bother: efforts of English Prime Minister Chamberlain to avert war by appeasing Hitler at the Munich conference of 1938.

FOR PADDY MAC

Fomorian: according to legend, the Fomorians were the first inhabitants of Ireland, pushed to the western edges of the island by the conquering Firbolgs.

Bran: a hero of early medieval Irish and Welsh literature; in Welsh literature, he is a god whose severed but living head presides over feasting and singing in the other world; in Irish literature he is the mortal who travels across the seas to the otherworld. Fallon seems to have joined the traditions.

Lever: Charles James Lever (1806–1872), Irish novelist.

Raftery: Anthony Raftery (1784–1835), the blind Gaelic poet of the folk tradition, who was admired for his eloquent capacity for praise and blame.

MALACODA

The title refers to a demon in Dante's *Inferno*.

ENUEG I

The title refers to a species of medieval French verse that is a catalog of annoyances.

Exeo: I depart (Latin)

Portobello: area on the south side of Dublin, near the Grand Canal.

Fox and Geese: southwestern suburb of Dublin.

Chapelizod: western suburb of Dublin. (The poet has obviously taken a long, despairing walk through the southern and western parts of the city.)

IRELAND

Clontarf: site in Dublin of the decisive battle (1014) in which Brian Boru defeated the Norse. The battle marked the end of the Viking wars in Ireland, and the establishment of a high degree of Irish political unity.

AN IRISHMAN IN COVENTRY

The Book of Kells: one of the masterpieces of early Irish art, an eighth-century illuminated manuscript translation of the Gospels; the designs are intricate and complex.

Lir's children: Aeife, the second wife of the Irish deity Lir, was jealous of the children of his first marriage, and had them turned into swans who could find shelter neither on land nor sea.

DUBLIN

O'Connell; Grattan; Moore: refers to statues in central Dublin of Daniel O'Connell (1775–1847), leader of the movement for Catholic Emancipation; Henry Grattan (1746–1820), leader of the Irish Volunteers, and prime mover in the establishment of the short-lived independent Irish parliament of the eighteenth century; Thomas Moore (1779–1852), popular poet and composer, author of Irish Melodies.

Nelson: a statue of the English admiral Nelson stood atop a tall pillar in O'Connell St., dominating the landscape of central Dublin until 1966, when it was destroyed by an explosion.

The Four Courts burnt: a reference to the attack on the Republican garrison in the Four Courts by Irish government forces in June 1922 that marked the beginning of the Irish civil war.

Fort of the Dane . . . : a summary of the various historical identities of the city of Dublin.

LOUGH DERG

The title refers to the island in County Donegal's Lough Derg, known as St. Patrick's Purgatory; it is still a place of pilgrimage and penance.

Merovingian centuries: the Frankish dynasty, sixth to eighth century; apparently a reference to the missionary zeal of the Irish monks of these times, who founded monasteries in France, Germany, Switzerland, and Italy.

ANK'HOR VAT

The title refers to a holy place of Buddhism, in Cambodia.

DAPHNE STILLORGAN

Stillorgan: a southeastern suburb of Dublin.

THE VETERANS

in the sixteenth year of the century: the Easter Rising of 1916.

POEM

Parnell: Charles Stewart Parnell (1846–1891), leader of the Home Rule movement.

Pearse: Padraic Pearse (1879–1916), leader of the Irish Volunteers in the insurrection of Easter 1916, executed by the British.

Raleigh: Sir Walter Raleigh (1552–1618), Elizabethan adventurer.

Lawrence: T. E. Lawrence (1888–1935), known as Lawrence of
  Arabia.
Childers: Erskine Childers (1870–1922), former British civil servant,
  convert to the cause of Irish nationalism, active in the Irish
  struggle for independence, and a member of the Republican
  faction in the Irish civil war. Executed by the Free State govern-
  ment in 1922.

THE POET

chaunt-rann: apparently a neologism combining, respectively, obso-
  lete English and Irish—"verse-chanter" is approximate.

GLOSS

Deirdre; Naisi; Conor: refers to the Irish myth in which Deirdre, the
  beautiful ward of the old King Conor (Conchubor) of Ulster,
  runs away with the young warrior Naisi. Conor relentlessly
  pursues them and kills Naisi. Deirdre then kills herself.
Dermot, Finn: a variant of the above myth in which the young
  woman is Grainne, the older man to whom she has been prom-
  ised is Finn MacCool, leader of the warriors who defend Ireland
  against invaders, and Dermot the handsome lover; Grainne,
  though heartbroken on Dermot's death, survives to become
  Finn's wife.

COPPER-BEECH AND BUTTER-FINGERS

en ti como sol: "within you like the sun" (Spanish).

THE BATTLE OF AUGHRIM

The title refers to a decisive battle in Irish history— July 12, 1691,
  at Aughrim in County Galway. The Irish and French army

supporting the Catholic cause of James II was defeated by the English and Dutch army supporting the Protestant William of Orange: the outcome of the battle had severe consequences for the Catholic population of Ireland for several centuries.

HIGH ISLAND

The title refers to a small island off the coast of Galway, owned by the poet.

BAGGOT STREET DESERTA

Baggot Street: a residential street in central Dublin.

CLARENCE MANGAN

The title refers to James Clarence Mangan (1803–1849), Irish poet born in the Dublin slums. His work has marked affinities with that of Edgar Allen Poe. He did extensive translations from Irish and German, and wrote memorable patriotic verse. He was highly praised by Yeats and Joyce.

A COUNTRY WALK

MacDonagh; McBride; Connolly; ironic invocation of the leaders of the Easter Rising in 1916.

RITUAL OF DEPARTURE

Dublin under the Georges: Dublin in the early nineteenth century after the Act of Union (1800) deprived Ireland of a parliament; George III and George IV occupied the throne of England until

1830. By mid-century at least a million Irish had died from star-vation and another two million had emigrated, mainly to the United States.

LAMENT FOR THE O'NEILLS

Annals of the Four Masters: the Gaelic chronicle of a thousand years of Irish history compiled by four historians. The collabora-tion of the four authors began in 1632, in Donegal.

Mountjoy: Lord Deputy of Ireland, the leader of Elizabeth's army when it defeated the Irish and their Spanish allies at the battle of Kinsale in 1601.

Chichester: Sir Arthur, the successor to Mountjoy as Lord Deputy of Ireland from 1606–1633.

Is uaigneach Eire: Ireland is lonely (Irish).

The Flight of the Earls: the departure into exile of Hugh O'Neill and Rory O'Donnell, princes of Ulster, with their followers in 1607, in the aftermath of the unsuccessful nine years war against Elizabeth; they sailed from Rathmullen, in Lough Swilly. Both are buried in Rome. Their departure signaled the virtual end of the Gaelic culture in Ireland, and the beginning of the Ulster plantation on a vast scale.

A NEW SIEGE

Bernadette Devlin: militant socialist leader of the civil rights move-ment in Northern Ireland, elected Member of Parliament for mid-Ulster (1969); a leader in the "new siege" of the Catholic Bogside area of Derry (in 1969) in which the inhabitants fought against the Ulster police force and its Protestant supporters. Even after the intervention of the British Army, the area ("Free Derry") remained a "no-go" area for police and army alike for the next three years. The details of the new siege are juxtaposed with those of the siege of Derry during the seventeenth century. The thirty thousand Protestant defenders of the walled city, loyal to the cause of William of Orange, were besieged for more than three months by the Catholic army of James II; the siege was relieved finally, on August 13, 1689. The triumph of the defenders of Derry greatly aided the Protestant cause in the war.

Creggan: a hillside rising above the city, the site of a Catholic housing project.

Roaring Meg: an ancient cannon used in the defense of the city.

Walker: a Presbyterian minister who provided a rallying point for the defenders of the city in 1689—his statue is referred to here.

Saracen: British Army armored car in widespread use in the current troubles in Northern Ireland.

Guildhall: seat of the municipal government in Derry, symbol to Catholics for many years of Protestant domination and of the virtual exclusion of the Catholic population from political power.

Cuchulain: ancient champion of Ulster. Here he seems to be ironically identified with the Protestant extremist Ian Paisley.

the Scarlet Whore: a personification of the Catholic church used by fanatical Protestants in Northern Ireland.

St. Columb: in the Catholic tradition, the founder of the city, though the cathedral that bears his name is Protestant.

Stormont: the seat of the Northern Ireland government; in 1972 the government was suspended by the British, who instituted direct rule.

Carson: a statue of Sir Edward Carson (1854–1935), leader of Ulster Unionists in setting up the state of Northern Ireland in 1920, stands outside the gates of Stormont.

THE CAVE OF NIGHT

Falls: Catholic working-class district in central Belfast, strongly Republican in character.

HERBERT STREET REVISITED

Herbert Street: residential street in Dublin.

SENIOR MEMBERS

Tadhg and Vincent are representative types of those Irishmen who emerged as leaders on the Irish political scene in the period following the achievement of independence. Tadhg is clearly the former I.R.A. man, a bullying countryman, and Vincent the smooth, city businessman who has inherited his uncle's conservative if nationalist politics. The "new politico" blends their outdated styles in order to keep up with the times.

ON SWEET KILLEN HILL

Mise: Irish for me, myself.

HISTORY

Fenian King: Finn MacCool, leader of the Fianna, a legendary band of warriors who protected Ireland's sovereignty.

Oisin: Finn's son who goes with the fairy queen Niamh to the Land of Eternal Youth.

Patrick: St. Patrick, to whom Oisin is recounting his adventures on his return to Ireland from the Land of Eternal Youth. Oisin has lived with Niamh for three hundred years and returns to find the Fianna long dead, and Ireland Christian.

THE DAY CONCLUDES BURNING

The "he" of the poem is the mythological Irish hero, Cuchulain, who in his last battle, suffering from mortal wounds, tied himself upright to a tree stump. His enemies were afraid to approach him until a crow (the shape taken by the goddess of war) landed on his shoulder, signifying that he was dead.

MY DARK FATHERS

Perished feet nailed to her man's breastbone: the author explains that this detail comes from a source that described the discovery of a man and a woman who had died from famine disease; the woman's husband had tried to warm her legs by putting them inside his own shirt.

the pit of doom: common burial ground for victims of the Great Famine of the 1840s.

REQUIEM FOR THE CROPPIES

Croppies: the Irish rebels of 1798, so nicknamed because their leaders wore their hair cropped after the fashion of the French revolutionaries with whose Republican political ideals they identified.

Vinegar Hill: site of the battle in Wexford where a large part of the rebel army, armed with scythes and pikes, was annihilated by the artillery of the English army.

LINEN TOWN

Young McCracken: Henry Joy McCracken (1767–1798), the most famous of the Northern leaders of the 1798 rebellion.

MOSSBAWN: TWO POEMS IN DEDICATION

Mossbawn: the townland in County Derry where Heaney grew up.

THE GRAUBALLE MAN

The title refers to the preserved body of an Iron Age man, found in a bog at Grauballe, in Central Jutland, Denmark; like other bog-people, he seems to have been a ritual sacrifice to fertility deities. His throat was cut.

the Dying Gaul: the famous bronze sculpture (third century B.C.) of the dying Celtic warrior found at Pergamon; the warrior is naked except for a torc around his neck, and his body is in a half-upright position on his circular shield.

TRIPTYCH

Brandon to Dunseverick: Brandon, County Cork, extreme south of Ireland; Dunseverick, County Antrim, extreme north.

Devenish; Boa; Horse Island: small islands in lower Lough Erne, County Fermanagh, the sites of early Christian churches. The stone carvings that remain are strongly Celtic in character, however.

Newry: probably a reference to the tension-ridden civil rights march in Newry, County Down, in the aftermath of the killing of thirteen civil rights marchers by British paratroopers in Derry city in January of 1972.

THE SINGER'S HOUSE

Carrickfergus: a town in County Antrim where salt was mined.

Gweebarra: a coastal area in County Donegal.

ENGLAND'S DIFFICULTY

England's difficulty with foreign enemies has traditionally been Ireland's opportunity. Persons of Republican sympathies in the North of Ireland consequently had mixed feelings about the German bombings of Belfast during World War II. The Free State (now the Republic of Ireland) was, of course, neutral.

the bitter Orange parts: refers here to Protestant districts of Belfast, so called because of their allegiance to the Orange Lodge (an organization devoted to the cause of Protestant supremacy in Northern Ireland and union with Great Britain).

Anahorish: place name in County Derry.

Haw Haw: an Irishman named Joyce from County Galway, nicknamed Lord Haw Haw. He broadcast propaganda for the Germans to England and was executed by the Allies after the war.

EXPOSURE

wood-kerne: a foot soldier in the Irish armies that waged guerilla
warfare from the woods against the Elizabethan armies of occu-
pation of the sixteenth and seventeenth centuries.

FLEADH

The title is Irish for a festival of traditional music.
Bodhran: the shallow goatskin drum played in traditional Irish music.

MAN LYING ON A WALL

L. S. Lowry (1887–1976): a British painter whose characteristic sub-
ject was the urban, industrial landscape of northern England
and its inhabitants.

NORTHERN IRELAND: TWO COMMENTS

Norwich Union: a large insurance corporation with headquarters in
Britain and branches throughout Britain and Ireland.

GLENGORMLEY

The title refers to a middle-class suburb of Belfast, overlooking
Belfast Lough.

I AM RAFTERY

Raftery was a blind, wandering Gaelic poet of the eighteenth cen-
tury. This is an updating of Raftery's poem, his retort on over-
hearing someone ask who the blind fiddler was.

394

AN IMAGE FROM BECKETT

Sorel, perhaps, or Kroger: refers to Julien Sorel and Tonio Kroger, the protagonists, respectively, of Stendhal's *The Red and the Black* and Mann's *Tonio Kroger*.

LUCINA SCHYNNING IN SILENCE OF THE NIGHT

Lucina: traditionally the goddess of childbirth, though Spenser connects her also with Diana, goddess of the moon.

CERNUNNOS

The title refers to a Celtic god with chthonic powers, and special affinities with animals, particularly the stag. The only image of him in Ireland is, rather incongruously, on a stone cross at the site of the monastic settlement of Clonmacnois.

MASTRIM: A MEDITATION

Mastrim: the original name of the Edgeworth estate in County Longford.
Maria: Maria Edgeworth (1767–1849), novelist; she is credited with running the estate first for her father and then her brother.

LANDSCAPE WITH MINUTE WILDFLOWERS

Downhill: a town on the coastline of County Derry, overlooking Magilligan Strand. The Mussenden Temple is on a nearby clifftop—it was built in 1783 by the eccentric bishop of Derry, the earl of Bristol.

ORNAMENTS

Council house: a house in a public housing project.

AMELIA STREET

Amelia Street was once a street of brothels, opposite the central railway terminus in Belfast.

ON DEVENISH ISLAND

Devenish Island is the site, in lower Lough Erne, of an early Christian monastic settlement. Most of the monastic settlements were plundered by the Norse in the ninth century.

THE INSULAR CELTS

The title refers to the Celts of Britain and Ireland as opposed to the Celts of the European continent.

ST CIARAN AND THE BIRDS

St. Ciaran: the poem does not differentiate between the various Irish saints of that name.

KNOCKMANY

The title refers to a hill in County Tyrone. The Irish placename means, literally, "hill of the monk."

FROM MY LAI THE THUNDER WENT WEST

My Lai: village in Vietnam; site of a notorious incident in the Vietnamese war in which many civilians were murdered by United States Army personnel.

WULF AND EADWACER

The Old English poem is found in the Exeter Book (tenth century). It is in the form of a dramatic soliloquy; the anonymous speaker is a woman, Wulf her lover, and Eadwacer her tyrannical husband.

KOHOUTEK

The title refers to the comet that passed close to the earth in 1975; it was discovered two years earlier by L. K. Kohoutek.

A WET NIGHT

Connemara: a mountainous coastal area of Galway.

ARMAGEDDON, ARMAGEDDON

Oisin: son of Finn MacCool, who on his return to Ireland after three hundred years in the Land of Eternal Youth, made the grievous mistake of touching the earth of Ireland. He was instantly transformed into an ancient old man.

DENIS DEVLIN:

"Lough Derg," "Ank'Hor Vat," "Wishes for Her," "Daphne Stillorgan," "Anteroom: Geneva," and "Renewal By Her Element," from *Collected Poems*, © Stephen Devlin 1964, by permission of The Dolmen Press; an extract from *The Heavenly Foreigner*, © Stephen Devlin 1967, by permission of The Dolmen Press.

W. R. RODGERS:

"The Net," from *Europa And The Bull*, by permission of Martin Secker & Warburg Ltd.; "Paired Lives," and "Scapegoat," from *Collected Poems*, © Oxford University Press 1971, by permission of Oxford University Press.

DONAGH MacDONAGH:

"A Warning To Conquerors" and "Just An Old Sweet Song," from *A Warning To Conquerors*, by permission of Iseult McGuinness and The Dolmen Press; "The Veterans" and an extract from "Charles Donnelly," from *Veterans And Other Poems*, by permission of the Irish University Press.

CHARLES DONNELLY:

"Poem," "The Tolerance of Crows," "Heroic Heart," and "The Flowering Bars," by permission of Joseph Donnelly.

VALENTIN IREMONGER:

"Hector," "Icarus," and "This Houre Her Vigill," from *Horan's Field and Other Reservations*, by permission of the author and The Dolmen Press.

PADRAIC FIACC:

"The Poet," "Gloss," and "Brendan Gone," from *By the Black Stream*, by permission of The Dolmen Press; "Haemorrhage," from *Odour Of Blood*, by permission of Goldsmith Press.

401

ACKNOWLEDGMENTS

ANTHONY CRONIN:

"Apology," "Anarchist," "Autumn Poem," "Surprise," and "The Elephant to the Girl in Bertram Mills' Circus," from *Collected Poems*, by permission of the author and New Writers Press.

PEARSE HUTCHINSON:

"Distortions," from *Expansions*, by permission of The Dolmen Press; "Into Their True Gentleness," from *Watching The Morning Grow*, "Copper-beech and butter-fingers," from *The Frost Is All Over*, by permission of Gallery Books.

RICHARD MURPHY:

"The Philosopher and the Birds" and "The Poet on the Island," from *Sailing To An Island*, and "High Island" and "Seals at High Island," from *High Island*, by permission of Faber and Faber Ltd. The above poems are also published in *High Island: New and Selected Poems*, © 1973, 1974 Richard Murphy, and are reprinted by permission of Harper & Row. An extract from *The Battle of Aughrim* is reprinted by permission of Faber and Faber; the same extract is reprinted from *The Battle of Aughrim and The God Who Eats Corn*, © 1968 Richard Murphy, by permission of Alfred A. Knopf, Inc. "Enigma" and "Trouvaille" are reprinted by permission of the author and *Irish University Review*.

RICHARD KELL:

"Fishing Harbour Towards Evening," from *Control Tower* and "Calypso" from *Differences*, by permission of the author and Chatto & Windus; "The Makers" by permission of the author.

THOMAS KINSELLA:

"Ritual of Departure," "Mirror in February," "A Country Walk," and "Wormwood," from *Nightwalker And Other Poems*, © 1965, 1967, 1968 by Thomas Kinsella are reprinted by permission of Alfred A. Knopf, Inc. The above poems and "Baggot Street Deserta," "Another September," "Clarence Mangan," and "Cover Her Face," are also published in *Selected Poems 1956-1968*, and are reprinted by permission of the author and The Dolmen Press. "Hen Woman" and "Death Bed," from *Notes From The Land Of The Dead And Other*

Poems © 1970, 1973 by Thomas Kinsella, are reprinted by permission of Alfred A. Knopf, Inc.; the same poems are also published in *New Poems 1973*, and are reprinted by permission of the author and The Dolmen Press. Poems XIX and XXIII from *A Technical Supplement* are reprinted by permission of the author and Peppercanister.

JOHN MONTAGUE:

"Wild Sports of the West," from *Poisoned Lands*, by permission of the author and The Dolmen Press; "All Legendary Obstacles" and "That Room," from *A Chosen Light*, by permission of the author; "Special Delivery" and "The Hag of Beare," from *Tides*, by permission of the author, The Dolmen Press, and The Swallow Press; "The Wild Dog Rose," "The Cage," "Lament for the O'Neills," "A Grafted Tongue," and an extract from "A New Siege," from *The Rough Field*, by permission of the author and The Dolmen Press; "Windharp" and an extract from "The Cave of Night," from *A Slow Dance*, "Walking Late" and "Herbert Street Revisited," from *The Great Cloak*, by permission of the author, The Dolmen Press and Wake Forest University Press.

SEAN LUCY:

"Senior Members," "Supervising Examinations," and "Longshore Intellectual," from *Five Irish Poets*, by permission of the author and The Mercier Press.

RICHARD WEBER:

"Envying the Pelican," "A Primer for Schoolchildren," and "The Poet's Day," from *Stephen's Green Revisited*, by permission of The Dolmen Press.

TOM MacINTYRE:

"On Sweet Killen Hill," "The Yellow Bittern," and "The Corrs," from *Blood Relations*, by permission of the author and New Writers Press; "Child," by permission of the author.

JAMES SIMMONS:

"Letter to a Jealous Friend," "Experience," and "Art and Reality," from *Selected Simmons*, by permission of the author and Blackstaff

Press; "Fear Test: Integrity of Heroes," from *West Strand Visions,* by permission of the author and Blackstaff Press; "John Donne," from *Judy Garland and the Cold War,* by permission of the author and Blackstaff Press.

JAMES LIDDY:

"The Voice of America" and "Thinking of Bookshops," from *In A Blue Smoke,* "The Republic 1939" and "Paean to Eve's Apple," from *Blue Mountain,* and "History," from *Corca Bascinn,* by permission of the author and The Dolmen Press.

DESMOND O'GRADY:

"Professor Kelleher and the Charles River" and "The Poet In Old Age Fishing at Evening," from *The Dark Edge of Europe;* "The day concludes burning" and "The pitch piles up in part," from *The Dying Gaul,* by permission of the author and MacGibbon & Kee/Granada Publishing Ltd.; "If I Went Away," from *Off License,* by permission of the author and The Dolmen Press.

BRENDAN KENNELLY:

"The Grip," from *Selected Poems,* by permission of the author; "The Thatcher," "Proof," "My Dark Fathers," from *New and Selected Poems,* by permission of the author and Gallery Books.

SEAMUS HEANEY:

"Digging," "Trout," and "In Small Townlands," from *Death of a Naturalist,* "Requiem for the Croppies," from *Door Into the Dark,* by permission of the author and Faber and Faber Ltd.; "Limbo," "A Northern Hoard" Parts I, II, and "Linen Town," from *Wintering Out* © 1972 by Seamus Heaney, by permission of Oxford University Press, New York, and Faber and Faber Ltd.; "Mossbawn," "The Grauballe Man," and "Exposure" from *North* © 1975 by Seamus Heaney, by permission of Oxford University Press, New York, and Faber and Faber Ltd.; "The Wanderer" and "England's Difficulty," from *Stations,* by permission of the author and Ulsterman Publications; "A Dream of Jealousy," "Triptych," "The Singer's House," and "The Badgers," by permission of the author.

ACKNOWLEDGMENTS

MICHAEL LONGLEY:

"Epithalamion," "Christopher at Birth," and "Emily Dickinson," from *No Continuing City*, by permission of the author; "Irish Poetry" and "Kindertotenlieder," from *An Exploded View*, "Desert Warfare," "Man Lying on a Wall," and "Fleadh," from *Man Lying On A Wall*, by permission of the author and Victor Gollancz Ltd.; "Peace" and "A Small Hotel," by permission of the author.

SEAMUS DEANE:

"Northern Ireland: Two Comments," "Derry," and "Elegy: Three," from *Gradual Wars*, by permission of the author and Irish University Press; "Fording the River" and "Scholar II," from *Rumours*, by permission of the author and The Dolmen Press.

MICHAEL HARTNETT:

"I Have Exhausted the Delighted Range," "All the Death Room Needs," "A Small Farm," "I Think Sometimes," "Marban, A Hermit, Speaks," and "For My Grandmother, Bridget Halpin," from *Selected Poems*, by permission of the author and New Writers Press; *The Retreat of Ita Cagney*, from *Cúlú Íde/The Retreat of Ita Cagney*, by permission of the author and The Goldsmith Press; an extract from "A Farewell to English" and "Death of an Irishwoman," from *Poems in English*, by permission of the author and The Dolmen Press.

DEREK MAHON:

"Glengormley" and "In Carrowdore Churchyard," from *Night-Crossing* © 1968 Oxford University Press, "An Image from Beckett," "I am Raftery," "Consolations of Philosophy," and "Ecclesiastes," from *Lives* © 1972 Oxford University Press, "The Snow Party, "Matthew V. 29–30," "Afterlives," and "A Disused Shed in Co. Wexford," from *Snow Party* © 1975 Oxford University Press, by permission of Oxford University Press; "A Departure," by permission ot the author.

EILEAN NI CHUILLEANAIN:

"Swineherd," "Dead Fly," and "Lucina Schynning in Silence of the Night," from *Acts and Monuments*, an extract from "Site of Ambush" and "Old Roads," from *Site of Ambush*, by permission of the author and New Writers Press. The above poems are also published in *The Second Voyage*, and are reprinted by permission of Wake Forest University Press.

STEWART PARKER:

"Health," "Chicago Allegory," and "Three Fitts," by permission of the author.

MICHAEL SMITH:

"The desolate rhythm of dying recurs," "Blond hair at the edge of the pavement," "At the appointed hour they came," and "Here is the abattoir where," from *Times and Locations*, by permission of the author and The Dolmen Press.

AUGUSTUS YOUNG:

"The Advice of an Efficiency Expert" and "Heritage," from *On Loaning Hill*, by permission of the author and New Writers Press; "Woman, don't be troublesome" and "She's my love," from *Danta Gradha/Love Poems from the Irish*, by permission of the author and Advent Books.

EAVAN BOLAND:

"New Territory" and "Athene's Song," from *New Territory*, by permission of the author; "The War Horse," "Child of Our Time," and "Song," from *The War Horse*, by permission of the author and Victor Gollancz, Ltd.

RICHARD RYAN:

"Knockmany" from *Ledges*, "Ireland," "From My Lai the Thunder Went West," and "Wulf and Eadwacer," from *Ravenswood*, by permission of the author and The Dolmen Press; "Kahoutek" and "A Wet Night," by permission of the author.

HUGH MAXTON:

"Cernunnos," from *Stones*, by permission of the author; an extract from "Mastrim, A Meditation," and "Waking," from *The Noise of the Fields*, by permission of the author and The Dolmen Press; "Dialectique" and "Landscape With Minute Wildflowers," by permission of the author.

FRANK ORMSBY:

"On Devenish Island," from *Ripe For Company*, "Amelia Street" and "Interim," from *Business As Usual*, by permission of the author and Ulsterman Publications; "Inferno," by permission of the author; "Ornaments," from *A Store of Candles* © 1977 Oxford University Press, by permission of Oxford University Press.

CIARAN CARSON:

"The Insular Celts," "St. Ciaran and the Birds," "The Car Cemetery," "The Bomb Disposal," and "Visiting the Dead," from *The New Estate*, by permission of Blackstaff Press and Wake Forest University Press.

PAUL MULDOON:

"Clonfeacle," "The Indians on Alcatraz," and "The Field Hospital," from *New Weather*, by permission of Faber and Faber Ltd.; "Mules" and an extract from "Armageddon, Armageddon," from *Mules*, by permission of Faber and Faber Ltd. and Wake Forest University Press.

Every attempt has been made to contact and to secure permission from the holders of copyright.

I owe a particular debt of gratitude to Dillon Johnston of Wake Forest University for permission to reprint copyright material from his excellent series of collections of the work of new Irish poets. I am also indebted to Terence Brown of Trinity College, Dublin, for encouragement and advice, to Thomas Dillon Redshaw of *Eire-Ireland* for his constructive criticism, and to Brenda McNiff and the *Irish Times* for furnishing me with many photographs of the poets. My thanks also for their help to Bill Dunlop and Nancy Crane of Bailey Library at the University of Vermont, and to my colleague Michael Stanton. I am indebted most of all to my wife Patty for her help at every stage of this undertaking. It should go without saying that I alone am responsible for errors and shortcomings.

INDEXES

INDEX OF POETS

INDEX OF POEMS

Hospital," "Canal Bank Walk," "Lines Written On a Seat On the Grand Canal, Dublin," "In Memory of My Mother," "To Hell With Common Sense," "October," and "If Ever You Go To Dublin Town," from *Collected Poems*, © Katherine B. Kavanagh, by permission of Martin Brian & O'Keeffe Ltd.

PADRAIC FALLON:

"Odysseus," "For Paddy Mac," "Pot Shot," "Weir Bridge," and "The Head," from *Poems*, by permission of The Dolmen Press.

BRIAN COFFEY:

An extract from "Missouri Sequence," "Odalisque," "Headrock," and "The Nicest Phantasies Are Shared," from *Selected Poems*, by permission of the author and New Writers Press; an extract from *Advent*, by permission of the author and *Irish University Review*.

SAMUEL BECKETT:

"Malacoda," "Enueg I," and "I would like my love to die," from *Poems in English*, © 1961 by Samuel Beckett, by permission of John Calder Ltd. and Grove Press, Inc.

JOHN HEWITT:

"Ireland," "Because I Paced My Thought," "An Irishman in Coventry," "Once Alien Here," and "The Spectacle of Truth," from *Collected Poems*, by permission of the author and MacGibbon & Kee/ Granada Publishers Ltd.; "A Minor Victorian Painter," from *Out Of My Time*, by permission of Blackstaff Press.

LOUIS MacNEICE:

"Dublin," "Snow," and an extract from "Trilogy for X," from *The Collected Poems of Louis MacNeice*, edited by E. R. Dodds, © The Estate of Louis MacNeice 1966, by permission of Oxford University Press, New York, and Faber and Faber Ltd.

ACKNOWLEDGMENTS

The editor gratefully acknowledges the permission of individuals and publishers to reprint the following copyright material:

THOMAS MacGREEVY:

"De Civitate Hominum," "Aodh Ruadh O'Domhnaill," "Recessional," "Homage to Marcel Proust," and "Nocturne of the Self-Evident Presence," from *Collected Poems*, by permission of Michael Smith and New Writers Press.

AUSTIN CLARKE:

"The Planter's Daughter," "Pilgrimage," "Night and Morning," "The Envy of Poor Lovers," "Tenebrae," "The Straying Student," "Three Poems About Children," "The Last Republicans," an extract from *Mnemosyne Lay in Dust*, "Inscription for a Headstone," "Mable Kelly," "Gracey Nugent," "Martha Blake at Fifty-One," "Dirge," and an extract from *Tiresias*, by permission of Nora Clarke, The Dolmen Press and Wake Forest University Press.

FRANK O'CONNOR:

"The End of Clonmacnois," and "Hope," from *Kings, Lords and Commons*, by permission of A.D. Peters & Co., Ltd; "On the Death of His Wife," and "The Angry Poet," from *The Little Monasteries*, by permission of the Dolmen Press.

PATRICK KAVANAGH:

"Shancoduff," "Stony Grey Soil," "To the Man After the Harrow," an extract from *The Great Hunger*, "Tinker's Wife," "Epic," "The

INDEX OF FIRST LINES